Gothic Histories

Related titles available from Continuum:

Gothic Readings
Rictor Norton

Horror Fiction
Gina Wisker

Pleasures of Horror
Matthew Hills

Gothic Histories

The Taste for Terror, 1764 to the Present

CLIVE BLOOM

continuum

Continuum International Publishing Group

The Tower Building   80 Maiden Lane
11 York Road   Suite 704, New York
London SE1 7NX   NY 10038

British Library Cataloguing-in-Publication Data
A catalogue record for this book is available from the British Library.

ISBN: 978-1-8470-6050-1 (hardback)
        978-1-84706-051-8 (paperback)

Library of Congress Cataloging-in-Publication Data
A catalog record for this book is available from the Library of Congress.

Typeset by Newgen Imaging Systems Pvt Ltd, Chennai, India
Printed and bound in Great Britain by Antony Rowe CPI

Romancer. Necromancer. I call up the dead. . . . I *am* the dead, and
their land . . . Stay, if your woman is a ghost, she doesn't know it.
William Gibson, *Neuromancer*, Chapter 21

At midnight four times in each year does her spright,
When mortals in slumber are bound,
Arrayed in her bridal apparel of white,
Appear in the hall with the Skeleton-Knight,
And shriek as he whirls her around.
Matthew Lewis, 'Alonzo the Brave
and the Fair Imogine', from *The Monk*, Chapter 9

Contents

Acknowledgements

The author would like to thank the Victoria and Albert Museum Theatre collection; the British Library Lord Chamberlain's collection; Annamaria Sofilla and Brandon Chew of New York University; Jacob Griswold, one of many insightful students at Notre Dame University; Alice Tyrell, Librarian, Notre Dame University; and P. Muralidharan, Newgen Imaging Systems Pvt Ltd, Chennai, India; as always, Lesley Bloom.

Chapter One
Now Welcome the Night:
The Origins of Gothic Culture

In 1555, a strange island was added to the coast of the New World. A Franciscan monk by the name of André Thevet claimed that he had made a journey to a mysterious place near 'Antarctic France' (Newfoundland) called Isola des Demonias – the Isle of Demons. There he had been assailed by 'a great clamour of men's voices', while on the island itself he was attacked by demons whom he kept at bay by repetition of the Gospel of St John. In 1558, Thevet wrote up his adventure, but even in a credulous age his tale was discounted. Nevertheless, Thevet had heard the tale from someone who had actually been there. This was Marguerite de La Rocque, niece of Jean-François de La Rocque, commissioned in 1540 to explore the east coast of Canada.

Marguerite had, however, fallen for an officer on board her uncle's ship with whom she had an affair, for which crime she and her lover, accompanied by a nurse, were abandoned on an island where they found themselves under attack from strange white creatures and demons, 'beasts or other shapes abominably and unutterably hideous, the brood of hell, howling in baffled fury', who attacked their hut but whom they beat back with readings of the New Testament and invocations of the Virgin. The lover and the nurse died, but Marguerite survived and was rescued. She met Thevet in Perigord and told him her alarming tale.[1]

Places like the Isle of Demons didn't exist, but they just might and if they did they were something to be shunned as one would shun Hell itself. This island represented an actual location, a place on the terrestrial map where the natural and the supernatural met: a geography of horrors. Two centuries later such fantastic localities had been banished from cartography, but not banished from a certain human need for the mysterious. The landscape of the Isle of Demons would from now on attract, rather than repel, the geography of imagination replacing the geography of trans-Atlantic exploration.

And if you were wealthy enough you might build your dream as a fairy castle, a ruined tower or haunted monastery, might dress servants as ghoulish monks and put lighted tapers in their hands to light you to bed, might even buy old suits of armour in hope that they might walk at night or old portraits whose sitters might descend spectrally from the frame; and if poorer you could imagine landscapes full of caverns and forests where bandits roamed and corpses rose from haunted graveyards. Getting to the Isle of Demons might make you sea sick; going to the land of ghosts would give you sensual vertigo.

This little book is about the gothic sensibility and about how that sensibility grew from an antiquarian interest in the peoples of the long distant past into one of the most influential artistic styles and artistic genres of the last four centuries affecting area as diverse as architecture, literature, photography, film, music, painting, computer games and even lifestyle; one which has readily adapted itself to almost every geography whether urban or rural and has found its expressions tailored to every culture.

The taste for gothic was always divisive: Dr Johnson thought it merely a liking for 'wild adventure and war', whereas William Lyon Phelps, in 1893, thought the whole thing synonymous with 'the barbarous, the lawless and the tawdry'; others such as Theodore Watts-Dunton saw the genre bringing a 'renaissance of wonder' to the British temperament. The gothic antiquarian Montague Summers suggested that in the gothic is to be found 'a revolt against . . . heavy materialism . . . dullness and drab actuality'. Whatever the response, a revolution in taste certainly happened in the middle of the Georgian period.[2]

The gothic is a 'feeling' expressed by certain formulas which have been readily expanded upon ever since the publication on Christmas Day, 1764 of Horace Walpole's *The Castle of Otranto*. These gothic feelings took shape in architecture, poetry, novels, short stories, pornography, romance and painting; they had political and ecclesiastical ramifications and formed a coherent philosophy of living.

The gothic sensibility takes pleasure in the bizarre and the wild, the magical and arabesque: in architecture, it was expressed in a revived taste for the medieval, while in literature and painting it was expressed by dealing in the supernatural, with the inexplicable monsters of the forest and castle – spooks, witches, damned souls and corpses that rise at midnight; it is interested in science and invention, but turned on their heads as the weird productions of necromancers – doctors in strange laboratories dealing in forbidden knowledge; it is fascinated with the abnormal and the hallucinatory – drug abuse, torture, terrorization, the fear of the victim – the pleasures of being insane!

> Gothic novels have conventionally been divided into the schools of terror and horror, schools which have been grouped under the names of Ann Radcliffe and Matthew 'Monk' Lewis. Terror seeks to evoke by suggestion, by suspense; horror displays in the hopes of producing disgust. Terror veils a potentially ghastly unknown and tempts the reader to peer through, to pull up a corner; horror marches readers through catacombs filled with violated nuns, with the rotting corpses of infants, with entombed lovers turned cannibal. Terror remains discrete and seeks a unity of tone; horror has an appetite for sudden variation, for the blackly comic, for the grotesque. And terror has been associated with the practice of women whilst horror has been judged the province of men, at least in the first . . . periods of Gothic.[3]

Such feelings, slow to be recognized as such at first, and mistaken for a certain jeu d'esprit by contemporary commentators, eventually grew into a whole cultural attitude: in architecture it was expressed in the dignity of ecclesiastical, parliamentary and university building, solidly dependable and conservatively British, while in literature and art that same gothicism was the prompt for eroticism, violence, melancholy and psychosis which used the muscularity of gothic architecture for decidedly un-muscular activities. One could quite easily be a Christian and a goth as Charles Maturin was to prove or an atheist and believe in hell as Matthew Lewis was to demonstrate. The ambiguity of the position became the expression of a mental universe so pervasive that it suffused the Victorian imagination where the most modern ideas were often decked out in 'gothic' medievalism.

The gothic was not merely a playground for the imaginative, it was also the very foundation of a new sense of the imagination. It was not merely a set of exterior devices through which to have cosy inglenook adventures, but a mechanism for describing not only the workings of the mind, but also the mind in relationship with the supernatural, the universal and the divine. The gothic, therefore, perforce dealt in the unspoken, the difficult and the painful in ways no other form of art could do. If during the eighteenth and nineteenth centuries progress was measured by technological change then it is in gothic literature that the first forms of modern mental alienation concomitant with that change are documented.

Much of Gothic fiction is also obliquely taken up with the confusions of the ontological and epistemological status of its subject matter: creatures who should be 'dead' are 'alive'; corpses may be made to walk; skeletons foretell the future; shadows do not accompany the bodies that should throw them; faces have no reflection; the phases of the moon may transfer a man into a wolf or a bat. It is precisely these confusions that allow the imagination to breach the border between the quotidian and the spectral land of weirdness and the supernatural where transgression and desire play upon the taboo.

The codification of the gothic mood and the creation of the vocabulary of that mood took the best part of 150 years to form. We have been playing variations ever since. The gothic mood took as its first vocabulary that of architecture on the one hand and of the wild on the other; confinement in dungeons and oubliettes and the confusion of the forest and the castle ruin. This new heightened emotionalism, which sought as its stimulus the sensational and the outré was nevertheless based on a certain long-standing revivalism which, over the 100 years separating the Commonwealth in the seventeenth century from the Georgians, had sought to define the gothic as the basic political, legal and ecclesiastical mental condition of the 'English'.

From these beginnings, so remote from the emotionalism at the end of the eighteenth century (as much from de Sade as from Wordsworth or Goethe), grew ever so insensibly, a feeling or a mood very different from that of the seventeenth and very early eighteenth century when horror was defused by the vulgarity of laughter.

No finer example exists of commonsensical humour, so antithetical to the gothic mood, than in Daniel Defoe's *Journal of the Plague Year*. Here he places the (purely fictional) tale of John Hayward and a poor drunk piper in what might later prove grounds for supernaturalism. Not here, not yet.

> It happened one night that this poor fellow, whether somebody had given him too much drink or no – John Hayward said he had not drink in his house, but that they had given him a little more victuals than ordinary at a public-house in Coleman Street – and the poor fellow, having not usually had a belly full for perhaps not a good while, was laid all along upon the top of a bulk or stall, and fast asleep, at the door in the street near London Wall, towards Cripple Gate; and that upon the same bulk or stall the people of some house, in the alley of which the house was a corner, hearing a bell which they always rang before the cart came, had laid a body really dead of the plague just by him, thinking, too, that this poor fellow had been a dead body, as the other was, and laid there by some of the neighbours.
>
> Accordingly when John Hayward with his bell and the cart came along, finding two dead bodies laying upon the stall, they took them up . . . from hence they passed along and took in other dead bodies . . . as soon as the cart stopped the fellow awaked and struggled a little to get his head out from among the dead bodies, when, raising himself up in the cart, he called out, 'Hey! Where am I?' This frighted the fellow that attended about the work; but after some pause John Hayward, recovering himself, said, 'Lord, bless us! There's somebody in the cart that is not quite dead!'. So another called to him and said, 'who are you?' the fellow answered, 'I am the poor piper. Where am I?' 'Where are you?' says Hayward. 'Why, you are in the dead-cart, and we are going to bury you.' 'But I an't dead though, am I?' says the piper, which made them laugh a little – though . . . they were heart-edly frighted at first.

Defoe's touch is light, anecdotal, urban (you can hear the London voices) and is full of the irreverent attitude of the cockney, but his whimsies aside, one may find in others the terrors that would later characterize the gothic. In Edmund Spencer's sixteenth-century

'Epithalamion', itself a poem in keeping with the new taste for the
dreary and for the expression of grief and sorrow, we find much that
is a blueprint for gothicism:

> Let not lamenting cryes, nor dolefull teares,
> Be heard all night within nor yet without:
> Ne let false whispers, breeding hidden feares,
> Brake gentle sleep with misconceiued dout.
> Let no deluding dreamses, nor dreadful sights
> Make sudden sad affrights;
> Ne let housefyres, nor lightnings helplesse harmes,
> Ne let the Pouke, nor other euill sprights,
> Ne let mishiuous witches with theyr charmes,
> Ne let hob Goblins, names whose sence we see not,
> Fray us with things that be not.
> Let not the shriech Oule, nor the Storke be heard:
> Nor the night Rauen that still deadly yels,
> Nor danmed ghosts cald vp with mighty spels,
> Nor griesly vultures make vs once affeard:
> Nor let th'unpleasant Quyre of Frogs still croking
> Make vs to wish theyr choking.

Here are owls and goblins, ghosts, vultures and reptiles, but they
are mere props, devoid of that attitudinal weight and the emotional
importance attached to them by the eighteenth century. Milton in
the seventeenth century could also indulge a taste for the depressive
and doleful. In 'Il Penseroso', written between 1631 and 1632, the
poet is already held in thrall to the world of that 'pensive nun' who is
herself 'divinest melancholy', the palette is 'black' and the world is
bathed in the light of a 'wand'ring moon' where 'contemplation' and
'silence' are the companions of the writer left to 'walk the studious
cloister's pale' and enjoy 'antique pillars' and 'storied windows'.

There were also later writers such as John Dyer who would
turn on the theatricals when required, as he did when composing
'Grongar Hill' in 1716 (but published 1726).

> Tis now the raven's bleak abode;
> Tis now th'appartment of the toad;

And there the fox securely feeds'
And there the pois'nous adder breeds,
Conceal'd in ruins moss and weeds:
While ever and anon there falls
Huge heaps of hoary, moulder'd walls.

Yet this was so much flimflam, so much theatrical prop. It would be another 50 years before the flame blew bright again.

Melancholic graveyard poetry was in vogue during the whole of the Georgian period. There was, of course, Thomas Gray, who in 1739 accompanied Horace Walpole on his continental tour and who wrote of the Grande Chartreuse, that it was 'not a precipice, not a torrent, not a cliff, but . . . pregnant with religion and poetry'.[4] Yet it was Robert Blair, the son of an Edinburgh cleric and author of only three published poems, who caught the spirit of graveyard terrors in his work 'The Grave':

See yonder hallow'd fane, the pious work
Of names once fam'd, now dubious or forgot,
And buried midst the wreck of things which were
There lie interr'd the more illustrious dead.
The wind is up: hark how it howls! Methinks
Till now I never heard a sound so dreary.
Doors creek, and windows clap, and night's foul bird,
Rook'd in the spire, screams loud! The gloomy aisles,
Black-plaister'd, and hung round with shreds of 'scutcheons
And tatter'd coats of arms, send back the sound,
Ladden with heavier airs, from the low vaults,
The mansions of the dead! Rous'd from their slumbers,
In grim array the grizly spectres rise,
Grin horrible, and obstinately sullen
Pass and repass, hush'd as the foot of night!
Again the screech owl shreeks – ungracious sound!
I'll hear no more; it makes one's blood run chill. . . .
Oft in the lone churchyard at night I've seen,
By glimpse of moon-shine, chequ'ring through the trees,
The schoolboy, with his satchel in his hand,
Whistling aloud to bear his courage up, . . .

> Sudden he starts! and hears, or thinks he hears,
> The sound of something purring at his heels.
> Full fast he flies, and dares not look behind him,
> Til, out of breath, he overtakes his fellows;
> Who gather round, and wonder at the tale
> Of horrid apparition, tall and ghastily,
> That walks at dead of night, or takes his stand
> O'er some new-open'd grave; and, strange to tell,
> Evanishes at crowing of the cock . . . .

While the poem catches the mood for goblins and spooks, catches the fashion for the revived folk tale told around a peat fire in a Highland croft and even gives a whiff of that romantic Celticism that so entranced Scottish antiquarianism and London's fashionable literati, it fails to have the substance, either narrative or emotional, of the true gothic tale. In short, it lacks that hard theoretical and philosophical core that saves the best tales from becoming mere anecdote or incoherent sensationalism. The great gothic tales are always emotionally coherent, if not always philosophically logical. Yet it was precisely emotionality, not philosophy that was needed. It would be Edmund Burke, in *A Philosophical Enquiry into the Origins of Our Ideas of the Sublime and the Beautiful* (1757), who would finally codify the gothic emotional experience.

> Whatever is fitted in any sort to excite the ideas of pain, and danger, that is to say, whatever is in any sort terrible, or is conversant about terrible objects, or operates in a manner analogous to terror, is a source of the *sublime*; that is, it is productive or the strongest emotion which the mind is capable of feeling . . .
>
> No passion so effectually robs the mind of all its powers of acting and reasoning as fear. For fear being an apprehension of pain of death, it operates in a manner that resembles actual pain. Whatever therefore is terrible, with regard to sight, is sublime too, whether the cause of terror, be endued with greatness of dimensions or not; for it is impossible to look on anything as trifling, or contemptible, that maybe dangerous . . .
>
> To make anything very terrible, obscurity seems in general to be necessary. When we know the full extent of any danger, when we can

accustom our eyes to it, a great deal of the apprehension vanishes. Everyone will be sensible of this, who considers how greatly night adds to our dread, in all cases of danger, and how much the notions of ghosts and goblins, of which none can form clear ideas, affect minds, which give credit to the popular tales concerning such sorts of beings.

It is this ideological bent that would influence much that was gothic and much that was gothicly inspired in the Romantics. Wordsworth, Coleridge and Keats exploited and enriched the descriptive vocabulary of Burke's sublime mood, Blake illustrated Robert Blair's poem, J. W. M. Turner and John Constable painted the landscape equivalent of the sublime, travelling to Stonehenge (Turner in 1825 and Constable in 1835) to capture the mystery of the ancient past, while others having read their Ann Radcliffe used Burke as if he were a philosophical tourist guide to the mountains and lakes of Italy, the forests of Germany, the Lake District (the English Alps) or the Scottish Highlands.

The new grand tour was a gothic grand tour and the new Goths (named as such as early as the 1750s) had to have their fair share of ruins, haunted inns, strange folk tales, dangerous mountain passes, cataracts and sublime views. It was a fashion that would not diminish until Jonathan Harker had tasted paprika for the first time in the wilds of the Carpathians on his way to Castle Dracula.[5]

Yet of all these influences none was more profound that that of Shakespeare, whose reputation had increased across the eighteenth century and whose, *Macbeth, Hamlet* and *Romeo and Juliet* (at least the more medieval and Italianate elements of the sub plot) fired many a gothic imagination. 'With all his faults', declared Alexander Pope in his preface of 1725, Shakespeare '[was]an ancient majestic piece of Gothic architecture'[but] compared with a neat modern building . . . [was] more strong and more elegant'. Walpole found reasons for the depiction of domestics (servants) in his very choice of subject matter precisely because it had already been tackled in Shakespeare and was therefore justified (by precedent) as an authentic part of the (gothic) genre Walpole was himself in the process of inventing. It was not merely a matter of good taste (although it was always that), but a matter of patriotic pride that Shakespeare outgunned Voltaire.

With regard to the deportment of the domestics . . . I will beg leave
to add a few words. The simplicity of their behaviour, almost tending
to excite smiles, which, . . . seems not consonant to the serious cast of
the work, appeared to me not only improper, but was marked design-
edly in that manner. My rule was nature. However, grave, important,
or even melancholy, the sensation of princes and heroes maybe, they
do not stamp the same affections on their domestics: at least the latter
do not, or should not be made to, express their passions in the same
dignified tone. In my humble opinion, the contrast between the
sublime of the one and the naiveté of the other sets the pathetic
of the former in a stronger light. . . . The great master of nature,
Shakespeare, was the model I copied. Let me ask, if his tragedies of
Hamlet and Julius Caesar would not loose a considerable share of
their spirit and wonderful beauties, if the humour of the grave
diggers, the fooleries of Polonius, and the clumsy jests of the Roman
citizens were omitted, or vested in heroics? Is not the eloquence of
Antony, the noble and affectedly-unaffected oration of Brutus, artifi-
cially exalted by the rude bursts of nature from the mouths of their
auditors? . . .

'No,' says Voltaire, in his addition Corneille, 'this mixture of
buffoonery and solemnity is intolerable,' Voltaire is a genius – but
not of Shakespeare's magnitude. (Horace Walpole, Introduction to
First Edition of *The Castle of Otranto*, 1764)

Part research, part dress-up, serious and comical by turns, the taste
for the antiquarian bore the seed of gothicism. Antiquarianism had
started even as the monasteries had fallen into ruins, scholars crawling over tumbled masonry or searching out the details of arcane
manuscripts. The glass painter Henry Gyles sketched the ruins of
Stonehenge, for instance, as early as the seventeenth century. Decay
brought the delights of forgotten as well as forbidden fruit. To take
an interest in 'the Gothes' was, as Sir Henry Wottton put it in 1624,
to revel in 'Reliques of [a] barbarous age',[6] which was not to say that
such revels did not produce their own residue of pleasure. Even as the
old gothic style gave way bit by bit against the new wave of classicism, brought on by Inigo Jones's proposals (in 1633) to give a
classical façade to Old St Paul's, so, perversely, the term became more
and more familiar through antiquarianism.

John Evelyn coming from Haarlem could comment in 1641 on the 'fairest churches of Gotiq design'. Indeed, he loves the word, spelling it variously as Gotiq, Gotick, Gotic and Gottic. The word was as moveable as its meaning, and as mysterious, being attributed in turn to Raphael, Vasari and Palladio, but whatever its origins it was clear what it meant: used as a means of expressing contempt for the past and the love of outdated and outmoded ways. The playwright Congreve in *The Way of the World* included this rebuff from one character to another who was old fashioned, 'Ah Rustick, ruder than Gothick'.[7] The gothic represented all the barbarisms and taradiddles which swept away the classicism of Rome. Thus while Evelyn might enjoy the gothic spires of Haarlem he still felt that the gothic style was a regression. One, nevertheless, that seemed to suit the barbarism of the present age.

> The Goths and Vandals, having demolished the Greek and Roman architecture, introduced in its stead a certain fantastical and licentious manner of building which we have since called modern or Gothic – of the greatest industry and expressive carving, full of fret and lamentable imagery.[8]

The gothic maintained a sentimental fascination with historians, churchmen and those of a legal bent. It would be a term used with great force by those interested in the origins of the common law and with constitutionalists and Anglicans and it would be a term hotly debated for at least a 100 years before the first neo-gothic stone was laid and before the first neo-gothic dream was dreamt by either poet or story teller.

Just after the Civil War in 1648, and meditating on the uniqueness of the English system, Nicholas Bacon could talk of that 'ancient Gothique law as this island hath'. This was a powerful myth to concretize in law the origins of the English and the right relationship the monarch might have with his people. In 1672, Sir William Temple called the English a 'branch of . . . [the] Gothic Nations'. It was one of the first rallying cries of Anglo-Saxonism and by 1719, Jonathan Swift would talk confidently of English politics as 'Gothic forms of government'. Oxford scholarship would play its part too. Between 1655 and 1707 when the Society of Antiquaries was re-established after being abolished during the reign of James I, a steady flow of antiquarian interest seeped out of Oxford into the counties of England. 'Many [Oxford men] looked back with longing to the Saxon period; there they found, they thought, a Church at once Catholic, English, episcopally governed, and spiritually independent'.[9]

Prolonged argument could not resolve the issue of whether the common law was 'immemorial' (that is, a creation of the Ancient Britons) or a creation of 'gothic' times or whether parliament was medieval or Saxon on origin. Theories of the English idea of a limited monarchy, given impetus by the accommodations of 1688, led to discussions regarding the usurpation of English rights by William the Conqueror, a debate which greatly influenced political agitators like Tom Paine and authors like Walter Scott, who was still arguing this idea in the pages of *Ivanhoe* in 1819, by which time the idea of Norman usurpation of English rights was commonplace.

> A circumstance which greatly tended to enhance the tyranny of the nobility and the sufferings of the inferior classes arose from the consequence of the Conquest by Duke William of Normandy. Four generations had not sufficed to blend the hostile blood of the Normans and Anglo-Saxons, or to unite, by common language and mutual interests, two hostile races, one of which still felt the elation of triumph, while the other groaned under the consequences of defeat. . . . all the monarchs of the Norman race had shown the most marked predilection for their Norman subjects. ... French was the language of honour, of chivalry and even of justice, while the far more manly an expressive Anglo-Saxon was abandoned to the use of rustics and hinds. (Chapter 1)

The impulse that had sent both Turner and Constable to Stonehenge also made men turn back to the most ancient of times in search of that historical security in immemorialism and ritual. The Green Knight in the tale of *Sir Gawain* seems to be associated with mysterious Neolithic barrows, and the antiquarians of the seventeenth century, for all their research, seemed to know little more than their forebears and regularly mixed up Neolithic people, the

builders of Stonehenge and the druids. Those who found comfort in
the ballads of the Celts, whether authentic or manufactured (by a
small industry of forgers) clubbed together to dress in what they
imagined were the robes of ancient priests and celebrated in all their
arcane detail rituals revived (but really invented) from antiquity. The
common law it was argued came from the Ancient Britons as
described by Caesar and Tacitus, and the Ancient Britons were not
only Celts but also a branch of a non-Roman stock or 'goths'. This
argument, first put forward by the Frenchman François Hotman
in 1573 gained increasing currency among Whigs in England
during the eighteenth century.[10] The Tory Viscount Henry St John
Bolingbroke also took no notice of the historical niceties of time or
place and made the Celts a branch of the gothic nations.

It was an age of clubs and societies and the revival of ancient
British (that is gothic) forms appealed. The Grand Lodge of the
Most Ancient Order of Druids was announced on Primrose Hill in
London on the autumnal equinox of 1717 and held its first meeting at the Apple Tree Tavern in Covent Garden. It was the brainchild
of John Aubrey who had done some digging at Stonehenge and
thought it might be a druid temple. He began working on a book
called *Templa Druidim* which was never published, but his
researches interested another antiquary called William Stuckley
who advanced the druid connection. Meanwhile yet another histo-
rian named John Toland had developed an interest in the druids to
the point where he had allegedly had a rather mysterious meeting
with 'druid' representatives with whom he had formed the Universal Druid Bond. The reverend Henry Rowlands followed with
Mona Antiqua Restaurata in which the druids were returned to the
sacred groves, but were given stone altars. For the most part the
druids were considered wise, nature worshipping and, above all,
patriotic.

Three years later in 1726, Toland published *History of the Druids*
and one year after that Jean Martin produced the first French work
to rehabilitate the leaders of the Gaulish nation. By the end of the
eighteenth century, druid societies were matched by Freemasons,
Rosicrucians, Hermetics, Illuminati and occultists across Europe
and many societies shared members. There were druidic societies in

London, Dublin and New York, and romantic nationalism visualized the Welsh nation persecuted and destroyed under the heal of Edward I. In the 1760s, the painter Richard Wilson had discovered the charms of Welsh ruins and landscape, turning Dolbadarn Castle into the sort of sublime, Italianate classical ruin that would attract Turner and others to make the long journey to Wales.

Thomas Gray's poem 'The Bard' was followed by a stream of visual representations of the last medieval bard committing suicide before the armies of the English. Thomas Jones painted *The Bard* in 1774, a picture that was to influence a generation. His rendition was followed by that of John Martin who made of the castle and cataracts he depicted a Mosaic tragedy. The first Eisteddford was organized by Thomas Jones in 1789 and elaborated on by Edward Williams (Iola Morganwg) who had held 'pagan' ceremonies on Primrose Hill. By 1796, LaTour D'Anvergne's *Origines Gauloises* had 'discovered' the word for Neolithic tombs and 'dolmen' has stuck ever since. By 1800, all dolmens, barrows and stone circles were considered druid, and druidism seemed comfortably at one with the medieval-ism of the gothic imagination, little more than picturesque, or so Walter Scott thought when he included a stone circle in the intro-duction to *Ivanhoe*.

> A considerable open space, in the midst of this glade, seemed formally to have been dedicated to the rights of Druidical supersti-tion; for, on the summit of a hillock . . . there still remained part of a circle of rough, unhewn stones, of large dimensions. Seven stood upright; the rest had been dislodged from their places, probably by the zeal of some convert to Christianity. (Chapter 1)

Alongside the continuous 'rediscovery' of an ancient past went reaction. By the time Edgar Allan Poe was completing 'Ligeia' (itself a partial pastiche of *Ivanhoe*) in 1838, gothic and druidic had become simply shorthand for the arabesque, disturbing and outré. Indeed the Lady Rowena is imprisoned in a room the shape of a pentangle, with a great gothic stained glass window where

> The ceiling, of gloomy-looking oak, was excessively lofty, vaulted, and elaborately fretted with the wildest and most grotesque

specimens of a semi-Gothic, semi-Druidical device. (Edgar Allan Poe, *Ligeia*)

This newer element of fear and revulsion seems to have set in by the mid-nineteenth century. Druidic culture was again reduced to the barbaric, mysterious, pagan and fearful under the onslaughts of imperialism and evangelism. While druidism was still seen as a wise, indigenous and patriotic tradition by Celtic nationalists this was confined to fringe attitudes. In England, Saxonism again triumphed. William Geller's popular 1832 print of Stonehenge showed blood-crazed crowds while Wordsworth could write in 1842 of 'priests and spectres grim and idols dire' ('Trepidation of the Druids'); Holman Hunt illustrated the early Christians hiding from druid wrath in a painting with no historical truth behind it; and in the newly decorated Houses of Parliament a picture of a druid sacrifice, one of three to illustrate ' ignorance [and] heathen superstition' was commissioned to illustrate Britain before the light of modernity.[11]

By the end of the century druidism was seen as much a part of a terrible past before the coming of the Romans as it was a warning of current fin de siècle decadence. The popular novelist Grant Allen musing before an excavation had this reverie.

I saw them bear aloft, with beating breasts and loud gesticulations, the bent corpse of their dead chieftain. . . .I saw the fearful orgy of mas-sacre and rapine around the open tumulus, the wild priest shattering with his gleaming tomahawk the skulls of his victims . . . the awful dance of blood-stained cannibals around the mangled remains.[12]

Yet the real fear in the discovery of this slaughter is the return of not only a long forgotten past but of a curse upon the discoverer, something echoed in the ghost tale and in the aftermath of the discovery of the tomb of Tutenkhamun.

Finally, the long task of heaping up . . . the earthen mound that was never again to be opened to the light of day, till ten thousand years later, we modern Britons invaded with our prying, sacrilegious mattock the sacred privacy of the cannibal ghost.[13]

The expression of this new fear was to emerge in the archaeological and antiquarian nightmares of the late Victorian and early Edwardian periods and in the fiction of Arthur Machen and M. R. James, whose own horror landscapes centred around the return of demonic forces from the Saxon and Celtic worlds respectively. After Darwin and Herbert Spenser such Celtic or Anglo-Saxon musings often suggested degeneracy.

Romantic fears were of a different order and things that caused unease in one generation were neutral in that of an earlier. Walter Scott could dress his Saxon swineherd as if he was a Neolithic man without cause to be queasy about the description.

> The eldest of these men had a stern, savage, and wild aspect. His garment was of the simplest form imaginable, . . . Composed of the tanned skin of some animal, on which the hair had been originally left, but which had been worn off in so many places that it would have been difficult to distinguish, from the patches that remained, to what creature the fur belong. This primeval vestment reached from the throat to the knees. . . . (*Ivanhoe*, Chapter 1)

This attitude to the distant past, nevertheless slowly hardened into one of fear, famously memorialized in Arthur Conan Doyle's gothic romance *The Hound of the Baskervilles* which he published in 1902. The tale is set in a bizarre landscape and one full of peculiar sounds and sights. Watson hears for the first time the 'boom' of the bittern, 'the weirdest, strangest thing that ever I heard in my life', before turning his attention to Grimpen Mire when Stapleton, soon to be unmasked as the psychopathic villain, but now posing as a naturalist, comments,

> 'It's rather an uncanny place altogether. Look at the hillside yonder. What do you make of those?'
>
> The whole slope was covered with grey circular rings of stone . . .
>
> 'What are they? Sheep-pens?'
>
> 'No, they are the homes of our worthy ancestors, Prehistoric man . . .'

Immediately prior to this there is a scene in which folk lore, the gothic and the murderous coincide. Watson and Lord Baskerville are alone on the moor when

> There arose suddenly out of the vast gloom of the moor that strange cry which I had already heard upon the borders of the great Grimpen Mire. It came with the wind through the silence of the night, . . . a rising howl. . . . The Baronet caught my sleeve and his face glimmered white through the darkness.
>
> 'My god, what's that, Watson?'
>
> 'I don't know. It's a sound they have on the moor. I heard it once before.' . . .
>
> 'Watson,' said the Baronet, 'it was a cry of a hound'.
>
> My blood ran cold in my veins, for there was a break in his voice which told of the sudden horror which had seized him.
>
> 'What do they call this sound?' he asked
>
> 'Who?'
>
> 'The folk on the countryside?'
>
> 'Oh, they are ignorant people. Why should you mind what they call?'. . . .
>
> 'They say it is the cry of the Hound of the Baskervilles'. (Chapter 9)?

What then emerges is nothing less than the return of the primeval, a Darwinian nightmare dressed up as a prehistoric man.

> Over the rocks, in the crevice of which the candle burned, there was thrust out an evil yellow face, a terrible animal face, all seamed and scored with vile passions. Foul with mire, with a bristling beard, and hung with matted hair, it might well have belonged to one of those old savages who dwelt in the boroughs on the hillsides. (Chapter 9)

Gothicism in literature or art, unlike gothic interests in history or architecture was always something to be wary of. Unlike its architectural cousin, it smelt of rebellion, chaos and slightly sulphurous, and those leading artists who did not embrace it were quick to condemn it. As late as 1797, Joshua Reynolds was still fighting a rearguard action against the iniquities of degenerate taste, his model was Raphael, but his target were those stubborn artists who could not be persuaded to give up the pernicious style, a style already quietly re-established alongside the classicism he advocated and which would become the leading mode in the next century. In the first of his *Discourses on Art*, Reynolds tells his audience:

> Raffaelle [Raphael], it is true, had not the advantage of studying in an Academy; but all Rome, and the works of Michael Angelo in particular, were to him an Academy. On the sight of the Capella Sistina, he immediately from a dry, Gothick, and even insipid manner, which attends to the minute accidental discriminations of particular and individual objects, assumed that grand style of painting, which improves partial representation by the general and invariable ideas of nature. (Sir Joshua Reynolds, *Discourses on Art*, Discourse 1)

It was the sentimental and degenerate taste of antiquarians, painters, medievalists, crypto-Catholics, poets and novelists that worried Reynolds as it would later worry Jane Austen fed up with those gothic emotional thrills which obscured her own very rational style. She would get her own revenge on its popularity in *Northanger Abbey* (1818) and warn against the influence of gothic titillation on young women.

> 'Dear creature! How much I am obliged to you; and when you have finished *Udolpho*, we will read *the Italian* together; and I have made out a list of ten or twelve more of the same kind for you'
>
> 'Have you, indeed! How glad I am! – What are they all?'
>
> 'I will read you their names directly; here they are, in my pocket-book. Castle of Wolfenbach, Clermont, Mysterious Warnings, Necromancer of the Black Forest, Midnight Bell, Orphan of the Rhine, and Horrid Mysteries. Those will last us some time'
>
> 'Yes, pretty well; but are they all horrid, are you sure they are all horrid?'
>
> 'Yes, quite sure . . .' (Chapter 6)

Yet young women and impressionable young men (if one believes the detractors) were reading and enjoying the thrills of the 'goblin-mongers'. Thomas Medwin, a school friend of Shelley, recalled that

> He was very fond of reading, and greedily devoured all the books which were brought to school after the holidays; these were mostly *blue* books. Who does not know what blue books mean? But if there should be anyone ignorant enough not to know what those dead darling volumes so designated from their covers, contain, be it known, that they are or were to be bought for sixpence, and embodied stories of haunted castles, bandits, murderers, and other grim personages – a most exciting and interesting sort of food for boys' minds.[14]

Shelley's favourite read was the 'banned' *The Monk* of Lewis. The novelist Charles Bucke recalled how such books were 'thumbed over, begged [and] borrowed' and how he himself had read *The Mysteries of Udolpho* nine times, Radcliffe's The *Romance of the Forest* four times and *The Italian* five times;[15] Hester Thrale thought William Beckford's *Vathek* a 'mad' book, but carried on reading it nevertheless; Thomas Green in his diary of 3 September 1799, recorded the pleasure he got from reading Walpole's *The Mysterious Mother* in which he enjoyed 'the raciness of [the] piece'; Elizabeth Carter, a famous translator, thought these 'wretched books' were ruinous to virtue but kept reading because such books were a 'pleasing relaxation'; Henry Crabb Robinson reread *Vathek* and *The Castle of Otranto* at intervals during the period between 1816 to 1829 and complained that though he 'ought not to have begun' them, he couldn't put them down.

Critics too were fascinated by the fashion for thrills, especially the reason for the continuance of the craze for gothicism. Anna Laetitia Aikin a poet and a democrat found the whole thing difficult to reconcile. Often critics were keen to compare and contrast such literature to the 'serious' novels of the period.

> The old Gothic romance and the Eastern tale, with their genii, giants, enchantments, and transformations, however a refined critic may censure them as absurd and extravagant, will ever retain a most powerful influence on the mind, and interest the reader independently of all peculiarity of taste.[16]

Coleridge, too close to the genre in his tastes and productions, was both fascinated and repulsed by 'hobgoblin-romance', while the critic T. J. Horsley Curties writing in 1801 could admonish women writers for their 'literary prostitution'. Many writers and most readers of gothic were women (at every social level) and Mrs Radcliffe in her own justification of her writing style was concerned to uphold the frivolity of a genre that nevertheless allowed readers a 'respite from the inexorable tyranny of facts'. It would be a defence used ever since to protect women's romance from its detractors. The trade of popular writing and therefore the new found working respectability of women novelists, however silly their stories, was to be defended.

> Upon the whole, romance writers ought to look jealously after their privileges, and prevent the use of apparitions from incurring proscription in these latter days of the scoffers, who think it is no great matter to take the bread out of the mouths of an hundred industrious persons in Grub Street, for the sake of shewing themselves above vulgar prejudices. Surely romance writers are far more numerous than philosophers, and might be well able to mob any prating son of Epicurus who attempted to undermine the credit of their machinery.[17]

Of course the gothic as a literary genre was easy to pastiche. The very pastiches over the years were incorporated into the narrative emotions they were attacking. From the 1790s to the great age of Hollywood gothic stories were satirized and sent up and serious productions would incorporate pastiche (as for instance in *The Bride of Frankenstein*). Both William Beckford and Edgar Allan Poe used pastiche and burlesque elements even in their most serious work. The work of Ann Radcliffe and Matthew Lewis were frequently satirized while satiric versions of the gothic were often published alongside serious works, especially during the 1790s. Thomas Love Peacock found the whole kit and caboodle of gothicism an excuse for a good laugh in *Nightmare Abbey*.

MARIONETTA

My cousin Scythrop has of late had an air of mystery about him, which gives me great uneasiness.

MR FLOSKY

That is strange: nothing is so becoming to a man as an air of mystery. Mystery is the very key-stone of all that is beautiful in poetry, all that is sacred in faith, and all that is recondite in transcendental psychology. I am writing a ballad which is all mystery; it is 'such stuff as dreams are made of', and is, indeed, stuff made of a dream; for, last night I fell asleep as usual over a book, and had a vision of pure reason. I composed five hundred lines in my sleep.

Yet it was the correspondent 'Jacobin' (possibly Coleridge) writing in the *Monthly Review* of 19 August 1797 who satirized the Radcliffe School of terror (and by implication the whole genre) to best effect.

In the first place, then, trembling reader, I would advise you to construct an *old* castle, *formerly* of great magnitude and extent, built in the Gothic manner, with a great number of hanging towers, turrets, and pinnacles. One half, at least, of it must be in ruins; dreadful chasms and gaping crevices must be hid only by the clinging ivy; the doors must be so old, and so little used to open, as to grate tremendously on the hinges; and there must be in every passage an echo, and as many reverberations as there are partitions. As to the furniture, it is absolutely necessary that it should be nearly as old as the house, and in a more decayed state, if a more decayed state be possible. The principal rooms must be hung with pictures, of which the damps have very nearly effaced the colours; only you must preserve such a degree of likeness in one two of them, as to incline your heroine to be very much affected by the sight of them, and to imagine that she has seen a face, or faces, very like them, or very like something else, but where, or when, she cannot *just now* remember. It will be necessary, also, that one of those very old and very decayed portraits shall seem to frown most cruelly, while another seems to smile most lovingly.

Great attention must be paid to the tapestry hangings. They are to be very old, and tattered, and blown about with the wind. There is a great deal in the wind. Indeed, it is one of the principal objects of terror, for it may be taken for almost any terrific object, from a banditti of cut-throats to a single ghost. The tapestry, therefore, must give signs of moving, so as to make the heroine believe, there is something behind it, although, not being *at that time* very desirous to examine, she concludes very naturally and logically, that is can be nothing but the wind. This same wind is of infinite service to our modern castle-builders. Sometimes it *whistles,* and then it shows how sound may be conveyed through the crevices of a Baron's castle. Sometimes it *rushes*, and then there is reason to believe the Baron's great grandfather does not lie quiet in his grave; and sometimes it *howls*, and, if accompanied with rain, generally induces some weary traveller, perhaps a robber, and perhaps a lover, or both, to take up their residence in this *very same castle* where virgins, and virtuous wives, were locked up before the invention of a *habeas corpus*. It is, indeed, not wonderful, that so much use is made of the wind, for it is the principal ingredient in that sentimentality of constitution, to which romances are admirabl[y] adapted.

Having thus provided such a decayed stock of furniture as may be easily affected by the wind, you must take care that the battlements and towers are remarkably *populous* in *owls* and *bats*. The *hooting* of the one, and the *flitting* of the other, are excellent engines in the system of terror, particularly if the candle goes out, which is very often the case in damp caverns.

And the mention of caverns brings me to the essential qualities inherent in a castle. The rooms *upstairs* may be just habitable, and no more; but the principal incidents must be carried on in *subterraneous* passages. These, in general, wind round the whole extent of the building; but that is not very material, as the heroine never goes through above half without meeting with a door, which she has neither strength nor resolution to open, although she has found a rusty key, very happily fitted to as rusty a lock, and would give the world to know what it leads to, and yet she can give no reason for her curiosity.

The building now being completely finished, and furnished with all desirable imperfections, the next and only requisite is a heroine, with all the weakness of body and mind that appertains to her sex; but, endowed with all the curiosity of a spy, and all the courage of a troop of horse. Whatever she hears, sees, or thinks of, that is horrible and terrible, she must enquire into it again and again. All alone, for she cannot prevail on the timid *Janetta* to go with her a *second time*; all alone she sets out, in the dead of night, when nothing but the aforesaid owls and bats are *hooting* and *flitting*, to resolve the horrid mystery of the moving tapestry, which threw her into a swoon the preceding night, and in which she knows her fate is awfully involved, though she cannot tell why. With cautious tread, and glimmering taper, she proceeds to descend a long flight of steps, which bring her to a door she had not observed before. It is opened with great difficulty; but alas! A rush of wind puts out the glimmering taper, and while Matilda, Gloriana, Rosalba, or any other name, is deliberating whether she shall proceed or return, without knowing how to do either, a groan is heard, a second groan, and a fearful crash. A dimness now comes over her eyes (which in the *dark* must be terrible) and she swoons away. How long she may have remained in this swoon, no one can tell; but when she awakes, the sun peeps through the crevices, for all subterraneous passages must have crevices, and shows her such a collection of sculls and bones as would do credit to a parish burying-ground.

She now finds her way back, determined to make a farther search next night, which she accomplishes by means of a better light, and behold! Having gained the fatal spot where the mystery is concealed, the tapestry moves again! Assuming courage, she boldly lifts up a corner, but immediately lets it drop, a cold sweat pervades her whole body, and she sinks to the ground; after having discovered behind this dreadful tapestry, the tremendous solution of all her difficulties, the awful word

HONORIFICABILITATUDINIBUSQUE!!!

Mr. Editor, if thy soul is not harrowed up, *I* am glad to escape from this scene of horror, and am,

Your humble servant,

A JACOBIN NOVELIST.

The critique was so acute it was long remembered, but it did little to diminish the craze for those 'silly books' which let us into a 'little silent world of fancy' as William Makepeace Thackeray recollected in 1840.[18] It is these silly dangerous books that this book is all about.

Chapter Two
Every True Goth: From Horace Walpole's Strawberry Hill to Thomas De Quincey's Opium Dreams

The rocky and tortured landscapes of Italy, Spain and Bavaria represented to English, Scottish and German writers not only an analogue of the mind but also a political landscape in which Spain, Italy and Germany usually stood for the chaotic and anarchic and England and France stood for sane manners and an ordered constitution. If de Sade suggested France was full of pederastic libertines he was an exception. Against this order was the primeval chaos of the wastelands of the Arctic, the Highlands of Scotland or the peat bogs of Ireland. Victor Frankenstein works on his female monster in the Orkneys and the monster himself vanishes into the frozen wastes of the Arctic. Curiously, despite the centrality of the arctic wastes to *Frankenstein* there was little interest in the area except from whalers, scientists or explorers looking for the North-West Passage. Walton, the overreaching hero at the beginning of the tale appears to be based upon William Scoresby, a real-life scientist obsessed with the Arctic. Scoresby was a scientist and explorer whose father had made a fortune in the whaling trade.

In 1819, Scoresby was elected a fellow of the Royal Society of Edinburgh and published 'On the Anomaly in the Variation of the Magnetic Needle'. He continued to write on the northern hemisphere, and in 1820, he published *An Account of the Arctic Regions and Northern Whale Fishery*.

The scientific interest in the glacial wastes of the Arctic and Antarctic produced no similar outpouring of artistic feeling. They simply were not considered particularly favourable to artistic depictions of the sublime or terrible. William Hodges had a go in the eighteenth century but felt better of it and painted over his canvas with a scene from Polynesia where previously there had been glacial cliffs, a fact only discovered with the help of an X-ray of the picture in 2008. It would be some years before Polar snow and ice would interest any painter.

These rocky and desolate outcrops, especially the romantic islands of Scotland did, however, after a blank period of about 40 years after Hodges, finally prove highly popular with artists and the general public who bought prints and dreamed about desolation. The inaccessible Fingal's Cave was memorialized by Felix Mendelssohn in his Hebrides Suite of 1830. They were nevertheless places on the edge of the world, Such places as the Polar caps were weird places on the very edge of consciousness itself where only God and wild birds lived and where writers like Poe might project fantasies of annihilation.

> Many gigantic and pallidly white birds flew continuously now from beyond the vale, . . . And now we rushed into the embraces of the cataract, where a chasm threw itself open to receive us. But there arose in our pathway a shrouded human figure, very far larger in its proportions than any dweller among men. And the hue of the skin of the figure was of the perfect whiteness of the snow. (*Narrative of A. Gordon Pym of Nantucket*, Chapter 25)

In complete contrast, the 'picturesque' garden had begun in an England that was searching for a corollary of its own imagined stability, discovered anew amidst the Palladian idyll of classical Rome and the Renaissance. Sweeping vistas, waterfalls and temples filled the landscape of the eighteenth century. Such gardens became de rigueur for the rich to be seen in. Charles Hamilton had bankrupted himself by 1773 modelling and remodelling the 250 acres of Painshill near Cobham in Surrey into a naturalistic landscape. Meanwhile Henry Hoare owner of Stourhead in Wiltshire, dammed the river Stour and built classical follies around his newly formed lake: the Temple of Flora and Temple of Apollo as well as gothic ruins filled the views from house and across water. Such sinuous and natural forms began, however, to give way to more fantastical designs which used optical illusion and rambling byways to create tension and surprise in those enjoying the grounds. This gardening was the latest fashion, but was ironically based on the antiquity of gothic ruination. Yet these waterfalls and temples were accompanied by another darker possibility. The fashion for follies, so prevalent in the eighteenth century, may have been based on classicism but it was expressed in medievalism tinged with the torturous architecture of Piranesi.

The first folly had appeared in 1530, built by Girolamo Genga as a ruined cottage for the Duke of Urbino in Italy and the first in England, a mystical building based on the Trinity built by Sir Thomas Tresham at Rushton Abbey in 1593. They were the pointless foibles to rich men's odd taste for the dramatic and it was this pointlessness which made the follies of ruined towers and abbeys so intriguing – odd excrescences in the landscape that told of a fictional past, an imagined history and the sense of a quite fake continuity with the land they were built upon. Follies also provided garden vistas with a point of contemplation, which closer up, as a fake grotto or cave, might prove a harbour for certain illicit liaisons otherwise under social interdict. Above all, such buildings were playful reminders to aristocrats that nothing lasts forever, ironically built at the very moment when such people thought their lifestyle was immune from threat.

> Contemplation, the action . . . most associated with ruins, is already an architectural act. A ruin is a *memento mori*, a reminder of the vanity of human ambitions, the fragility of human powers, and the transience and mutability of things. Like tombstones, they allow us both to sympathise with the poor, superseded past to which they bear witness, and to imagine our own demise, while congratulating ourselves that it is still, for us, sweetly, in the offing. Chateaubriand articulates what had become the conventional view: 'All men have a secret attraction to ruins. This feeling belongs to the fragility of our nature, and a secret conformity between these destroyed monuments and the fleetness of our own existence'.[1]

Thomas Whateley, in his *Observations on Modern Gardening* of 1770, considered that

> All remains excite an enquiry into the former state of the edifice and fix the mind in contemplation on the use it was applied to . . . they

suggest ideas which would not arise from the buildings, if entire . . . Whatever building we see in decay, we naturally contrast its present to its former state and delight to ruminate on the comparison.[2]

Horace Walpole along with most of the gentry of Britain fell for the romance of ruin. Walpole went with friends to visit Netley Abbey near Southampton and came away with the feeling he had been to 'paradise'. The whole edifice only needed making more romantic by the planting of 'cypresses'. Thomas Gray was struck by the legends of the place and wrote in 1764 about a ferryman who rowing him towards the ruins, but admitted that although 'a lusty young lad . . . [he] would not for all the world pass a night at the Abbey, there were such things seen near it!'

Netley was a ruin among ruins and was immortalized by William Pearce in an opera which played at Covent Garden during 1794. His cynical character Phenegan McScrape nevertheless had the cheek to remark that 'it must cost . . . a great deal to keep those ruins in a continuous state of decay'. In 1795, Richard Warner published *Netley Abbey*, a novel about 'a mystery of a horrible nature'. Gray thought the place evoked the sort of fantastic imagination that conjured ghosts at 'noon-day' and of course the whole structure and its history was pregnant with ghosts and curses. The ruins may have been one inspiration for Jane Austen's *Northanger Abbey* and its 'horrible', yet romantic story led the painters Turner and Constable to visit. By the nineteenth century tourists were demanding tea, music and dancing which were provided by some wily cottagers living nearby.

The crowds were drawn perhaps in the hope of seeing the 'grey lady' or 'the nun' who were meant to haunt the site and who had been made famous by the humorous verses of Reverend Richard Barham whose *Ingoldsby Legends* had appeared in *Bentley's Miscellany* edited by Dickens.

> And there was an ugly hole in the wall
> For an oven too big for a cellar too small
> And I said ' Here's a nun has been playing some tricks'
> That horrible hole! It seems to say
> I'm a grave that gapes for a living prey!

Like others, the poetess Susan Evance was drawn to write a sonnet after her experience. It was in the graveyard tradition and called 'Sonnet Written at Netley Abbey'.

> Why should I fear the spirits of the dead?
> What if they wander at the hour of night,
> Amid these sacred walls, with silent tread,
> And dimly visible to mortal sight!
> What if they ride upon the wandering gale,
> And with low sighs alarm the listening ear;
> Or swell a deep, a sadly-sounding wail,
> Like solemn dirge of death! Why should I fear?
> No! seated on some fragment of rude stone,
> While through the Ash-trees waving o'er my head
> The wild winds pour their melancholy moan,
> My soul, by fond imagination led,
> Shall muse on days and years for ever
> flown, And hold mysterious converse with
> the dead!

Ruins were high fashion. The Germans even had a word for the potentiality of ruin in buildings only just built: 'ruinenwert', the china manufacturer Spode produced a 30- piece tableware set of crockery decorated with blue patterned ruins between 1805 and 1815 and Byron applied the idea of ruin to mankind as 'a ruin amidst ruins' in 'Child Harold's Pilgrimage' (l. 4).

The problem was that there was never enough of the medieval to go round; not enough castles, abbeys, manuscripts, silverware, armour. Indeed, the first really systematic armour collection was not started until the 1820s when Sir Samuel Meyrick published his three-volume history, *A Critical Inquiry into Antient Armour*, a study of the armour he had collected. In such short supply were such literary and warlike artefacts that they had to be reinvented anew in a type of Druidic-Celtic-Anglo-Saxon-medieval mélange. The poet Thomas Chatterton sat up faking medieval ballads as did James McPherson, whose mock Celtic forgery 'Ossian' (supposedly discovered by him in 1761) became the watchword of eighteenth-century poets and artists and inspired Napoleon.

In England it all started with Walpole and his obsession with a medieval past that could be 'recreated' in bricks and mortar. For Walpole the past and therefore the dead were 'empty', husks in which to reanimate whatever contemporary fantasy one could afford, which is not to say that Walpole was not serious in his enterprise, just tongue-in-cheek in its execution in the manner of the rich and self assured.

Horace Walpole was born on 24 September 1717, the third son of Sir Robert and Catherine Walpole. His father was the first prime minister of Great Britain. His father and mother were separated and the young Walpole spent most of his time with his mother to whom he was devoted. In 1727, he duly went to Eton where he met Thomas Gray, and in 1735 did the journey from Windsor to Cambridge to study for a degree he did not finally take. In 1739 he went with Gray on a grand tour, imbibed the taste for classicism, met various scandalous women and quarrelled with his travelling companion. Thereafter he was bought sinecure positions in government offices by his father and settled down to the life of a gentleman and a scholar, although one sometimes tinged with strange shadows. Walpole was rather effeminate in appearance, was probably homosexual and his private life was such that the political opposition accused him of being a 'hermaphrodite'; an accusation left unanswered.

In 1747, Walpole purchased Strawberry Hill, a modest house near Twickenham and set about remodelling it in the medieval taste that had begun to fascinate him and Gray. The house itself was a modest country retreat built originally in 1698 and called Strawberry Hill Shot and had once been lived in by the poet laureate Colley Cibber, and in the 1740s it was still a modest house owned by 'three minors of the name of Mortimer' and lived in by a Mrs Chenevix, the wife of a toy shop proprietor. Walpole sublet and began thinking about his grand plans to turn this respectable, but modest house into 'the most celebrated Gothic House in England'. By his death in 1797 Walpole had spent a staggering £20,000 in realizing his fantasy.

To build his dream of 'future battlements' and to turn his 'small capricious house' into a 'Gothick castle', Walpole formed a Committee of 'Taste' with John Chute and Richard Bentley and an advisory group consisting of the builder William Robinson and the Swiss painter Johann Heinrich Muntz, his 'resident artist', who were to scour the cathedrals and ancient sites of England for models and antiques with which to furnish the dream. The house itself was like Walpole's personality, a fay illusion held up by paper and plaster. On 12 June 1753, Walpole wrote to Sir Horace Mann a description of the work completed so far.

> Now you shall walk into the house. The bow-window below leads into a little parlour hung with a stone-coloured Gothic paper and Jackson's Venetian prints . . . From hence under two gloomy arches, you come to the hall and staircase, which is impossible to describe to you, as it is the most particular and chief beauty of the castle. Imagine the walls covered with (I call it paper, but it is really paper painted in perspective to represent) Gothic fretwork: the Gothic balustrade to the staircase, adorned with antelopes (our supporters) bearing shields; lean windows fattened with rich saints in painted glass, and a vestibule [the Armoury] open with three arches on the landing place, and niches full of trophies of old coats of mail.

Walpole's house was followed by the more substantial crenellated pile of Kingsgate Castle, which had been built on the romantic cliff line just outside Broadstairs in Kent by Henry Fox, First Baron Holland. Kingsgate remains typical of the mock gothic that became the taste of every gentleman.

Alongside such taste was an archaeological desire to renovate and discover. Real castles were rebuilt on romantic lines. Alnwick castle in Northumberland had stood since 1309, but it did not stop Elizabeth and Hugh Smithson redecorating the place in the latest 'gothick' style when they came to live there. The castle and its surroundings were improved by Robert Adam and Capability Brown. Such fashionable interest could mean anything from an act of preservation on a ruin such as that of the castle in Eynsford in Kent to the grandeur of the restoration of the medieval fortifications of Carcassonne by Viollet-le-Duc in 1853, where the architect actually had demolished medieval buildings in order to 'restore' the town to its former glory.

Discoveries also excited the archaeological imagination. Thus when excavations in 1804 exposed a shell grotto in Margate, it was immediately thought of as druidic or Roman. Further excavations in

1837 'exposed' rooms that did not appear to have existed in the original find and suggested improvers were at work on what has proved subsequently to be a seventeenth-century Catholic chapel – in other words, the very essence of the gothic. Yet the most spectacular gothic build was the most modern of all and it was the brainchild of a rich West Indian plantation owner.

William Beckford was the son of William Beckford, one of the richest plantation owners in the West Indies and one of the most powerful men in the City of London whose collection of art was housed at Fonthill House in Wiltshire, a mansion rebuilt in the Palladian style during the 1750s, and renamed Splendens for the splendid things it contained. With all his wealth and position as Lord Mayor of London, Beckford was still nouveau riche, but that did not stop him jockeying for social position, something that the son may have obtained if his decidedly strange lifestyle had not offended polite society. Yet when you were 'England's wealthiest son' the rules simply did not count. To express his love of the eccentric rather than the gothic, Beckford decided to rebuild Fonthill. It would be its third incarnation and this time it would be built as an 'abbey'.

Fonthill 'Abbey' in Fonthill Gifford literally towered above the Beckford estate. It was extravagant and monumental, intended by its owner to rival Salisbury Cathedral, whose restorer James Wyatt was to be employed on the project and whose budget of near on half a million pounds would ensure a work both of unprecedented grandeur and mystery, for although the gothic style was well established by 1796, it had never been employed with such abandon for so eccentric and dangerous an owner. Building and rebuilding continued until 1822. The scale of the building ensured that it was painted or engraved by numerous artists including Turner for whom the edifice was a form of the man-made sublime.

The building itself was built to a Hollywood scale: its cruciform structure imitated medieval cathedrals, but retained, despite its monumental scale, the feeling of a domestic house, even if one it would be hard to live in; its great western hall was 120 feet high and had a ceiling buttressed and decorated with spurious heraldry and contained a staircase so vast in its proportions that it dwarfed visitors; two wings extended 400 feet either side; the whole was topped by a great octagonal tower rising 276 feet in the air and dominating the landscape around like the residence of some Tolkienesque wizard. It was, as Kenneth Clark pointed out in 1928, not a gothic building but the product of 'megalomania' and 'the bored eighteenth century'.

This it may have been, but it was also the unconscious model for every vast Hollywood castle interior built during the 1930s and 1940s for the likes of *Dracula*, *Frankenstein* or *The Wolf Man* and like the sets on the Universal backlot the whole affair was an illusion. The tower was built too fast and without proper foundations and fell down. It fell down more than once. There was, in the end, no substance to Fonthill. It was like a dream edifice, a Ruritanian fantasy placed in an English setting for which it was unsuited, because, despite its pretensions to the gothic there was something arabesque in its grandeur that could only be expressed in visionary fiction. The house partly fell down and was partly pulled down. Virtually nothing remained except the dream memory of the place recuperated in Beckford's foray into gothic literature, *Vathek*.

The tale itself is a mock Arabian fable in imitation of Voltaire, Samuel Johnson and others who had filled the eighteenth century with dreams of the east. Originally written in French, Anglophone reader has access to the text through the translation of Samuel Henley who finally published the work as a tale from the old 'Arabian', the whole charade much to Beckford's annoyance.

> [Vathek] is . . . a megalomaniac in everything: and, after a course of comparatively harmless luxury, devotes himself, partly under the influence of his sorceress mother, Carathis, to the direct service of Eblis [Hell]. Crime now follows crime; and, though, in his journey towards the haunted ruins of Istakar (the site of the purgatory of Solomon and the inferno of Eblis himself), he conceives an at least human and natural passion for the beautiful Nouronihar, she is as much intoxicated by the prospect of supernatural power as he is himself. They are at last introduced, by a subordinate fiend, to the famous hall of Eblis, where, after a short interval, they meet with their due reward – the eternal torture of a burning heart – as they wander amid riches, splendours, opportunities of knowledge and all the other treacherous and bootless gifts of hell.[3]

That *Vathek* was influential cannot be denied, but whether it was in good taste might be disputed and it might be disputed all the more because of those the book influenced (Aubrey Beardsley and Oscar Wilde among others). George Saintsbury, writing as late as 1921, thought that

> It cannot be denied that a great part of Beckford's celebrity is derived from, and has been always maintained by, sources which appeal to the more vulgar kinds of human interest. His wealth, which, even at the present day, would be reckoned great, and which, for his time, was immense and almost incredible; his lavish and fantastic expenditure of it; his pose as a misanthropic, or, at least, recluse, voluptuary; his eccentricities of all sorts; his distinguished connections; and even his long life – were powerful attractions of this kind to the vulgar.[4]

In the eighteenth century, the gothic became the alternative to classicism with follies, grottoes, coach houses, grand houses and mock castles, but it was in the nineteenth century that the style went from a rich man's whim to one of British patriotic architecture that would dominate the century. University, parliamentary and ecclesiastical buildings promoted the idea of contemporary thinkers, but dressed them in the bricks and mortar of the thirteenth century. The medieval stood for an ideal of chivalrous 'Catholic' knighthood, gentlemanly behaviour towards women and the lower orders, muscular upright leadership, and proper behaviour in a conservative (if not necessarily in a Tory) manner.

It was Walter Scott in his home at Abbotsford rather that Horace Walpole who turned what was a mere fashion into a tradition that somehow stood for the essence of gentlemanly living. And it was heraldry that proved you had made it into the ranks of those who counted.

> The arms of the leading Border families run round the cornice; the arms of Scott's ancestors run along the crest of the vault. It was scarcely surprising that the reviving interest in chivalry led to a revival of heraldry. . . . now . . . people were increasingly anxious to show that they were connected with the Middle Ages, there was no better way of doing it than by heraldic display. King Edward's Gallery in William Beckford's Fonthill was decorated with 72 coats of arms, . . . such a display helped to conceal the fact that the Beckford's themselves . . . were . . . of very dubious origin. . . . In 1825 Sir Samuel Brydges, . . .

published a book called *Stemnata Illustria* in which the supposed glories of his ancestry were illustrated by a shield containing no fewer than three hundred and sixty quarterings.[5]

Bricks and mortar, stucco and papier mache could transform a perfectly good modern house into medieval pastiche. Gothic remodelling sprang up all over Britain and was often accompanied by the purchase or revival of ancient titles or the adding of 'de' before a plain name, such as de Winton for the more plebeian Wilkins of Walter Wilkins whose gothic pile was erected in Radnorshire. Interminable war with France brought a renewed interest in ballads and medieval tales and French versus Anglo-Saxon chivalry, but it also proved a boom time for castle builders. This lasted about 20 years from 1798 to 1820 in England and includes the work of John Nash and Robert Smirke; in Ireland castles were built by architects such as Francis Johnson; while in Scotland the style was down to Gillespie Graham and Archibald Elliott; William Atkinson rebuilt Abbottsford for Scott in the 'Scottish baronial' style.

Great gates and towers, a symmetry of design, a solidity of material declared that these buildings stood for the rights of those in power, guarded against change by a fake portcullis and a dubious coat of arms. George III had his own castle which was nicknamed 'the Bastille' and was demolished on his death. Every sort of imaginary castle was built and every castle demanded tapestries, armour, heraldry and paintings. Mock castles and castellated mansions were the playthings of the rich, and domestic architecture predated the emergence of other forms of gothic space. Nevertheless, churches were soon being decked out in neo-gothic.

Craftsmen and artists produced volumes of mock medieval tapestry, stained glass and silverwork. Charles Inwood worked on Westminster School, designed chalices and flagons and plate; Charles Leslie, the biographer of John Constable, produced paintings and book bindings; it was Thomas Rickman, a chemist first and architect second, who invented the term 'Early English'; Lewis Vulliamy designed paper houses for noblemen; William Butterfield produced a profusion of chalices, churches and altar crosses in silver and gold; William Burgess, antiquary and architect designed private houses and furniture in the medieval style, his iconography found in mock castles such as that at Cardiff; Sir Gilbert Scott was the designer of Liverpool cathedral at the end of the century.

It was an age of revival with a host of lesser designers, architects, craftsmen and artists all trying their hand at medieval finery: men like Thomas Willement, heraldic designer to George IV; W. G. Rogers wood carver at Kensington Palace and the Brighton Pavilion; Sara Losh, a Cumberland woman who designed and built a church for her village and who employed a local boy William Hindson to do symbolic carving or Moritz von Schwind and his colleagues in Munich who won a competition to design new windows for Glasgow cathedral, but with the proviso that nothing Roman Catholic was allowed to creep into their design. And in 1834 with the wreckage of parliament needing redesigning, it was to Charles Barrie and Augustus Pugin that the committee turned for gothic splendour and modern amenities.

Alongside the craze for medieval building and ecclesiastical silverware there came, imperceptibly at first, a renewed interest in knightly gallantry which translated itself into the code of the gentleman. In 1822, Kenelm Digby produced a manual for chivalrous behaviour called *The Broad Stone of Honour* which contained 'Rules for the Gentlemen of England'. It was an instant hit with expansions and new editions in 1828 and 1829, 1844 to 1848 and had become five volumes by 1877. Digby had become chivalry-mad like many an adolescent with the publications of Scott's romantic poems. His father had even built a wooden abbey as a mausoleum for his dead pets.[6]

The publication of the book meant that Digby could vent his spleen on everybody whom he did not consider a gentleman, which included 'atheists, deists, rationalists, radicals, Americans, utilitarians and supporters of both dictatorship and democracy'.[7] Regardless of his distaste for democrats and radicals the spirit of chivalry quickly assimilated itself into the world of street politics with knights in full armour led the procession which supported Queen Caroline against her husband George IV. Digby may not have thought that dressing up as knights in Arthur's court appropriate to the life of an English gentleman, but others disagreed.

The eccentric and reclusive Charles Lamb created the 'Kingdom of Winipeg', a set of mock medieval hutches for his many hundred guinea pig pets. Lamb constructed an elaborate narrative into which he wove the lives of his pets for whom he created elaborate pedigrees; Queen Cavia and the Knight of Kilgynger lived and died in elaborate castleated mansions with names such as 'cabbage castle . . . the ancient residence of the Counts of Valoise and Cabbage' or were recorded in pen and ink drawings of guinea pig armorial bearings or guinea pigs dressed for war in full armour.[8]

Lamb's half brother, Archibald Montgomerie, thirteenth Earl of Eglington, was bemused by the menagerie but convinced by the chivalry, and so in 1839 decided to hold a full-blown tournament. There was already a craze for the idea of seeing knights in combat, *Ivanhoe* had run in five separate theatrical versions during the 1820s, and suits of armour, if not available from some dusty attic could be bought from Samuel Pratt's showrooms in Lower Grosvenor Street which housed its wares in a gothic apartment. 'To gaze on the plumed casque of the Mailed Knight equipped for the Tournament. . . . encrusted with the accumulated rust of centuries, cannot fail to inspire admiration for the chivalrous deeds of our ancestors' ran the catalogue. The first successful auction of armour had been at Christies during 1789 after which wealthy men would trick out baronial halls with armour retrieved, borrowed or bought, as Lord Lytton did at Knebworth during the 1840s when he transformed the house into a mock Tudor pile complete with armour-filled baron's hall.

Eglington Castle was in Ayrshire and the great and good complete with servants, medieval fancy dress and Grosvenor Street armour travelled up there during a week which threatened rain, in order to reinforce the ideological standpoint of the aristocratic and landowning class of England sorely threatened by the spectre of reform. The hosts blackballed anyone who was not a 'Tory'. The guests were assembled, the knights in place, the heralds ready and the Queen of Beauty about to mount her horse when a clap of thunder announced a storm. The first day was a farce, with heralds, knights and ladies fair drenched and the evening ball ruined: not lances but umbrellas, not helmets but top hats covered the embarrassment of the rich which cartoonists of the day greatly enjoyed. Even Queen Victoria, who did not attend, thought the whole affair 'a great absurdity' in her diary entry for 2 September 1839.

The weather, of course, improved, and knights and fair ladies disported themselves accordingly. Indeed the tournament was lively to the extent that at least two aristocrats fought as if the whole thing were real and not fancy dress!

At least nine artists followed the flower of England to Ayrshire. There was even the painter Edwin Landseer and the pioneer photographer Octavius Hill among them, the result being yet another surge of bad history paintings of which none now merit attention and some of the earliest photographs, taken not at a modern railway station or cotton mill, but of mock-medieval knights dressed for glory. Around 1850, J. O. Fairlie was still happy to dress up for the photographer in the suit of armour he had worn at Eglington.

Victoria and Albert may not have attended the celebrations in the north, but that did not stop them from showing that they could put on a medieval banquet unrivalled by any aristocrat's pretensions. During 1842, the Queen conceived of a fancy-dress ball to be held at Buckingham Palace. Victoria would come as Queen Philippa and Albert as Edward III. It was one of the most expensive royal events ever staged, successful, but pointless. The prime minister saw no reason for the gothic charade, but Prince Albert was full of the medieval and its Germanic sensibility. It was Albert who was the chair of the Royal Commission that decided on the design of the Houses of Parliament in 1841 and it was he that agreed the painted panels of King Arthur in the Queen's Robing Room in the House of Lords. It would be Albert's short stay on the British stage, the aftermath of his death and Victoria's pathological grieving that would put the stamp of medievalism on everything from royal monuments to town halls and railway stations.

They were still jousting in July 1912 when six knights fought at the Royal Tournament as part of the celebrations for the tri-centenary celebrations of 'Shakespeare's England', celebrations conceived by Lady Randolph Churchill and which included a Queen of Beauty carried in a litter with purple plumes. Lord Ashby St Legers won the gold cup from Viscountess Curzon who played the Queen of Beauty.[9]

While the gothic flourished as the key-note style of respectability, another more insidious style took shape, quite other than mock Anglo-Saxon or faux medieval, quite other than clear in its meaning. Gothic orientalism, a strange mixture of chinoiserie, Arabism and Hinduism floated into the late eighteenth century as a psychic disorder. Those who came under its spell were opium eaters, sodomists, pleasure seekers and sensualists. The very word hedonist had only just been invented to describe those who took drugs for 'voluptuous pleasure'.

William Beckford even characterized his secretive homosexual life in terms of Arabian fantasy. In 1807, he had taken to calling himself Barzaba, a play on the Syriac word for voluptuary, and referred to the Seven Dials slum near Covent Garden as 'the Holy Land' where he could look for boys who were willing to 'kiss the relics' (1 July 1812). Beckford was ever on the look out for young men as if they were objects d'art. He finds a tight-rope walker who takes his fancy, but he vanishes. Not to be put off Beckford sets his 'friend' Franchi to 'find the earthly paradise'. 'Many have sought in vain' sighs Beckford, 'some in Syria or Mesopotamia, some in Abyssinia others in Ceylon', but (Beckford, following the scent like a connoisseur after rare antiquities) tracks his amour down to 'Bristol'. On his travels he was accompanied by an Albanian called Ali-dru who enjoyed the illicit pleasures of The Turkish Bath with him and Beckford named his second house near Bath 'Baghdad' and topped it with yet another phallic tower (but unlike Fonthill, one that stayed erect).

The pleasures of eighteenth-century cottaging were nothing compared to the heroic walks of repressed poets. Walking one day from Porlock to Lynmouth in November 1797, on one of his marathon hikes with William Wordsworth was Samuel Taylor Coleridge who was considering a monumental 'prose-tale' or 'verse-romance' as the two hiked along. The two poets passed by the coastal scenery (the Valley of the Rocks) that would form the basis for 'Kublai Khan', the most famous of all romantic oriental excursions. On the way, Coleridge was seized with stomach cramps brought on by dysentery which forced him to rest at a nearby farmhouse. While there he took two grains of opium and fell asleep for three hours during which time he sleep-hallucinated 'between two and three hundred lines of poetry' which came to his senses not as ideas but as 'things', of which he recollected and transcribed 54 lines before that tiresome 'person . . . from Porlock' made him forget the rest. Coleridge recognized it for a 'psychological curiosity', the workings of the unconscious mind under the influence of bodily persuasion which had produced a string of hallucinatory and surreal images made up of the fragments of

Coleridge's reading both of *Purchas His Pilgrimage*, from whence comes 'Cublai Can', and Maurice's *History of Hindostan*, from whence the 'sunny pleasure dome' and 'caves of ice'. Embedded within the orientalist framework is however a gothic nightmare straight out of Gottfried Burger, the author of the gothic horror poem, 'Lenore' (see Chapter Three).

> But oh! That deep romantic chasm which slanted
> Down the green hill athwart a cedarn cover!
> A savage place! As holy and enchanted
> As e'er beneath a waning moon was haunted
> By woman wailing for her demon-lover!

If poor poets could only dream of pleasure domes, rich men could build them and in 1783, George, Prince of Wales was advised to take the waters at the small fishing village of Brightonstone. He bought a house in which he could recuperate and entertain his mistress Lady Fitzherbert with relative discretion. The house soon proved too small, and in 1787 Henry Holland was commissioned to rebuild the modest farm into a neo-classical building. It was now known as the Marine Pavilion, although this eventually proved unsatisfactory and John Nash was called in 1815 to remodel the whole into an oriental fantasy. The Moghul exterior with its dome and minarets was to be complemented by an interior of rococo chinoiserie, the whole called 'Indo-Saracenic' and to include the barbarous and the sensual and to have a level of bizarrerie that would be both entrancing and phantasmagorical. Despite the fact that the workmanship was at first so shoddy the roof-leaked, the affair was completed by 1823.

Inside was as weird and as exotic as the outside: The music room was lit by nine lotus-shaped chandeliers under which Italian operas would entertain guests; the walls were of a Chinese red, decorated with fantastic Chinese scenes; the banqueting hall was surmounted by one gigantic candelabra fitted into a palm tree design and held in place by a winged dragon clamp; the royal apartments more restrained but decorated with Chinese wallpapers; the kitchens, meanwhile, opulently appointed with four cast iron columns disguised as palm trees, were so grand that visitors were escorted round them – fitting tribute to a palace of sensual appetite.

This appetite for eastern promise would be increased with the appearance of Byron's *Don Juan*, whose licentious scenes outraged some and titillated others. The poem was endlessly plagiarized and pirated by radical booksellers finding it hard to make a living out of revolution and who turned increasingly to pornography in the years around 1817. Byron's harem section was what caused all the fuss, and it was this section of the poem that stimulated the erotic fascination with the seraglio that had started with *Vathek* and was to continue for another 100 years.

With its assortment of eunuchs, slaves, and odalisques as well as hookahs, hashish, and perfumes, the harem evoked endless sexual fantasies in the West that revolved around violent incarceration and limitless sensuality.[10]

The idea of the vampire certainly owes some of its origins to Byron's oriental poem 'The Giaor'.

> A turban carved in coarsest stone,
> A pillar with rank weeds o'ergrown,
> Whereon can now be scarcely read
> The Koran verse that mourns the dead,
> Point out the spot where Hassan fell
> A victim in that lonely dell.
> There sleeps as true an Osmanlie
> As e'er at Mecca bent the knee;
> As ever scorn'd forbidden wine,
> Or pray'd with face towards the shrine,
> In orisons resumed anew
> At solemn sound of "Alla Hu!"
> Yet died he by a stranger's hand,
> And stranger in his native land;
> Yet died he as in arms he stood,
> And unavenged, at least in blood.
> But him the maids of Paradise
> Impatient to their halls invite,
> And the dark Heaven of Houris' eyes
> On him shall glance for ever bright;

They come – their kerchiefs green they wave,
And welcome with a kiss the brave!
Who falls in battle 'gainst a Giaour
Is worthiest an immortal bower.

But thou, false Infidel! shall writhe
Beneath avenging Monkir's scythe;
And from its torments' scape alone
To wander round lost Eblis' throne;
And fire unquench'd, unquenchable,
Around, within, thy heart shall dwell;
Nor ear can hear nor tongue can tell
The tortures of that inward hell!
But first, on earth as Vampire sent,
Thy corse shall from its tomb be rent:
Then ghastly haunt thy native place,
And suck the blood of all thy race;
There from thy daughter, sister, wife,
At midnight drain the stream of life;
Yet loathe the banquet which perforce
Must feed thy livid living corse:
Thy victims ere they yet expire
Shall know the demon for their sire,
As cursing thee, thou cursing them,
Thy flowers are withered on the stem.
But one that for thy crime must fall,
The youngest, most beloved of all,
Shall bless thee with a *father's* name –
That word shall wrap thy heart in flame!
Yet must thou end thy task, and mark
Her cheek's last tinge, her eye's last spark,
And the last glassy glance must view
Which freezes o'er its lifeless blue;
Then with unhallow'd hand shalt tear
The tresses of her yellow hair,
Of which in life a lock when shorn
Affection's fondest pledge was worn,
But now is borne away by thee,

Memorial of thine agony!
Wet with thine own best blood shall drip
Thy gnashing tooth and haggard lip;
Then stalking to thy sullen grave,
Go – and with Gouls and Afrits rave;
Till these in horror shrink away
From Spectre more accursed than they!

Byron's own exoticism inspired Caroline Lamb's novel, *Glenarvon*, from which John Polidori in his turn stole the name Ruthven for the Byronic vampire of his short story, 'The Vampyre'. Byron, partly in his poetry, partly in the company he kept, but especially in his life, exemplified the exotic and the decadent and the seductively wicked.

George Noel Gordon, the man who would inspire nearly as many biographies as Napoleon, was born on 22 January 1788. Byron was born with a famous club foot, a disability much remembered, but little commented upon, because it was relatively unnoticeable, by his closest friends. At the age of ten, the boy inherited his great uncle's estate at Newstead Abbey and happily played among its decay and ruination until whisked off to school at Dulwich and later Harrow where, as with many others, he formed homosexual attachments.

By 1808, Byron was already feeling the effects of moral corruption in 'an abyss of sensuality' and had fallen in debt. When he turned 21 he took his place in parliament and went on the grand tour, especially enjoying Greece and Turkey and writing 'Childe Harold', which proved a sensation when published on his return to England in 1811.

In 1814 he married Anne Isabella Millbanke, got drunk a lot, fought a lot, lost money and separated in short order. By this time his relationship with Lady Caroline Lamb and the hints of incest with his sister Augusta Leigh were enough to send him into exile never to return. And it was on these travels that Byron settled at the Villa Diodati with the ménage that included Shelley, Claire Clairmont, John Polidori and Mary Godwin.

More books made Byron more famous and more infamous, the sale of Newstead Abbey made him debt free and adventurous, spending the next little while in Italy where he was contacted in 1823 by the London Greek Committee, which was at that time trying to form an army of liberation against the Turks. In Greece, Byron raised troops and returned to that homosexual lifestyle that Polidori hints at in 'The Vampyre'. A hero to the Greeks, but reviled at home, when Byron died of a fever in 1824 he was refused a memorial in Westminster Abbey. Thus died the one person who in his life's spirit exemplified the gothic and in whose strange tastes the gothic found material and imaginative form.

> [The Countess of] Blessington reports in Conversations, that Byron had a mild prepossession for worms and special predilection towards vampires. 'Do you know' said Byron 'that when I look on some face that I love, imagination has often figured the changes that death must . . . produce . . . the worm rioting on lips now smiling, the features and hues of health changed to the livid and ghastly tints of putrefaction . . . this is one of my pleasures of imagination'.[11]

Many years later Herbert Read thought Byron to be 'the only English poet who might conceivably occupy . . . the position held by the Marquis de Sade'. But Byron left a legacy of doomed aristocracy rather than debauched libertinism.[12] His grandson recalled that his grandfather 'had a fancy for some oriental legends of pre-existence, [that] took up the part of a fallen or exiled being, expelled from Heaven or sentenced to be a new avatar on earth for some crime; existing under a curse'.[13] The arabesque was Byron and Byron was arabesque and he knew it and played to it.

Byron was drawn to oriental decadence, and a favourite decadent novel of his was *Zofloya* by Charlotte Dacre, a tale of murder and sexual longing set in and around Venice. Indeed, it was Venice rather than any other European city that exemplified many the gothic spirit, something which Thomas Mann took up in the plague-ridden novella, *Death in Venice*, and that was still fascinating writers as late as Daphne du Maurier's *Don't Look Now* of 1970. Venice was a city of intrigue, dissembling and masquerade, a city of dangerous liaisons and murderous assassins. Even to the Venetians their palazzos and strange waterways were intriguing and slightly forbidding.

In tune with the spirit of the city and the times, Piero di Cosimo came up with this amusing idea as early as the fifteenth century for a masqued progress in the crowded byways of the city.

The triumph was a huge chariot drawn by buffaloes, black all over the painted with human bones and white crosses, and over the chariot was a huge figure of Death, with scythe in hand and all around the chariot were a large number of covered tombs; and at all the places where the triumph halted . . . these tombs opened, and from them issued figures draped in black cloth, on which were painted all the bones of a skeleton on their arms, breast, backs, and legs: and all this, . . . struck the eye as fearsome and horrible. And the dead, at the sound of certain muffled trumpets with harsh and mournful tones, came forth from the tombs and seating themselves upon them sang to music full of melancholy . . . This dreadful spectacle . . . filled the whole city both with terror and with wonder.[14]

Thus by 1806, when Dacre came to write *Zofloya*, Venice had long been a decadent, mind-altering and subversive space. In the city she situates a story of passion that subverts and reverses the moral narrative style of Ann Radcliffe by infusing it with elements from de Sade and Matthew Lewis: cruelty, deceit and above all female dreams of sexual freedom and power predominate. But more subversive of all is the heroine's desire for the black servant *Zofloya*, where 'uncommon sensations filled [Victoria's] bosom as she observed her proximity to the Moor' (Chapter 20) and whose 'eyes wandered with admiration over the beauty of his form' (Chapter 19) but whose nobility disguises (but also reinforces) the fact that he is Satan himself.

Dacre herself was as exotic, free-willed and mysterious as her characters. She was actually named Charlotte and was the daughter of one Jonathan King, himself born Joseph Rey (possibly of Sephardic Jewish origin) in 1771 or 1772, and published her first poems in 1798 under the name of Rose Matilda in the complex Della Crusca School fashion of the late eighteenth century. Thereafter she became the mistress of Nicholas Byrne, the editor of the *Morning Post*, with whom she had three children before getting married on 1 July 1815. Byrne himself was actually murdered under circumstances worthy of a gothic novel.

One winter's night, or rather morning, nearly forty years ago, when Mr. Byrne 'was sitting alone in his office, a man entered unchallenged from the street, and made his way to his room. He wore a

crape mask, and rushing upon his victim stabbed him twice with a
dagger. The wounds proved mortal but no London paper reported
the murder. Herd concludes that 'we must assume . . . that the attack
did take place . . . and that no one outside of the office knew anything about it. We must further assume that knowledge of the attack
was limited to one or two trusted members of his staff, and that
Bryne was still sufficiently master of himself to command them at
once to silence about the affair'.[15]

Thereafter Charlotte Byrne vanishes from history, dying in 1825,
her literary output entirely forgotten. Her female characters,
alternatively palpitating with 'voluptuous pleasure' or seething with
'bitterest hatred', and who have no time for 'female delicacy', but
instead take who they want or kill who is in their way; who have no
feelings for loving parents, who are not afraid to become mistress to
those they may not marry or become the lovers of Satan, such women
were too strong for all but Byron's taste and soon vanished with the
appearance of the heroines of Jane Austen and her ilk.

Yet perhaps the most haunting landscape was that of Egypt, which
since Napoleon's invasion and discovery of the Rossetta Stone had
taken a marked hold of the Western mind. The discovery of a 'new'
style of Pharoanic architecture soon attracted British architects.
Antiquarians like Sir John Soane were willing to pay over the asking
price (and outbid the British Museum) for a gem of Egyptian funerary ware. Although never as pervasive as the neo-classical or gothic,
the Egyptian taste was to be found across England in buildings as
diverse as public halls, theatres and cemeteries.

London's Mansion House had its banqueting hall designed in the
Egyptian style by George Dance the Elder, although this was a space
that was Egyptian in name only as the design was called Egyptian
from the arrangement of columns as laid down by Palladio. Far more
Egyptian was the Egytian Hall in Piccadilly, a theatre and exhibition
space designed by G. F. Robinson in 1812. Here customers were
greeted by a façade reminiscent of an Egyptian temple and inside
treated to the spectacle of such human freakery as 'the human
skeleton', 'the Siamese twins', 'Tom Thumb', 'Millie Christen',
the 'two headed nightingale' (black American co-joined twins) and
'the Missing Link', a man-monkey who was in fact an acrobat in an

outfit! There were also exhibitions such as Bonaparte's carriage and collections of natural history.

Nevertheless, what attracted the imagination were ancient Egyptian tombs, sarcophagi and mummies which seemed both mysterious, and attractive and forbidding. At first the taste for such things was relatively comic in tone with characters such as Carathis, Vathek's mad mother and literature's first mad scientist, happy to invoke all the demons of hell with a little mummy powder.

> By secret stairs, contrived within the thickness of the wall, and known only to herself and her son, she first repaired to the mysterious recesses in which were deposited the mummies that had been wrested from the catacombs of the ancient Pharaohs. Of these she ordered several to be taken. From thence she resorted to a gallery where, under the guard of fifty female negroes, mute and blind of the right eye, were preserved the oil of the most venomous serpents, rhineoceros' horns, and woods of a subtile and penetrating odour procured from the interior of the Indies,. Together with a thousand other horrible rarities.

Mary Shelley would compare European mountains to 'shining pyramids' in Frankenstein and even suggest that the monster himself was a reanimated mummy.

> Over him hung a form which I cannot find words to describe – gigantic in stature, yet uncouth and distorted in its proportions. As he hung over the coffin, his face was concealed by long locks of ragged hair; but one vast hand was extended, in colour and apparent texture like that of a mummy. (Chapter 24)

What finally set the architectural tone for the Egyptian, which was a fashion always slightly modish and decidedly freakish was a morbid interest in funerary fashion and ritual which began with the need for an architectural style for the private cemeteries which sprung up in the 1840s and 1850s. The apotheosis of this interest in funerary architecture was Highgate Cemetery, where an Egyptian Avenue was constructed in 1851.

The avenue, still there today, is reached through a Pharoanic arch and the tombs themselves consist of small rooms with shelves to 'house' the dead. When reading *Dracula* it is here that readers often suppose the location of the tomb of the vampire Lucy Westernra. The belief is erroneous but that hasn't stopped film makers using the site (or its recreation) for numerous horror movies. This is especially so with the Hammer remake of *Dracula*, which in 1958 started the trend and nor has it scotched rumours of real vampires lurking in the ruins, the last panic being during the 1970s. The Egyptian Avenue has in a 100 years gone from a symbolic place of peace to a place of popular horror.

Literary interest did not die out and by the 1830s, Poe was having fun with a 'Conversation with a Mummy', but the full potential of the applicability of Egyptian models for gothic sensation were not to emerge until the discovery of Tutankhamen's tomb in1922 and the subsequent journalistic spin of ancient curses. From then on the world of ancient Egypt would become as exotic as the world of Transylvania. The notion of curses, arcane rituals, the walking dead and the winding chambers of the pyramids would be sufficient to offer ideas to a whole industry of 1920s American pulp writers.

H. P. Lovecraft, most famous of all pulp writers, was commissioned to write a piece on Egypt involving the adventures of Harry Houdini, which he completed for *Weird Tales* as a substitute for a honeymoon. The piece, called 'Imprisoned with the Pharoahs' was published in May 1924 and focussed on the gothic scenario of being incarcerated in the labyrinth below the pyramids, a labyrinth in which nameless horrors worship at 'terrible altars' of an 'Unknown One before ever the known gods were worshipped'. It leads to one unmistakable conclusion.

The monstrosities were hailing something which had poked itself out of the nauseous aperture to seize the hellish fare proffered it. It was something quite ponderous, even as seen from my height; something yellowish and hairy, and endowed with a sort of nervous motion. It was as large, perhaps, as a good-sized hippopotamus, but very curiously shaped. It seemed to have no neck, but five separate shaggy heads springing in a row from a roughly cylindrical trunk; the first very small, the second good-sized, the third and fourth equal and largest of all, and the fifth rather small, though not so small as the first. . . . The Great Sphinx! – that idle question I asked myself on that sun-blest morning before . . . *what huge and loathsome abnormality*

was the Sphinx originally carven to represent? Accursed is the sight, be
it in dream or not, that revealed to me the supreme horror – the
unknown God of the Dead, which licks its colossal chops in the
unsuspected abyss, fed hideous morsels by soulless absurdities that
should not exist. (Imprisoned with the Pharoahs)

For Lovecraft, the horror of pyramidal life was the suggestion
of extra-terrestrial life. The idea, though potent never caught the
imagination as well as another implication from Ancient Egypt – the
reanimation of a mummy. The idea was put to extensive use in Bram
Stoker's novel, *The Jewel of the Seven Stars*, in which the taboo of
interfering with the dead finds full expression, but it was not until
the Universal movie of 1932 that the tale took on its modern shape.
Here an expedition from the British Museum (excavating in 1921)
finds and accidentally reanimates the mummy of Im-Ho-Tep (played
by Boris Karloff), who wanders the environs of Cairo in search of his
lost love, the 'corpse bride' Princess Anck-es-en-Amon whom he left
behind millennia ago and whom he hopes to resurrect through the
'rebirth' of a living woman, the supposed reincarnation of his
original lost love. This is what makes this version of the story, with its
exotic backdrop of 1920s or 1930s Cairo, its idea of a fated British
museum expedition, the back story of ancient Egypt, the sense of evil
waiting to be reborn, the romantic love story and imprisonment in
the Pyramids, the first gothic tale that had a life as a movie screenplay
rather than an adaption of an older novel.

Fantasies of the Orient were different from the realities of the
Middle or Far East which had a strange way of turning up at the
English gentlemen's door. Eastern visions fascinated and terrified
Western imaginations. Coleridge was so traumatized by his childhood reading of 'the tale of a man who was compelled to seek for a
pure virgin', which he found in *The Arabian Nights*, that he could not
stop reading even though it caused both waking fantasies and nightmares. His father was eventually forced to burn the book.[16]

There was always Thomas De Quincey, lowly born, a runaway
from his school in Manchester, a tramp, a dosser on floors in
London, a friend of prostitute and Jews and a self-styled 'opium-
eater' at seventeen. He is a man for whom the east was a morbid
procession of nightmare images of pure otherness. De Quincey

relates a strange tale of the east in *The Confessions of an English Opium Eater*. He is in his cottage in the Lake District, disturbed one day by a knocking on his door, which when opened reveals a Malay 'seaman' standing in the doorway. The Malay does not speak; he wears 'loose trousers and a turban'. It is a great mystery. Why is he there so far from a port, unable to speak a single word of English? The servant girl (Barbara Lethwaite) thinks him from some distant planet or a 'demon' whom her master can 'exorcise'; De Quincey tries out the only eastern word he knows (in Turkish), it is the word for opium, but gets no response so he tries some odd lines from the Iliad spoken in Greek. Still he gets no response. The Malay lays down and sleeps the night. In the morning De Quincey offers him some grains of opium.

> I presented him . . . with a piece of opium. To him, as a native of the East, I could have no doubt that opium was not less familiar than his daily bread; and the expression of his face convinced me that it was. Nevertheless, I was struck with some little consternation when I saw him suddenly raise his hand to his mouth, and bolt the whole, divided into three pieces, at one mouthful. The quantity was enough to kill some half dozen dragoons. ('The Pleasures of Opium')

And yet who or what was this mysterious Malay – hallucination or tangible phantom?

> The mischief, if any, was done. He took his leave, and for some days I felt anxious; but, as I never heard of any Malay, or of any man in a turban, being found dead in any part of the very slenderly peopled road between Grasmere and Whitehaven. ('The Pleasures of Opium')

During the Spring of 1818, that wily Malay returned to haunt De Quincey's dreams, not by appearing in them, but by acting as the motivational force behind them. De Quincey's nightmares are filled with 'Asiatic scenery' which terrifies and paralyses his senses. In his delirium, partly brought on by drinking laudanum, China, India and Egypt coalesce and the teeming life of Asia crystallizes into the antediluvian mud of the Nile. Everything comes to life and that which should not move *moves*.

> If I were compelled to forego England, and to live in China, among Chinese manners and modes of life and scenery, I should go mad. The causes of my horror lie deep, and some of them must be common to others. Southern Asia, in general, is the seat of awful images and associations. . . . No man can pretend that the wild, barbarous, and capricious superstitious of Africa, or of savage tribes elsewhere, affect him in the way that he is affected by the ancient, monumental, cruel and elaborate religions of Hindostan. The mere antiquity of Asiatic things, of their institutions, histories, above all, of their mythologies &c, is so impressive, that to me the vast age of the race and name overpowers the sense of youth in the individual. A young Chinese seems to me an antediluvian man renewed. . . . most swarming with human life, the great *officina gentium*. . . . In China, over and above what it has in common with the rest of Southern Asia, I am terrified by the modes of life, by the manners, by the barrier of utter abhorrence placed between myself and *them,* by counter-sympathies deeper than I can analyse. I could sooner live with lunatics, with vermin, with crocodiles or snakes. . . . I brought together all creatures, birds, beats, reptiles, all trees and plants, usages and appearances, that are found in all tropical regions, and assembled them together in China or Hindostan. From kindred feelings, I soon brought Egypt and her gods under the same law. I was stared at, hooted at, grinned at, chattered at, by monkeys, by paroquets, by cockatoos. I ran into pagodas, and was fixed for centuries at the summit, or in secret rooms; I was sacrificed. ('The Pains of Opium')

The uncanny came in Oriental guise and it brought both personal and philogenic fears. Such fears combined the fear of the other and the fear of psychic invasion. In the end, the Orient would even define a type, the master criminal bent on world domination. Dracula himself comes from the 'east as is the epitome of the master criminal'.

> The Count is a criminal and of a criminal type. Nordau and Lombroso would so classify him, and qua criminal he is of an imperfectly formed mind. (Chapter 25)

Such too is Sax Rohmer's Dr Fu Manchu, the character he created in 1913 as an amalgam of German evil and Chinese cunning, born near a graveyard and imbued with a brow like Shakespeare, waiting like a spider in the depths of Limehouse to destroy the Empire. Such too is Ian Fleming's Dr No, working in the laboratory for SPECTRE, his hands replaced by pincers, gliding silently towards world domination.

Chapter Three
With Raven Wings: Ann Radcliffe, German Horrors and the Divine Marquis

In March 1796, readers of the popular *Monthly Magazine* were treated to a translation of an original German ballad called 'Lenore', but in the translation of William Taylor transmuted to the rather more anglicized 'Lenora'. The poem was a sensation with several translators vying to be first in print and translations being made continuously into the twentieth century, the poem influencing the whole of the Romantic movement.

The narrative concerned a long and protracted war from which the knights were only now returning. Lenore watches for the return of her William, but to no avail. She despairs and despite her mother's pleas abjures God. William mysteriously returns in the night and, although evidently 'dead', carries off Lenore in her night shirt to be his bride. As they reach the graveyard the morning comes up and William enters the tomb and turns to a skeleton while his horse vanishes. Lenore is left dying with the spooks of the graveyard around her awaiting the judgement of Heaven.

> And when hee from his steede alytte,
> His armour, black as cinder,
> Did moulder, moulder, all awaye,
> As were it made of tinder.
>
> His head became a naked skull;
> Nor haire nor eyne had hee:

His body grew a skeleton,
Whilome so blithe of blee.

And att his dry and boney heele
No spur was left to be;
And inn his withered hande you might
The scythe and hour-glasse see.

The poem had been written by Gottfried August Bürger. The poet, the son of a Lutheran pastor, was born on New Year's Day in 1748. Seen as a wayward child, Bürger was sent to study theology, but changed his mind twice, first to the law and then to literature. By 1771 things had improved and Bürger was not only a new district magistrate, but also a poet with a growing reputation. In 1773, 'Lenore', a ballad based on Bürger's love of all things English-folksy, and especially on the English taste for the border ballad revival, was published in the collection *Musensalmanach* for that year, and Bürger's fame, at least locally, was assured. It was assured in Anglo-German circles as well, and translations of his work, both poetry and short stories, soon appeared in Britain. Walter Scott translated Bürger's 'Der Wilde Jäger' and had a major success with 'The Wild Huntsmen' which he published in Matthew Lewis's *Tales of Wonder* in 1796. Lewis provided his own version of Lenore in 'The Ballard of the Water King' which he included in Chapter Eight of *The Monk*.

With gentle murmur flowed the Tide,
While by the fragrant flowery side
The lovely Maid with carols gay
To Mary's Church pursued her way.

The Water-Fiend's malignant eye
Along the Banks beheld her hie;
Straight to his Mother-witch He sped,
And thus in suppliant accents said:

'Oh! Mother! Mother! now advise,
How I may yonder Maid surprize:
Oh! Mother! Mother! Now explain,
How I may yonder Maid obtain.'

The Witch She gave him armour white;
She formed him like a gallant Knight;
Of water clear next made her hand
A Steed, whose housings were of sand.

The Water-King then swift He went;
To Mary's Church his steps He bent:
He bound his Courser to the Door,
And paced the Church-yard three times four.

His Courser to the door bound He,
And paced the Church-yard four time three:
Then hastened up the Aisle, where all
The People flocked, both great and small.

The Priest said, as the Knight drew near,
'And wherefore comes the white Chief here?'
The lovely Maid She smiled aside;
'Oh! would I were the white Chief's Bride!'

He stept o'er Benches one and two;
'Oh! lovely Maid, I die for You!'
He stept o'er Benches two and three;
'Oh! lovely Maiden, go with me!'

Then sweet She smiled, the lovely Maid,
And while She gave her hand, She said,
'Betide me joy, betide me woe,
O'er Hill, o'er dale, with thee I go.'

The Priest their hands together joins:
They dance, while clear the moon-beam shines;
And little thinks the Maiden bright,
Her Partner is the Water-spright.

Oh! had some spirit deigned to sing,
'Your Partner is the Water-King!'
The Maid had fear and hate confest,
And cursed the hand which then She prest

But nothing giving cause to think,
How near She strayed to danger's brink,

Still on She went, and hand in hand
The Lovers reached the yellow sand.

'Ascend this Steed with me, my Dear;
We needs must cross the streamlet here;
Ride boldly in; It is not deep;
The winds are hushed, the billows sleep.'

Thus spoke the Water-King. The Maid
Her Traitor-Bride-groom's wish obeyed:
And soon She saw the Courser lave
Delighted in his parent wave.

'Stop! Stop! my Love! The waters blue
E'en now my shrinking foot bedew!'
'Oh! lay aside your fears, sweet Heart!
We now have reached the deepest part.'

'Stop! Stop! my Love! For now I see
The waters rise above my knee.'
'Oh! lay aside your fears, sweet Heart!
We now have reached the deepest part.'

'Stop! Stop! for God's sake, stop! For Oh!
The waters o'er my bosom flow!'
Scarce was the word pronounced, when Knight
And Courser vanished from her sight.

She shrieks, but shrieks in vain; for high
The wild winds rising dull the cry;
The Fiend exults; The Billows dash,
And o'er their hapless Victim wash.

Three times while struggling with the stream,
The lovely Maid was heard to scream;
But when the Tempest's rage was o'er,
The lovely Maid was seen no more.

Warned by this Tale, ye Damsels fair,
To whom you give your love beware!
Believe not every handsome Knight,
And dance not with the Water-Spright!

'Lenore' remained popular throughout the nineteenth century, being re-translated by Dante Gabrielle Rossetti and directly affecting the tales and poetry of Poe and Longfellow. The ballad was even recalled by Bram Stoker, who gives a line of the poem to a Carpathian peasant on the first encounter with Dracula in the Borgo Pass.

'You cannot deceive, my friend; I know too much, and my horses are swift, as he spoke he smiled, and the lamp light fell on a hard-looking mouth', with very red lips and sharp-looking teeth, as white as ivory. One of my companions whispered to another the line from Bürger's 'Lenore': –

'Denn die todten reiten schnell' – ('for the dead travel fast.') (Chapter 1)

Bürger's success was due to the growing internationalization of the gothic style in literature. Whereas neo-gothic architecture was an essential English style (which spread in the nineteenth century to America and was later adopted to the peculiarities of the Scottish baronial), gothic thrills knew no particular national boundaries. In 1790, the Scots poet Robert Burns found celebrity with the tongue-in-cheek tale of a drunk who encounters the devil and a coven of witches. 'Tam O'Shanter' became instantly famous combining as it did a satire on Scottish attitudes, broad Scots dialect and a sly wink towards the new-found interest in Celtic ballads and folk tales.

> Inspiring bold John Barleycorn!
> What dangers thou canst make us scorn!
> Wi' tippenny, we fear nae evil;
> Wi' usquabae, we'll face the devil!
> The swats sae ream'd in Tammie's noddle,
> Fair play, he car'd na deils a boddle,
> But Maggie stood, right sair astonish'd,
> Till, by the heel and hand admonish'd,
> She ventur'd forward on the light;
> And, wow! Tam saw an unco sight!
>
> Warlocks and witches in a dance:
> Nae cotillon, brent new frae France,
> But hornpipes, jigs, strathspeys, and reels,

Put life and mettle in their heels.
A winnock-bunker in the east,
There sat auld Nick, in shape o' beast;
A towzie tyke, black, grim, and large,
To gie them music was his charge:
He screw'd the pipes and gart them skirl,
Till roof and rafters a' did dirl. –
Coffins stood round, like open presses,
That shaw'd the Dead in their last dresses;
And (by some devilish cantraip sleight)
Each in its cauld hand held a light.
By which heroic Tam was able
To note upon the haly table,
A murderer's banes, in gibbet-airns;
Twa span-lang, wee, unchristened bairns;
A thief, new-cutted frae a rape,
Wi' his last gasp his gabudid gape;
Five tomahawks, wi' blude red-rusted:
Five scimitars, wi' murder crusted;
A garter which a babe had strangled:
A knife, a father's throat had mangled.
Whom his ain son of life bereft,
The grey-hairs yet stack to the heft;
Wi' mair of horrible and awfu',
Which even to name wad be unlawfu'.
Three lawyers tongues, turned inside oot,
Wi' lies, seamed like a beggars clout,
Three priests hearts, rotten, black as muck,
Lay stinkin, vile in every neuk.

Many European, Scandinavian and American authors tried their hand at the genre if only once. In Germany there was Karl Theodor Korner, Johann Karl August Musaus, Johan Apel, Alois Wilhelm Schreiber and plenty of anonymous writers whose stories such as the 'The Hall of Blood', 'The Spectre Barber' and 'The Fatal Marksman' were quite enough to thrill adults and juveniles alike, with their melodramatic and often misleading woodcut frontispieces acting as a cheap come-on. Respectable German authors also tried their

hand: Johann Wolfgang von Goethe produced 'The New Melusina';
Friedrich von Schiller, 'The Ghost-seer' and Johann Ludwig Tieck,
'The Bride of the Grave', while E. T. A. Hoffman produced a collection of truly weird short stories from 1816; Mozart's *Magic Flute* is
itself shot through with 'gothic' elements.

In France there were François Buculard D'Arnaud, Charles
Pigault-Lebrun, Eugene Sue and even Donatien Alphonse François
de Sade (the Marquis de Sade), as well as a host of scribblers who
remained anonymous, while Scandinavia produced works with titles
such as 'Valdwulf or The Fiend of the Moor' and Italy the anonymous 'Maredata and Guilio'. America was also entranced by gothic
ruins, although it had none, and soon adapted the genre to its
peculiar circumstances. Washington Irving and Charles Brockden
Brown were the first of a number of writers including Nathaniel
Hawthorne, Charles Hoffman, Sutherland Menzies (who wrote the
first werewolf story) and Edgar Allan Poe.

The Germanic taste was partially home grown and partially
imported (mainly from Britain). Even before the defeat of Jena and
the humiliation of French occupation, German academics had been
exploring the folk tales of greater Germany. Jakob and Wilhelm
Grimm collected folk tales both from middle class as well as folk
sources and progressively worked them up into their *Kinder- und
Hausmarchen* which they perfected over several editions between
1812 and 1857 and wrote up in several rough versions from 1810
onwards. The first version in English was edited by Edgar Taylor
soon after. The history of the tales shows a certain reciprocity between
the gothic and the fairy story and while Grimm's tales are both
instructional and moral, aimed at children, progressively Christian
and imbued with a happy ending, the body of many of the tales, with
their journeys into an ambiguous world of forests, witches, woodcut-
ters, wolves and wicked stepmothers conjures up the terrors of gothic
abandonment. Such dangers are minimized and made humorous in
the werewolf tale 'Little Red-Cap' (Little Red Riding Hood), but are
left strange and disturbing elsewhere. In the 1810 Olenberg manuscript of (Hansel and Gretel) we meet the threat at the heart of the
forest in the person of the witch.

> The old woman, however, had only pretended to be friendly. She was
> really a wicked witch on the lookout for children, and had built the

house made of bread only to lure them to her. As soon as she had any children in her power, she would kill, cook and eat them. It would be like a feast day for her. Now, witches have red eyes and cannot see very far, but they have a keen sense of smell, like animals.[1]

These 'naïve' tales for children fitted the general literary taste for the weird and uncanny and could be exploited by contemporary writers to suggest, at one and the same time, the distance and the similarity between children's stories and those for adults; children's fears upgraded to adult neurotic or psychotic states:

It is a wicked man who comes after children when they go to bed and throws handfuls of sand in their eyes, so that they jump out of their heads all bloody, and then he throws them into his sack and carries them to the crescent moon as food for his little children, who have their nest up there and have crooked beaks like owls and peck up the eyes of naughty children. (ETA Hoffman, 'The Sandman')

Moreover the fairy story beginning was almost an analogue of the beginning of all fiction which dealt with the fantastic.

'I tormented myself to begin [the story] in a significant . . . fashion. 'Once upon a time' – the loveliest opening for any story'. ('The Sandman')

The English rediscovery of the 'folk' ballad fitted a 'völkisher' mentality that was quick to associate the gruesome passages in Shakespeare with the 'folk' tales of the Black Forest. Shakespeare, at least for a time, spoke German to his listeners. From this joint German and Anglo-Scottish interest in all things romantically strange, including such peculiarities as 'the corpse bride', the 'Wandering Jew', the 'living' portrait, the spectre-haunted graveyard and the 'wilde jager' or hunt of the dead, emerged a new so-called German gothic school of horror.

This style infiltrated English gothic and mixed with the sentimental tale of terror that Ann Radcliffe had made popular, in which most of the terrors are explained and a happy ending with reunited lovers prescribed. Indeed, it was tales of terror, rather than German horror, that characterized British gothic writing up to the 1790s and it was

Radcliffe and her followers who exemplified the style best. Radcliffe was born in Holborn on 9 July 1764, just a few months before the publication of Walpole's *Otranto* and the invention of the genre in which she would find fame. She was the daughter of a haberdasher and his well-connected wife and as she grew up she was able to mix with London's literary celebrities. In 1787 she married William Radcliffe, the owner and co-editor of the *English Chronicle*, changed her name from Ward to Radcliffe and began to write. Radcliffe stopped writing in 1797 after *The Italian* perhaps unable to compete in the harsher 'school of horror' then coming from Germany, perhaps because she was depressed, but not because she was insane through writing too many gothic books as her contemporaries believed.

Radcliffe may have stopped writing but the fashion for Radcliffe-style sublime landscapes went on regardless. It got on the poet Shelley's nerves. In a review in *The Ant-Jacobin Review and Magazine* of January 1812, he wrote of one of her imitators,

Had not the title-page informed us that this curious 'Romance' was the production of 'a gentleman,' a freshman of course, we should certainly have ascribed it to some 'Miss' in her teens; who, having read the beautiful and truly poetic descriptions, in the unrivalled romances of Mrs. Ratcliffe [*sic*], imagined that to admire the writings of that lady, and to imitate her style were one and the same thing. Here we have *description run mad;* every uncouth epithet, every wild expression, which either the lexicographer could supply, or the disordered imagination of the romance-writer suggest, has been pressed into . . . service . Woe and terror are heightened by the expressions used to describe them. Heroes and heroines are not merely distressed and terrified, they are 'enanguished' and 'enhorrored.'

Nor are the ordinary sensations of *joy* or even *delight,* sufficient to gratify such exalted beings. No, when the hero was pleased, not only did he experience 'a transport of delight'; *burning ecstasy revelled through his veins; pleasurable coruscations were emitted from his eyes.* Even hideous sights acquire an additional deformity under the magic of this 'gentleman's' pen. We read of 'a form more hideous than the imagination is capable of portraying, whose proportions, gigantic and deformed, were seemingly blackened by the *inerasible traces of the thunderbolts of God.*'[2]

German gothic was stranger, more metaphysical, supernatural and creepy than English 'terror'; more interested in the occult, pseudo-science and weird societies and concerned not with female sensibilities but with brooding and dangerous Byronic anti-heroes whose mesmeric gaze was an invitation to the delights of Hell. It was a literature of shudders, well suited, despite its peculiar taste for graveyards and corpses, to psychological exploration of irrational states and to the idea of the soul without God.

Even its national settings were different from those of Radcliffe, no longer France and Italy, but Spain and Germany. The ascriptions 'from the German' or 'translated from the German' were quite enough to whet the British appetite for 'Germanic' ghouls and scenes of torture. Mary Shelley, Matthew Lewis and Charles Maturin were greatly influenced by German ideas of the sublime and horrible as was Poe in America. This newer hardening of the attitude towards gothic thrills may be seen in the replacement of the menaced female by the appearance of the 'corpse bride' or 'bleeding nun' which superseded her.

A figure entered, and drew near my bed with solemn measured steps. With trembling apprehension I examined this midnight visitor. God almighty! It was the bleeding nun! It was my lost companion! Her face was still veiled, but she no longer held her lamp and dagger. She lifted up her veil slowly. What a sight presented itself to my startled eyes! I beheld before me an animated corse. (*The Monk*, Chapter 4)

This taste for everything macabre, whether 'Italian' in origin or 'German', even extended to people's funerary arrangements and their own homes. Lady Elizabeth Nightingale's tomb in Westminster Abbey is a fine example of a very early goth monument in an age of rococo. It was designed by Louis-François Roubiliac in 1761 and influenced by Bernini. Nevertheless, the grotesqueness of the monument, complete with a very realistic skeleton emerging from an open vault to aim his spear at the deceased, owes less to the influence of the great Italian than to the eighteenth-century taste for the graveyard picturesque. The whole effect is a masterpiece of terror and of a certain 'Catholic' taste for torment and suffering, is grisly rather than consolatory.

The eccentric architect and collector Sir John Soane whose house was already full of broken Roman fragments, sarcophagi and pictures by Fuseli (Johann Heinrich Füssli), completed the eccentricity of his dwelling in Lincoln's Inn Fields with a 'crypt' set aside for the imaginary monk 'Padre Giovanni' which not only included his skull but also his grave (actually the burial place of Soane's dog). This little suite of rooms was called the monk's parlour and cell, and guests were ushered in by candlelight to participate in this rather unusual and satiric entertainment. For the most part, and despite the tongue-in-cheek attitude taken to the genre, German gothicism was taken very seriously by many authors.

The two poles of 'German' gothic horror are Hell and mental torture, the one exemplified by Matthew Lewis's *The Monk* (1794), the other by Charles Maturin's *Melmoth the Wanderer* (1820); the ruling image is of death, the central symbols cosmic annihilation (*Frankenstein* [1818]) and the invasion of supernatural otherness beyond rational consciousness (*Dracula* [1897]); the underlying theme: the withdrawal or non-existence of God and the long night of the soul beyond salvation. All 'German' gothic writing in the English style is balanced between these poles and these four books, whether authors are writing in imitation or in rejection.

The gothic did not develop all at once but evolved in phases and by multiplication and development of its originating tropes: from 1764 to the 1820s when it was concerned with external threats, such things as graveyards, ghostly monks, medieval coats of armour, curses and banditti; from the 1830s when psychological terrors turned the landscape inward and into a hallucinatory phantasmagoria fuelled by opium and wild dreams, erotic and horrible by turns; and with the coming of film, at first silent, then with sound, in which the directors of Hollywood and Germany invented a new gothic with light and shadow and sound.

By the 1820s the major tropes of the genre, except the werewolf, were in place. From then on there really has been only variation and intensification, of which the move from tales which were 'terror-filled' burlesques to tales which were psychologically serious was the most significant and remains the longest lasting. The literary gothic lost a certain ironic humour in the Romantic period which it never regained, *Melmoth the Wanderer* signifying the plunge into the tortured night of the soul.

It is often forgotten that the tropes of the genre developed slowly and discontinuously. The original tales were concerned as much with

Horace Walpole's castles as with William Beckford's arabesque, with Ann Radcliffe's pseudo-horrors of Italy, with Mary Shelley's Arctic wastes, with Matthew Lewis's and Charles Maturin's horrors of the Spanish monastery, the 'corpse bride' or 'the Wandering Jew'. Not yet for them the floating spectre in the twilight mist nor the Transylvanian undead (John Polidori's vampire is associated with ancient Greece and Scotland) nor the old dark house of American imagination nor yet the psychopathic stalker or terrified teenager. These were in the future as was the infusion of Freudian themes. Yet these later developments were really analogues of the literary tropes invented between 1764 and 1820 and the legal, religious and political tropes that preceded them.

The tropes of the gothic while usually confined to tales of terror or 'horror' lent themselves to other modes of writing, namely the detective story, the thriller and women's romance, and anticipated these sub-gothic genres in plotting and characterization. At the heart of gothic fiction is a mystery, as it is in these other genres, whether the mystery be of death or love. Later gothicism allowed writers to produce villains who might not be supernatural but criminal, heroes whose honour was a result of moral fibre and who did not have to be aristocrats disguised as peasants, locked-room mysteries which no longer required the room to be either a dungeon or a monk's cell.

Peculiarly, it was Ann Radcliffe writing at the very height of the first wave of Romantic gothicism who realized, in books like *The Mysteries of Udolpho* (1794), that gothic tropes could be used to banish gothic atmospheres and dispel the irrational. Fifty years later, during the 1840s, the first modern fictional detective banished the evil conjured up by gothic atmospheres. Here in a crumbling corner of the Faubourg St Germain, Edgar Poe's C. August Dupin and his narrator companion rent their strange home.

> I was permitted to be at the expense of renting, and furnishing in a style which suited the rather fantastic gloom of our common temper, a time-eaten and grotesque mansion, long deserted through superstitions into which we did not enquire . . .
>
> Had the routine of our life at this place been known to the world, we should have been regarded as mad men . . . Our seclusion was perfect. We admitted not visitors. . . . We existed within ourselves alone.

It was a freak of fancy in my friend . . . to be enamoured of the
Night for her own sake; and into this *bizarrerie*, . . . I quietly fell. . . .
at the first dawn of the morning we closed all the massy shutters of
our old building; lighted a couple of tapers which strongly perfumed,
threw out only the ghastliest and feeblest of the rays. By the aid of
these we then busied our souls in dreams. . . . ('The Murders in the
Rue Morgue')

Gothic horror on the other hand is about that which should *not*
be, whose comprehension is the end of sanity and the opening of the
abyss, in which cursed state of knowledge of the forbidden becomes
manifest, the veil is withdrawn and the fabric of the material universe
falls to dust. For that which 'should not be' to manifest itself to
consciousness, making visible the otherness of cosmic indifference, is
a profoundly disturbing, terrifying and sublime moment, but it is
also play, masquerade, toying, a delicious fiction by which we fake
our own terror for the sake of mere pleasure.

The gothic went from being merely a set of despised literary
and architectural devices to a way of life and a way of thinking
about the self which spread with the coming of European Romanticism. Its modus operandi was however still defined by the literary.
Indeed, its adherents struck poses that they had learned from the
books they had read and these books were a prescription for psychological states that remained without classification until the twentieth
century.

At its most extreme, gothicism is the antithesis of the rational but,
curiously, it is also the rational testing its limits both as carnival and
as revolution. Its obsession is with death. This death masquerades at
first as that prescribed by the Church, but by degrees the notion loses
its idea of Heaven and comes much closer to annihilation. Hell
remains triumphant still (at least in British novels) to 1800, but the
withdrawal of the spiritual and the advance of the material leaves the
space of religious belief devoid of God, dogma or priest but also
leaves a residual ritualism and fascination with arcana and the occult
which dominates the Romantic period and beyond. Death is moreover now tied to an erotic element in which the erotic value of death/
sex is the ultimate experience, worked out obsessively in the visions
of de Sade or the bite of the vampire.

The gap, which existed between attraction and repulsion, manifested itself in the eighteenth century when the aristocratic imagination first toyed with the possibility of its own annihilation. The medieval world conjured up in the hothouse gothic of the middle- to late eighteenth century was not a return to the flowering of Catholic Europe, but a worm-ridden nightmare of corpses, tombstones and ruined cloisters. The 'trellised' sky of Burgundian illustration was replaced by jagged lightening bolts and clashing thunder, the City-on-the-Hill was replaced by dark Teutonic forests, heaving cataracts and storm-filled skies.

Yet this was mere toying, but toying with a sinister foreboding of actual doom. In the tales of Radcliffe it is no longer social standing that counts. For this daughter of a Holborn draper it would no longer be sufficient just to be an aristocrat, one would now have to earn moral superiority, and the way in which her heroine's combine moral bearing and physical resilience aligns them with the virtuous peasants who inhabit her landscapes and stand in contrast to those dissolute and stupid aristos or the nouveaux riche whose money means crassness and vulgarity. For de Sade, of course, it was the very wealth of the rich that made them 'barbarians' and 'libertines' who could prey with impunity on the poor and whose wealth protected them against the prosecutions of justice. For both de Sade and Radcliffe aristocracy represented a trap.

Even the homes of the wealthy were built to catch the virtuous. Such dwellings are the belly of the beast. Radcliffe's Emily, wandering in the depths of Montoni's castle in *Udolpho*, fears that she might 'again lose herself in the intricacies of the castle' and de Sade's Justine (in his novel *Justine*) is continuously trapped in the aristocratic labyrinth of which a monastery remains the foremost exemplar, at once castle, prison, harem and brothel. One of the inmates explains to Justine that,

> The church and the pavilion form what is properly called the monastery; but you do not know where the building we inhabit is situated and how one gets here; 'tis thus: in the depths of the sacristy, behind the altar, is a door hidden in the wainscoting and opened by a spring; this door is the entrance to a narrow passage, quite as dark as it is long, whose windings your terror, upon entering, prevented you from

noticing; the tunnel descends at first, because it must pass beneath a moat thirty feet deep, then it mounts after the moat and, leveling out, continues at a depth of no more than six feet beneath the surface; thus it arrives at the basements of our pavilion having traversed the quarter of a league from the church; six thick enclosures rise to baffle all attempts to see this building from the outside, even were one to climb into the church's tower; the reason for this invisibility is simple: the pavilion hugs the ground, its height does not attain twenty-five feet, and the compounded enclosures, some stone walls, others living palisades formed by trees growing in strait proximity to each other, are, all of them, at least fifty feet high: from whatever direction the place is observed it can only be taken for a dense clump of trees in the forest, never for a habitation; it is, hence, as I have said, by means of a trap door opening into the cellars one emerges from the obscure corridor of which I gave you some idea and of which you cannot possibly have any recollection in view of the state you must have been while walking through it. This pavilion, my dear, has, in all, nothing but basements, a ground floor, an entresol, and a first floor; above it there is a very thick roof covered with a large tray, lined with lead, filled with earth, and in which are planted evergreen shrubberies which, blending with the screens surrounding us, give to everything a yet more realistic look of solidity; the basements form a large hall in the middle, around it are distributed eight smaller rooms of which two serve as dungeons for girls who have merited incarceration, and the other six are reserved for provisions; above are located the dining room, the kitchens, pantries, and two cabinets the monks enter when they wish to isolate their pleasures and taste them with us out of their colleagues' sight; the intervening story is composed of eight chambers, whereof four have each a closet: these are the cells where the monks sleep and introduce us when their lubricity destines us to share their beds; the four other rooms are those of the serving friars, one of whom is our jailer, another the monks' valet, a third the doctor, who has in his cell all he needs for emergencies, and the fourth is the cook; these four friars are deaf and dumb; it would be difficult to expect, as you observe, any comfort or aid from them; furthermore, they never pass time in our company and it is forbidden to accost or attempt to communicate with them. Above the entresol are two seraglios; they are identical; as you see, each is a large chamber edged by eight cubicles; thus, you understand, dear girl, that, supposing one were to break through the bars in the casement and descend by the window, one would still be far from being able to escape, since there would remain five palisades, a stout wall, and a broad moat to get past: and were one even to overcome these obstacles, where would one be? In the monastery's courtyard which, itself securely shut, would not afford, at the first moment, a very safe egress. A perhaps less perilous means of escape would be, I admit, to find, somewhere in our basements, the opening to the tunnel that leads out; but how are we to explore these underground cellars, perpetually locked up as we are ? were one even to be able to get down there, this opening would still not be found, for it enters the building in some hidden corner unknown to us and itself barricaded by grills to which they alone have the key. However, were all these difficulties vanquished, were one in the corridor, the route would still not be any the more certain for us, for it is strewn with traps with which only they are familiar and into which anyone who sought to traverse the passageways would inevitably fall without the guidance of the monks. (Chapter 21)

The aristocratic mind may have embraced the gothic as a 'jeu d'esprit, but revolutionary democrats took up the genre as an act of class war. Both Victor Frankenstein and his monster are democrats.[3] 'The republican institutions of our country have produced simpler and happier manners than those which prevail in the great monarchies that surround it', muses Victor (Chapter 6), while the monster watching the comings and goings of his adopted 'peasant' family hears of 'the division of property, of immense wealth and squalid poverty' (Chapter 13) leading him to consider his own monstrous democratic body. With the gothic aesthetic, democrats pushed the aristocratic to its limits and took a foible of the literary and artistic fancy and made it central to it is vision of sublimity.

The gothic split into the fanciful and the furious but failed to recognize its two aspects, thereafter confusing readers and reviewers alike. The gothic was, all at once, aristocratic burlesque and serious middle-class writing. Gothicism was now not merely a form of low entertainment but a low entertainment whose 'high' and democratic message could shake the very concept of social cohesion. At its core, as entertainment and as ontological enquiry was the central destructive sense of annihilation (of virtue, of sanity, of existence) which *raises* our awareness and presents us with the frisson of our own mortality. In the gothic mode, democratic romanticism with its deification of the plain and humble, rural and rustic, ordinary and mundane found a voice for difficult political and epistemological questions.

Democratic gothicism replaced the playful, but actual power of aristocratic gothicism, with a concern for the 'will to power', but this drive had as its goal only destruction. Here gathers democratic 'man' spurred on by the quest for forbidden knowledge where he becomes a 'moral' aristocratic, whose own journey to the gates of Hell is determined by the accidental discovery of occult formulae, lost diaries, curious liquids or secret passageways. In rising above the mass and in experiencing the exquisite tortures of destruction, the adventurer in arcane realms rises to a transcendence of feeling denied to the rest of us, in the gutter but looking at the stars, as Oscar Wilde had it.

The archetypal democratic 'aristocrat' is the bachelor professor, the wayward archaeologist, the mad doctor or the haunted inheritor and each comes to inhabit the endless corridors, the ruined chambers and the crazy and alchemical laboratories of the abandoned space of the real aristocrat. Once such doomed adventurers step into the forbidden they transmogrify from the professional and bureaucratic servants of the everyday whose hobby is merely the outré, into the frightened amateurs who have seen too much and whose destiny is death. In going 'beyond', such characters obtain moral transcendence in an age of the banal and join the select ranks of 'those who have witnessed': an aristocracy of fellow sufferers.

Relieved of their everyday function, gothic heroes and heroines lose their role in society (they are often only children or orphans) only to gain acute self-awareness and the exquisite knowledge of the beyond, forming thereby a superior caste, above and beyond the mundane. This is the perfect gothic attitude, but it carries the danger of a rift with the real, stranding gothic characters in scenarios they cannot escape precisely because they have imagined them into reality. The worry over imagination is exemplified by the character Emily in Radcliffe's *Mysteries of Udolpho*. Emily's father even warns his daughter against that excessive sensitivity to life which would otherwise overwhelm reason. Emily, it turns out, nevertheless, has exactly what it takes to be a gothic heroine. Her father just does not get the point, not realizing that he exists, not in life as the voice of Enlightenment good sense, but in a book of gothic sensation.

> Your sorrow is useless. Do not receive this as merely a common-place remark, but let reason therefore restrain sorrow. I would not annihilate your feelings, . . . I only teach you to command them. (Chapter Two)

In warning against the 'false philosophy' of sentiment and emotional extravagance, Emily's father misunderstands that these are necessary virtues in a daughter of the gothic. It is through the usual contradictions of gothic literature that this very sensibility, so useless in life, but so handy in fiction, saves our heroine from the fate of her common-sense aunt, Madame Cheron, imprisoned in an Italian castle at the hands of the wicked Count Montoni.

For Radcliffe the whole atmosphere of her books was charged with excessive sensibility, but while the atmosphere is almost alive with actual emotion or its analogues (music, footsteps, voices), the message is conservative and restrained. Again and again the author reminds us that this is fiction and in fiction, unlike life, there is much that is permissible. Her conservative message to her readers of recuperated and conserved energy is in contrast to that of Matthew Lewis for whom the gratification of desire *in real life* is the consequence of reading the excessive in fiction.

The prevailing feeling of the typical gothic heroine is melancholic. A head filled only with images of the grand, sublime and terrible and with banditti and noble peasants is bound to become 'melancholy', a word that, in all its variations, fills almost every page of the work of Radcliffe. There is 'melacholy charm', 'pensive melancholy', 'delicious melancholy', 'unaffected melancholy' and every variation between, in fact so many analogues of sublimity and romance, that the repetition becomes a type of grammar or ritual wordplay.

Exquisite melancholy was not English, however, but German and it filled the European mind with a new and morbid vision of the sensitive soul. This new sensibility came from Goethe's novella *Die Leiden des Jungen Werther* (*The Sorrows of Young Werther*) of 1774 and it caught a universal mood among sensitive types.

The hero is a young man typical of the alienated over-educated intelligentsia that the German states found so difficult to employ constructively. At the beginning of the book he comes to the country to recuperate from various pressures and miseries. He is charmed by the sunshine and simplicity around him. . . . [He] dallies with Charlotte a delightful local girl who shares his taste in poetry. But she is betrothed to Albert, and in an attempt to avoid confrontation, Werther leaves . . . snubbed by the petty aristocracy and deeply in love he . . . returns to Charlotte, who rejects him. Now he . . . reflects despairingly on life . . . [all] appears stormy and cruel. [Finally] Werther shoots himself with a pistol lent by Charlotte and Albert.[4]

The emotional appeal of this story was immense and seemed to open floodgates of dangerous emotion. Not only suicide à la Werther but murder à la Werther became fashionable; not only suicides, but murderers with Werther in their pocket. Napoleon, who suffered from energy and ennui all his life felt the prevailing mood. At seventeen he was writing how, 'I return home to dream by myself, and submit to the liveliness of my own melancholy: what turn will it take today? Towards Death . . .'[5] It was a state of mind that would last for at least the ten years from Austerlitz to Waterloo.

Werther was also one of three books that Frankenstein's monster reads and it exemplifies his despair.

Sorrows of Young Werter [*sic*], beside the interest of its simple and affecting story, so many opinions are canvassed and so many lights thrown upon what had hitherto been to me obscure subjects that I found in it a never-ending source of speculation and astonishment. The gentle and domestic manners it described, combined with lofty sentiments and feelings, which had for their object something out of self, accorded well with my experience among my protectors and with the wants which were forever alive in my own bosom. But I thought Werter himself a more divine being than I had ever beheld or imagined; his character contained no pretension, but it sank deep. The disquisitions upon death and suicide were calculated to fill me with wonder. I did not pretend to enter into the merits of the case, yet I inclined towards the opinions of the hero, whose extinction I wept, without precisely understanding it. (Chapter 15)

It is 'Werther' which occasions the monster's meditation upon his own condition, his own abandonment by his maker seals him inside a mental straightjacket which is more and more identifiable with the isolated artistic temperament, foreshadows the life and deaths of artists as diverse as Thomas Chatterton and Tchaikovsky and the fictional moodiness of a character such as Heathcliff. The monster's self-questioning is the first real expression during the nineteenth century of the existential crisis of those who felt that they were abandoned by God and who sought revenge for this abandonment. The problematic sentiments worried Mary Shelley (who 'Christian-ized' later editions) as they did movie audiences when *Frankenstein* was turned into film in 1931 and 1935.

I learned from Werter's [sic] imaginations despondency and gloom . . . I applied much personally to my own feelings and condition . . . I was dependent on none and related to none. 'The path of my depar-ture was free,' and there was none to lament my annihilation. My person, was hideous and my stature gigantic. What did this mean? Who was I? What was I? Whence did I come? What was my destina-tion? These questions continually recurred, but I was unable to solve them. (Chapter 15)

Such problematic musings were the product of the nature worship that had grown into a cult since the French Revolution and that obsessed the Romantic poets and philosophers of the sublime such as Burke. Radcliffe is full of the imagined 'romantic scenery' she would not visit but that would send tourists scurrying to the Alpine regions of Italy or France or their native equivalent in the English Lake District.

Emily could not restrain her transport as she looked over the pine forests of the mountains upon the vast plains, that, enriched with woods, towns, blushing vines, and plantations of almonds, palms and olives, stretched along, till their various colours melted in distance into one harmonious hue, that seemed to unite earth with heaven. Through the whole of this glorious scene the majestic Garonne wandered; descending from its source among the Pyrenees, and winding its blue waves towards the Bay of Biscay.

The ruggedness of the unfrequented road often obliged the wanderers to alight from their little carriage, but they thought themselves amply repaid for this inconvenience by the grandeur of the scene; and, while the muleteer led his animals slowly over the broken ground the travellers had leisure to linger amid these solitudes, and to indulge the sublime reflections, which soften, while they elevate, the heart, and fill it with the certainty of a present God! Still the enjoyment of St Aubert was touched with that pensive melancholy, which gives to every object a mellower tint, and breathes a sacred charm over all around. (*The Mysteries of Udolpho*, Chapter 3)

It is precisely here in this meditation which gives to the landscape its 'sublime' aspect and where the 'sacred charms' of the scenery prove the existence of 'a present God' that a hidden danger may lie. What 'transports' Emily is NATURE not God, who is a mere inference of the landscape. What would prove to be the study of nature would not be theology but science.

Romantic Gothicism had unwittingly discovered the path to Hell and no one knew that road better than the Marquis de Sade whose *Justine* was published in 1791 and reissued continuously until 1801 when the orders of Napoleon put a temporary end to its career. *Justine* still is scandalous and if not gothic at least one of the major influences on *The Monk* and *Melmoth the Wanderer* and a hidden influence on *Frankenstein* (where natural justice does not prevent a second Justine being guillotined for a murder she has not committed) as well as a commentary on all of Radcliffe's oeuvre.

In *Justine*, the heroine does not win through on virtue alone nor enjoy a virgin's peace at the novel's happy ending. Instead she is debauched, sodomized, raped, crucified and branded for the sake of her virtue, finally cut to pieces by a lightening strike. At the heart of the novel, however, is not sex but nature and the impulses of nature, a survival of the fittest nightmare world. 'Is this existence other than a passage each of whose stages ought only, if he is reasonable, to conduct him to that eternal prize vouchsafed by Virtue'? Asks the deluded Justine, 'who will avenge us if not God?' she cries in despair.

'No one. . . absolutely no one' answers one of her torturers. Another makes it quite clear that nature is cruel and blind and actually opposed to Christianity. 'The Doctrine of brotherly love is a fiction we owe to Christianity and not to Nature', exclaims one of the monks in the Abbey in which Justine is incarcerated.

These were just the extreme views of those whose minds had found an equilibrium with revolutionary times and they could hardly have gone unnoticed by those who cared and who wished to refute Atheism, nature worship, Deism or Unitarianism. Revisionists found their voice in a clergyman who knew about science. William Paley was commissioned to prepare a refutation of 'atheism' and scientific enquiry by the Bishop of Durham and in 1802 published *Natural Theology*, a book whose central metaphor of the 'dropped watch' was intended to suggest the design of the universe by a maker, albeit a maker no longer present. God was diffused throughout nature. So far the argument may have satisfied Deists and Pantheists alike. So far, so good and Paley was happy to employ the language of automata, hydraulics and mechanics to prove his point.

It was an argument which might almost have satisfied Erasmus Darwin, then one of the most industrious thinkers and scientists of his age, to whom Paley's watchmaker was nothing less than the 'Great Architect' of the universe. Darwin is actually mentioned in the Preface to *Frankenstein* as a radical scientist who believed artificial life at least possible. The fact that Mary Shelley immediately refutes the claim on which the whole of 'The Modern Prometheus' is based suggests special pleading. This is a work of 'fancy' not merely based on scientific musings but also a commentary on those musings which confused contemporary critics looking either for a moral or at least an unambiguous ending. Shelley may have been hedging her bets or merely running out of fictional options for her to leave religious ambiguity behind. Such ambiguity was dangerous in a work which also espoused republican sentiments.

What if you are a man-made monster like Frankenstein's creation – a mechanical man made from various bits of dead tissue, but ontologically whole, imbued with moral sense, knowing your designer, but not his purpose, and the only creature on earth whose circumstances of birth are not natural but who seems to possess a soul nevertheless? The result is nature which turns on man, kills its maker, and murders God. 'He is dead who called me into being' raves the monster in despair; the 'fallen angel becomes a malignant devil' and nature freezes over in the wastes of the Arctic circle, the least hospitable place for human existence.

Gothic heroes and heroines worry about everything, and so they might in their circumstances, because everything is or could be significant in the scheme of their narratives: an abandoned piece of paper covered with poetry; a closed cabinet; a creaking door which is locked on the outside; a portrait which is veiled or distant music or footsteps thrill and terrify which give notice of the sublime and exquisite faculties of mind of the central character. Indeed, it is almost a central requirement of the heroine (or hero) that they 'resonate' with the vibrations of nature. Empathy is essential. Henry Clerval, Victor Frankenstein's best friend and a man who has dedicated his life to scholastic learning rather than the business of the counting house of his father is 'a being formed in the "very poetry of nature"' and he will die at the hands of a monster barred from the balm of nature.

This mental and emotional flight from quotidian realities ensures gothic heroes and heroines have such acute hearing, taste and feeling that even life itself becomes painful, because it is imperfect and unutterably dull. It is the origins of ennui, that curious mental disease of the mid-nineteenth century that affects everyone in gothic writing from Roderick Usher (with his 'hysteria' and 'hypochondria'; his sensitivity to sound and colour) to Sherlock Holmes (with his cocaine, shag tobacco and violin) and even Dracula, who although undead and beyond hope, may still hear the wolves' howl and remark wistfully, 'listen to them – the children of the night. What music they make', a most cadenced and poetical response and one dreamily beyond mundane concerns! (Chapter 2)

The 'sensitive' attitude would be adopted universally by artists at the end of the nineteenth century and by artistic types ever since. The perfect mentality for gothic shocks is also the one that travels nearest the borderline with that cosmic madness that will eventually overwhelm it, as E. T. A. Hoffman demonstrates.

Nathaniel was running about on the gallery, raving and leaping high into the air, and screaming: 'Spin, spin, circle of fire! Spin, spin, circle of fire!'. People came running at the wild screaming and collected below; among them there towered gigantically the advocate Coppelius, who had just arrived in the town and had made straight for the market-place. Some wanted to enter the tower and overpower the mad man, but Coppelius laughed and said: 'Don't bother: he will soon come down by himself,'. . . . Nathaniel saddening stopped as if frozen; then he stooped, recognised Coppelius, and with the piercing cry: 'Ha' Lov-ely *occe!* Lov-ely *occe!*' he jumped over the parapet.

As Nathaniel was lying on the pavement with his head shattered, Coppelius disappeared into the crowd. ('The Sandman')

No one knows more about ontological crises than the characters that inhabit gothic fiction. Their personalities and actions are, to use the word in its most general sense, modern. That is, they represent a type of person whose existence becomes codified during the eight-eenth century, but remains with us today. This 'new' person is defined by being 'holistic', in possession of that essential term 'inalienable rights'. Such persons represent a world of equality, where republican-ism coalesces with the democratic. In becoming unique individuals, the citizens of the new democratic idea also become the embodi-ment of ordinariness: liberty, equality, fraternity and sorority make their appearance. Yet the idea of inalienable rights (offered first to a wide world in *The Declaration of Independence* and embodied in pro-gressive human rights legislation ever since) also left a feeling of unease that everything was capable of being 'alienated', detached, unhinged.

When Thomas Jefferson and the signatories of *The Declaration of Independence* enshrined the primary condition of human nature as endowed with inalienable rights the words are already haunted by the terror of those rights that are inherently *alienable*. Rather than just a declaration of independence from the ancient regime, Jefferson's formulation is both prediction and nostalgia: a prediction of the new free and independent individual and nostalgia for a golden age before the age of alienation. Independence brought on an existential crisis, of cosmic aloneness or alienation. The whole free man was now the most alienated, once history has no other sign except the human. Jefferson declared the beginning of that 'post' history which came to its apotheosis in France with the beheading of Louis XVI. Inalienable rights are declared only in an age where such rights are actually alienable.

Anna Letitia Barbauld, Ann Radcliffe, William Godwin, Coleridge, Percy and Mary Shelley, John Polidori, Lord Byron and Charlotte Smith among others were advocates of radical politics and supported the French Revolution. *The Anti-Jacobin Review* considered the gothic to be an effeminate, revolutionary and French, and de Sade concluded rather disingenuously that the gothic was 'the inevitable fruit of the revolutionary shocks felt by the whole of Europe'. It was however, the anonymous 'Jacobin' in his letter to the editor of *the Monthly Magazine* who summed up the background to the advent of horror tales by comparing literature to the current political climate. In 'The Terrorist System of Novel-Writing', the correspondent suggested that there had been a profound change in the writing of novels since 'Monsieur Robespierre, with his system of terror . . . taught our novelists that fear is the only passion they ought to cultivate [and] that to frighten and instruct were one and the same'.[6]

The embodiment of rights was already compromised by the possibility of its divisibility. 'Despondency and melancholy' were from now on, if one is to believe Wordsworth, the lot of those poets and others too sensitive for the world. Dorothy Wordsworth, Mary Lamb, Samuel Taylor Coleridge and Friedrich Hölderlin were among the victims of this new sensitivity to life.

Coleridge became increasingly obsessed with the relationship between mental, imaginative, emotional and physical states. In May 1801 he told a friend Thomas Poole his self-diagnosed problems in great detail, while in a letter of 1804 he could write that, '[he was] heart-sick and almost stomach-sick of speaking, writing, and thinking about myself'.[7] Such morbid interest in the self led Coleridge to invent a word for his woes: 'psychosomatology'. His interest in the imagination which he explored in great detail in *Biographia Literaria* also led Coleridge to formulate a theory that equated the 'I' of self with the self-contained 'I' of God. Yet this equation was riven with anxiety. Coleridge had begun taking laudanum (opium in solution – usually wine) as early as 1796, a decade later he was an opium addict and in December 1813 so deranged by the addiction that he feared the sort of mental collapse that might confine him to a straightjacket.

An indefinite, indescribable, TERROR[*sic*], as with a scourge of ever restless, ever coiling and uncoiling SERPENTS drove me on from behind . . . From the sole of my foot to the crown of my head there was not an inch in which I was not continually in torture.[8]

It was an age of madmen during the reign of that Hanoverian who was himself a mad king. The old 'history' of theological conflict ended in the American and French republican experiments. From now on 'history' would be about the conflict of political ideologies. Yet, 'post history' was also the age of modern psychology and existential aloneness.

The progressive landscape of Romanticism also contained its opposition, the dark response of modern alienation. For Matthew Lewis and Charles Maturin, perhaps taking their licence from the latent anti-papism of the British as well as the anti-religious bias of the early French Revolution, the supreme other of good taste as well as Englishness was the Spanish Catholic in their guise as inquisitor, monk or nun: characters on whom every sin of sadism and debauchery could be projected. It is often overlooked that English gothic from 1790 to 1820 is less 'Germanic' and far more intimately tied to the southern European, to banditti, convents, Catholic cathedrals, relics and the dungeons of the Jesuits. This was the natural home, at least for English writers of terror, sublimity and erotic torment. This was the landscape par excellence of sexual perversity and of otherness. Protestant unease and bourgeois sentiment coupled itself with 'nostalgia' for a Catholic, monarchical, autocratic sentimentalism, that could be revisited to oppose modernity itself.

The impulse to 'transcend' the mundane was coupled with the left-over religiosity of an age alienated from salvation. To be haunted by ghouls, pursued by zombies, howled at by moonstruck werewolves is a means of imaging an 'elsewhere' into which we step as readers. This world lay in a landscape of ruins, Here was the ready-made landscape of the picturesque which aristocratic literary tourists added to their collection of experiences on grand tours. This same landscape soon ceased to be merely picturesque and entered the imaginative realm of the sublime, now not only beautiful but beautifully terrifying as an inspiration for transcendent experience.

What was left was a fear of annihilation, dismemberment and madness and these fears required physical as well as psychological embodiment: castles and corridors, long moon shadows cast through barred windows across curtains and hangings, broken tombs and abandoned chapels, the oubliette or long drop of the elevator shaft in the haunted skyscraper, the long-forgotten lane to the American gothic mansion, fog across fens and moors or crawling down the byways of New York or Victorian London, forests of dead trees: all haunted dreamscapes mutating by analogy through literary history.

This was a historical landscape reclaimed as a fantasy fairyland and as an imaginative corollary to that disturbance of mind necessary to the aesthetics of that late Romanticism that emerged during the Napoleonic Wars. This late Romantic aesthetic was an ideal state which had mutated from the progressive 'humanist' phase of Romanticism that had accompanied the French Revolution. The second phase in its gothic form abandoned progress for transcendent annihilation, the very opposite of its own roots. As an oppositional aesthetic, the gothic stood for 'refusal' and clothed itself in the garb of disturbing imagery and unpalatable thoughts, mixed up in a sort of erotics of death. Such an aesthetic found in the ruins of the English and Italian landscapes provides a perfect image of the self in crisis.

Gothic experience is a certain heightening of feeling by exciting the passions of fear and torment. This is the nightmare world of torture, both mental and physical and of inevitable entrapment in a universe of terrorization. This too had its origins in an aristocratic ennui seeking thrills before the coming of the guillotine and the Terror of the French Revolution. It is essentially erotic in content and displaced into a sensuous geography. Yet its revolutionary double is more murderous and more sadistic. The social rituals of the ruling élite are now replaced by the occult rituals of the Romantic self, guardian of nothing except its own transcendent ego. Such rituals confirm the apartness of the self and its unique structure, sensibility and space. Each in turn offers itself for penetration and violation, bereft of the social formation whose only fear is the anarchy of social collapse. Romantic fear is anarchic, a libertarian free-for-all where the endlessly repeated concern is not of social collapse (the ultimate fear of aristocracy), but of psychic collapse.

The gothic is the imbuing of the mundane with a forbidding and foreboding atmosphere.

> Last night I dreamt I went to Manderley again. . . . Like all dreamers, I was possessed of a sudden with supernatural powers and passed like a spirit through the barrier before me. The drive wound away in front of me, twisting and turning . . . Nature had come into her own again and, little by little, in her stealthy, insidious way had encroached upon the drive with long, tenacious fingers. The wood, always a menace even in the past, had triumphed in the end. It crowded, dark and uncontrolled . . . The beeches with white, naked limbs leant close to one another. Their branches intermingled in a strange embrace, making a vault above my head like . . . a church. . . . I would recognise shrubs . . . that had gone native now, rearing to monstrous height without a bloom, black and ugly as the nameless parasites that grew beside them. *Rebecca* (Chapter 1)

The gothic developed into a mode of representation for a new sensibility, and bits of this sensibility may be hijacked for other projects which retain gothic tropes but empty them of their philosophical content in order to find a new uses for 'gothic' language. In this respect, the language of ruin has always been ruinous itself. Gothic is the map of a border, a mapping of the edge always illuminated by the shadow of night and the rays of the moon. It is a night-world filled with dark dreams.

The triumph of the 'human' in the years of revolution was accompanied by the alignment of human nature to the natural per se. The effect was to ennoble the idea of self and then to categorize that ennoblement. The self became the world and by doing so became a natural force motivated by the organ of imagination which resided in a mind filled with the inner unknowable violence of nature itself. No sooner had the idea of the 'imagination' been discovered (an ideological function of the Romantic world view) than it became filled with demons as an unknowable and fearful centre for self-hood. Thus it was found that the inner self was not only good and creative, but also violent, wilful and self-destructive. Psychoanalysis merely confirmed what the gothic already knew of the self as an unknown territory.

Gothic horror (the end effect of gothic atmosphere) has little to do with religion and much to do with the borders of the material. The state of 'personhood' implies physical and spiritual boundaries. When these boundaries of privacy are breached, the self becomes imperilled. It is in the confrontation with the 'not me' that the self becomes subject to spiritual angst. The gothic represents that continual confrontation with absolute otherness. The monstrous demons of gothic fiction are not only projections of the self but also imaginings of the not-self engaged in a struggle at the border of experience.

Chapter Four
Land of Shadows: Melmoth the Wanderer *to* Sweeney Todd

Charles Maturin, the curate of Saint Peter's, Dublin was an elegant, almost foppish literary type who if he had not been ordained would have been an actor; he expected his wife, Henrietta, to dress in the height of fashion and never be seen out without rouged cheeks; he himself liked to look around decaying houses that he found on his long walks or dance French quadrilles at parties. It was all odd behaviour for a church minister who declared himself a 'high Calvinist', but, then, Charles Maturin was odd – a well-dressed, almost over-dressed party animal by day, gay and talkative, but by night a writer who indulged in the excesses of human misery, who fuelled himself on brandy and water (the same concoction that kept Thomas Paine going all night), who felt that his life had been 'wasted' in 'labour, distress and misery', who dwelt on the gloomy facts of poverty, 'in which your children ask for food, and you have no answer', for whom the release of death by opium suicide was a pleasant reverie ('by reposing on a bed of eastern poppy flowers, where sleep is death') and who released the 'criminals of the mind' to play among his writings in the small hours before dawn. From such midnight musings emerged the story of *Melmoth the Wanderer* in 1820, the last great gothic novel of the Romantic era, and perhaps, the last truly gothic novel, which after going underground for 70 years emerged again triumphant in the pages of *Dracula*, by a later graduate of Trinity College, Bram Stoker.

Maturin was born in Dublin in 1782, and at 21 went into the Church of Ireland. His passion, however, was not for sermonizing but for 'being a writer of romances' and playwrighting, embarrassing traits in a clergyman for which he apologizes in the preface to *Melmoth*. In 1807, he had written the first of a steady flow of novels: *The Fatal Revenge* was published in 1807; *The Wild Irish Boy* in 1812; *Woman, or Pour et Contre* in 1816; but no money from sales meant that Maturin turned to his first love, the stage, and in 1816, *Bertram* was acted by Edmund Kean at Drury Lane. Maturin, Henrietta and the children moved precipitously to London. His next two plays failed. Slowly the family sank into poverty. Maturin, always a maverick, somewhat schizophrenic in his lifestyle, naturally prone to a moodiness that became more paranoid as his life turned bad, poured his regrets and annoyance into a new book where the 'creaking voice of his dreams' could at last be given vent, with nothing to lose.

He was a man who must have long brooded on the unfairness of life, and who told Walter Scott that his pages reflected the 'shade of obscurity and misfortune under which his own life had been wasted'. He was looking for something other than gothic thrills. There would be no Radcliffe-style terrors or suspense, nor would there be the 'Schauer–romantik' horrors of Monk Lewis with his emphasis on pollution, corruption and decay. The gothic machinery, borrowed from over 20 years of experimentation would be borrowed certainly and there would be the terrors of the Inquisition, dungeons, mad monks, imprisonment, torture, 'the Wandering Jew', curses, old mansions and weird portraits, but such symbols had long been flexible, abler to be emptied of their older meanings and reworked with new symbolic significance. It was this new language that Maturin was seeking in a novel at whose core was the nihilism and despair that was many miles away from Lewis's Germanic horror burlesques. *Melmoth* is the product not of the youthful exuberance of Beckford, Lewis or Shelley, but of a lifetime's brooding on perceived human indifference and institutional cruelty. Despite Maturin's avowed Calvinism, the work is so extreme in its tests of religious practice and institutionalism that it reads almost as if, in those small lonely hours of brandy and water, faith had been tested only to be shattered. Ironically, the germ of the book had come from a sermon on salvation where Maturin had asked, almost to himself,

> Is there one of us present, however we may have departed from the Lord, disobeyed His will, disregarded his word, is there one of us who would

at this moment, accept that all man could bestow, or earthy afford, to resign the hope of his salvation? – No, there is not one – no such a fool on earth, were the enemy of mankind to traverse it with the offer.

(Introduction to First Edition)

Such a challenge already smelled of brimstone and sulphur, already was temptation and Maturin's brooding, philosophic novel was to explore the consequences of such a pact in a deeper way than Lewis and in a parallel way to the influential work of Goethe whose reworking of *Faust* influenced generations of writers, poets and composers through the nineteenth century.

The story itself begins when John Melmoth goes to visit his dying uncle in his house by the cliffs in Ireland; the servants are degenerate; the uncle a miser; the mansion crumbling. In a locked chamber is an ancient and forbidding portrait, its sitter walks the corridors, 150 old, unable to die, because he took the devil's bargain. He is the ancestor of the present John Melmoth – Melmoth the Wanderer. The rest of the tale is a convoluted history of Melmoth's ancestor and his attempts to offload his burden (as with the Ancient Mariner) on any poor passing and potential victim. We follow Melmoth as he destroys an Englishman in the seventeenth century and then causes mayhem during the Spanish Inquisition. A strange tale concerning a Rousseau-istic child of nature whom Melmoth the 'undead' seduces and abandons finally brings up the end of the narrative before Melmoth, at the end of his own tether, throws himself from the cliffs to his doom.

Yet what marks the story as very different from *The Monk* and other tales of mad monks and Faustian pacts is the obsessive anti-Catholicism that drives the story. Indeed, the horrors come not from anything supernatural, but from the casual cruelty and violence that Maturin sees as inherent in a bureaucratic and institutional world such as the Catholic Church. As such the novel is almost rabidly prejudiced, an Irish protestant rant that coincided with the founding of the Orange of Order. Nevertheless, in scrutinizing the cruelty of institutions, the story rises above its prejudices and comes near to the despair inherent in de Sade, the only British novel to do so. Indeed, so convoluted and difficult does Maturin make the theological discussions that one is inclined to see him as wholly atheistic.

Either way, the last of the great gothic novels is also the genre's highest achievement, foreshadowing books such as *1984* or even *Catch 22*.

By the time *Melmoth the Wanderer* was published, the first wave of writers were now very old or dead: Matthew Lewis had died in 1818, coming home from his West Indian plantations, buried at sea; Charles Maturin was dead by 1824, only four years after the triumph of *Melmoth*; Ann Radcliffe had abandoned writing for over 20 years before her death in 1823. It was true that Mary Shelley still wrote, but the fire had gone and she continued to produce more or less forgotten historical novels until her own death in 1851. Byron was dead from fever contracted while fighting the Turks. As for Coleridge, he had forgotten his influence on the gothic, become its implacable opponent, a Unitarian and a sage-like bore. William Beckford lived on until 1844, a faded reminder of regency decadence as he paraded with his dwarf servant through the streets of Bath. Cyrus Redding visited the old man in Bath, during the mid-1830s, by which time Beckford had gained a reputation among the populace for being both eccentric and solitary; Redding approached Beckford's house at Landsdowne Terrace still thinking of these rumours.

> But I forget that his dark-complexioned dwarf porter, Pero, as broad as he was long, had opened the door of his house to me – my companions had disappeared, and I was alone. A second servant led the way up to the library, the prolongation of which was over the arch . . . This the people of Bath gave out was the habitation of the mysterious dwarf. They knew, as I have said, as little of Mr Beckford as if he dwelt fifty miles away. The servant announced my name, and retired.
>
> The author of *Vathek* was sitting before a table covered with books and engravings. He rose, and, bowing with all the ease of a gentleman of the old school, began conversation without further ceremony. He was then in his seventy-fourth year, but did not look anything like as old. . . .
>
> '*Vathek*', I observed, 'made a great sensation when it appeared?'
>
> 'You will hardly credit how closely I could apply myself to study when young. I wrote *Vathek* in the French, . . . at twenty-two years of

age. It cost me three days and two nights of labour. I never took off my clothes the whole time. It made me ill'. . . .

'Your mind must have been deeply imbued with a love for Eastern literature?'

'I reveled day and night … in that sort of reading. It was a relief from the dryness of the old classical writers'.[1]

Edgar Allan Poe was neither dead nor sliding into genteel retirement. Poe was born on 19 January 1809, in Boston, to parents who were actors and whose perambulations left him homeless and finally an orphan at the age of two. He was adopted by a childless couple, the Allans of Richmond, Virginia, who took their new-found and ill-loved child to visit Scotland and England where Poe stayed until he was eleven. Returning to America, Poe finished his schooling at the University of Virginia, where gambling debts forced his removal before his eighteenth birthday. He began writing, which was published, went to West Point Military Academy, but was dismissed in 1831; he was finally alienated from his foster parents and forced at the point of starvation to earn his living as a journalist. He married, which gained him a live-in mother-in-law and a cat, took up editing, but barely scraped a living. In 1842 he left Philadelphia where his little ménage had settled under the cloud of his wife's illness, a burst blood vessel, which unable to repair itself burst one more and final time in 1842. Poe went temporarily insane, recovered, but luck trickled away and he collapsed in a gutter in New York in mysterious circumstances on 8 October 1849. The sexton, George W. Spence placed a sandstone marker numbered '80' on his grave and there it stayed until 1874 when a permanent memorial was finally erected.

Poe is the best-known and most recognizable of all the gothic writers, but the obscurity of his upbringing, the manner of his squalid death and the weirdness of his vision has led to him variously being accused of being a drunk, a drug addict, obsessional and impotent. He may have been all of these things or he may not. What he was able to do was to harness internal drives with the emerging journalistic concerns of his day in order to produce a new fiction in which personal neuroses were sublimated to the universal (and often prurient) interests of a reading public hungry for sensation literature which purported to be truthful. Poe was a jobbing author quite willing to take up snippets of information or journalistic anecdotes relating to technology ('The Balloon Hoax'), murder and detection ('The Murder of Marie Roget') or medical experiment ('The Facts in the Case of M. Valdemar') which exploited the general fascination with mesmerism and with the after life, and even had medical men fooled despite its horror ending.

> As I rapidly made the mesmeric passes, amid ejaculations of "dead! Dead!" absolutely *bursting* from the tongue and not from the lips of the sufferer, his whole frame at once – within the space of a single minute, or even less, shrunk – crumbled – absolutely *rotted* away beneath my hands. Upon the bed, before that whole company, there lay a nearly liquid mass of loathsome – of detestable putridity. ('The Facts in the Case of M. Valdemar')

Yet his true achievement was to combine what psycho-medical knowledge he could cull from text books and the encyclopaedia with insights into the emerging concerns of the mid-nineteenth century with regard to cosmic ennui and alienation. In this way his tales go beyond the older gothic tropes and start to explore those inner demons that would haunt the century, its thinkers and artists. In a series of tales including 'the Man of the Crowd', 'The Imp of the Perverse', 'Ligeia', 'The Fall of the House of Usher' and 'The Black Cat' Poe began an exploration of the psychology of obsessional psychosis that was only categorized in the twentieth century. In 'The Fall of the House of Usher', the tale of which covers Roderick Usher's peculiar mental landscape and Madeline's equally strange 'catatonia', Poe embedded a poem he had previously written called 'The Haunted Palace' to exemplify the central character's psychosis – madness conquers all:

> In the greenest of our valleys
> By good angels tenanted,
> Once a fair and stately palace-
> Radiant palace- reared its head
> In the monarch Thought's dominion-
> It stood there!
> Never seraph spread a pinion
> Over fabric half so fair!

Banners yellow, glorious, golden,
On its roof did float and flow,
(This- all this- was in the olden
Time long ago,)
And every gentle air that dallied,
In that sweet day,
Along the ramparts plumed and pallid,
A winged odor went away.

Wanderers in that happy valley,
Through two luminous windows, saw
Spirits moving musically,
To a lute's well-tunèd law,
Round about a throne where, sitting
(Porphyrogene!)
In state his glory well-befitting,
The ruler of the realm was seen.

And all with pearl and ruby glowing
Was the fair palace door,
Through which came flowing, flowing, flowing,
And sparkling evermore,
A troop of Echoes, whose sweet duty
Was but to sing,
In voices of surpassing beauty,
The wit and wisdom of their king.

But evil things, in robes of sorrow,
Assailed the monarch's high estate.
(Ah, let us mourn!- for never morrow
Shall dawn upon him desolate!)
And round about his home the glory
That blushed and bloomed,
Is but a dim-remembered story
Of the old time entombed.

And travellers, now, within that valley,
Through the red-litten windows see
Vast forms, that move fantastically

To a discordant melody,
While, like a ghastly rapid river,
Through the pale door
A hideous throng rush out forever
And laugh- but smile no more. ('The House of Usher')

It is through the satiric tale 'The Mad Tryst of Sir Launcelot Canning', which explodes the old medieval gothic tale once and for all, that Poe brings about the denouement of the 'The Fall of the House of Usher' when the lady Madeline returns from premature burial to fall in a final sex/death liebestod on her brother Roderick – the last of the old gothic machinery also finally dies. Poe's tales are psychological, not supernatural and his worlds essentially hallucinatory nightmares where reality and the imagination combine; his horrors are those of the mentally ill, the dreamer and the drug addled; the world of Poe's gothic paraphernalia is merely the trappings of a diseased mind.

Nowhere is this derangement of mental space typified in greater depth than in 'Ligeia' in which an idealized and exemplary wife, one perhaps not actually there but hallucinated, is replaced with a real wife, the first wife returning over the corpse of the second in the last spectral insane vision of the narrator. This, of course, is yet another take on the bride-corpse of 40 years previous, but it is changed into phantasmagoria through the introduction of an unreliable narrator who 'in the excitement of . . . opium dreams' and 'a vivid imagination', rendered morbidly active by the terror of the lady [his second wife Rowena who is dying] conjures up his original 'spouse' (Ligeia) from the 'corpse' of the second. In the tale 'Berenice', the 'realities of the world' affect the narrator 'as visions only'.

The origin of Poe's spectral women actually lay in an obscure passage in that even more obscure book, by Charlotte Dacre, the forgotten *Zofloya*, a book that Poe may have come across in his youth. In it the delusional dream hallucinations of one of the characters is brought rudely into reality when he awakes not to his 'flaxen' haired love, the virginal Lilla but instead awakes next to the 'raven' haired seductress Victoria.

Scarce could his phrenzied gaze believe the sight which presented itself. – Not the fair Lilla, the betrothed and heart-wedded wife of his bosom, but Victoria! Appearing Lilla no longer, blasting his strained eyes with her hated image! – Sleep still overpowered her senses, unconscious of the horror she inspired – those black fringed eyelids, reposing upon a cheek of dark and animated hue – those raven tresses hanging unconfined – oh, sad! Oh, damming proofs! – Where was the fair enamelled cheek – the flaxen ringlets of the delicate Lilla? – (Chapter 29)

Yet if Lilla sounds like Ligeia and the situation exactly replicates that of the menage of Poe's narrator, the raven-haired Ligeia and the unfortunate flaxen locks of Rowena, it is nevertheless where any resemblance leaves off. Such occurrences have ceased to be mere narrative conveniences. The intensity and peculiarity of Poe's vision alongside the psychological particulars of the narrator's psychosis means that the death and resurrection of spectrally beautiful women have ceased to be a device in Poe, they are now the morbid obsession upon which the narrative hinges. And this morbidity tends in one direction without hope of happy ending or salvation: 'There is a countenance which haunts me . . . There is a hysterical laugh which will forever ring in my ears' as the narrator of the 'Oblong Box' concludes at the end of a tale of burial at sea.

If anglophone readers took Poe to be merely a good retailer of horror tales (or not: T. S. Eliot thought his writing 'adolescent') and his characters as merely stock lunatics, French readers, nevertheless, through the translations of Baudelaire, took his depictions of morbidly obsessed, over-sensitive types as models for the new idea of the doomed and self-destructive 'artist', one whose obsession with the erotics of death would influence painters and writers into the twentieth century and itself be the foundation of the Symbolist movement of the late nineteenth century with its 'diseased' sickly hues of acid green, yellow or purple, the very foundation of the nineteenth-century's idea of the modern artist.[2]

Surely, man had never before so terribly altered, in so brief a period, as had Roderick Usher! It was with difficulty that I could bring myself

to admit the identity of the wan being before me with the companion
of my early boyhood. Yet the character of his face had been at all
times remarkable. A cadaverousness of complexion; an eye large,
liquid, and luminous beyond comparison; lips somewhat thin and
very pallid, but of a surpassingly beautiful curve; a nose of a delicate
Hebrew model, but with a breadth of nostril unusual in similar
formations; a finely-moulded chin, speaking, in its want of prominence, of a want of moral energy; hair of a more than web-like
softness and tenuity; these features, with an inordinate expansion
above the regions of the temple, made up altogether a countenance
not easily to be forgotten. And now in the mere exaggeration of the
prevailing character of these features, and of the expression they were
wont to convey, lay so much of change that I doubted to whom
I spoke. The now ghastly pallor of the skin, and the now miraculous
luster of the eye, above all things startled and even awed me. The
silken hair, too, had been suffered to grow all unheeded, and as, in its
wild gossamer texture, it floated rather than fell about the face,
I could not, even with effort, connect its arabesque expression with
any idea of simple humanity. ('The Fall of the House of Usher')

If the odd-remembered scenario from older gothic books is to be
found reworked in Poe, it is nevertheless in Thomas De Quincey's
'ruby–coloured laudenum' decanter and its accompaniment, 'a book
of German metaphysics' that the whole philosophy of Edgar Poe is to
be found, as is his vision of the artist.

In that state, crowds become an oppression to him; music, even,
too sensual and gross. He naturally seeks solitude and silence, as
indispensable conditions of those trances, or profoundest reveries,
which are the crown and consummation of what opium can do
for human nature. ('The Pleasures of Opium' in *The Confessions of an
English Opium Eater.*)

'The vivid imagination, rendered morbidly active . . . by . . . opium'
which falls in 'large drops of . . . ruby coloured fluid' in Poe's story
'Ligeia' is never far away from those arcane and sometimes invented
volumes that line the libraries of mad men and their narrators.

Our books – the books which, for years, had formed no small portion of the mental existence of the invalid – were, as might be supposed, in strict keeping with this character of phantasm. We pored together over such works as the *Ververt et Chartreuse* of Gresset; the *Belphegor* of Machiavelli; the *Heaven and Hell* of Swedenborg; the *Subterranean Voyage of Nicholas Klimm* by Holberg; the *Chiromancy* of Robert Flud, of Hean D'Indagine, and of De la Chambre; the *Journey into the Blue Distance of* Tieck*; and the *City of the Sun of* Campanella. One favourite volume was a small octavo edition of the *Directorium Inquisitorum* by the Dominican Eymeric de Gironne; and there were passages in *Pomponius Mela*, about the old African Satyrs and AEgipans, over which Usher would sit dreaming for hours. His chief delight, however, was found in the perusal of an exceedingly rare and curious book in quarto Gothic – the manual of a forgotten church – the *Vigilar Mortuorum Chorum Ecclesie Maguntinae* ('The Fall of the House of Usher')

Even Poe's lugubrious prose (also partly borrowed from De Quincey), so derided in America and England was now seen (by Baudelaire) as the first flourish of the European prose poem. And of Poe's women, spectral, mysterious, present and absent at the same time and always somehow moribund or indeed 'dead' in their beauty, of these women who have taken the place of the corpse bride, the canvasses of the Symbolists and the pages of decadent writers are full by the end of the century, not least of which those by Bram Stoker.

Before turning in we went to look at poor Lucy. The undertaker had certainly done his work well, for the room was turned into a small *chapelle ardent.* There was a wilderness of beautiful white flowers, and death was made as little repulsive as might be. The end of the winding-sheet was laid over the face; when the professor bent over and turned it gently back, we both started at the beauty before us, the tall wax candles showing a sufficient light to note it well. All Lucy's loveliness had come back to her in death, and the hours that had passed, instead of leaving traces of 'decay's effacing fingers,' had but restored the beauty of life, till positively I could not believe my eyes that I was looking at a corpse. (*Dracula*, Chapter 13)

France embraced Poe and France embraced Walter Scott. It was in France among the imitators of Scott, those who had read his medieval romances in the translations of Defauconpret, that the next innovation of the gothic would occur. Victor Hugo, looking to 'out-Scott' Scott, published *Notre Dame de Paris* (*The Hunchback of Notre Dame*) in March 1831, hoping in so doing to explain not only the Parisian medieval world on the brink of modernity, but also the seeds of the coming revolution in that world. To tell his tale, Hugo took a playwright, a king, a gipsy girl, a satanic monk and a deformed bell ringer and placed them in the teeming streets of Paris and the packed environs of the Ile de la Cité. At the centre of the novel is a long description of the cathedral of Notre Dame and at its centre is the bell ringer Quasimodo, that compilation of brutish and malicious parts that is itself a metaphor for the heterogeneous insensitivity of city life. It is Quasimodo riding the great bell that is the demonic heart of the cathedral, itself the demonic centre of Parisian life.

> Now, suspended over the abyss, borne to and fro by the formidable swinging of the bell, he seized the brazen monster by the ears – gripped it with his knees – spurred it with his heels – and redoubled, with the shock and weight of his body, the fury of the peal. Meanwhile, the tower trembled; he shouted and gnashed his teeth – his red hair bristled – his breast heaved and puffed like the bellows of a forge – his eye flashed fire – the monstrous bell neighed panting beneath him. Then it was no longer either the great bell of Notre-Dame, nor Quasimodo – it was a dream – a whirl – a tempest – dizziness astride upon clamour – a strange centaur, half man, half bell – a spirit clinging to a winged monster . . . the presence of this extraordinary being seemed to infuse the breath of life into the whole cathedral. . . . the old cathedral seemed to be a docile and obedient creature in his hands; waiting his will to lift up her mighty voice; being filled and possessed with Quasimodo as with a familiar spirit. One would have said that he made the immense building breath. (Book 4, Chapter 3)

Here then is a new sense of the gothic. It is no longer to be located in a house, a cell, a monastery, but now fills a city as if the demonic was the essence of city life and that all the city could offer. The city was corruption, as Mrs Radcliffe might hint without knowing why, but now it was laid bare and minutely dissected. In Hugo's novel, everything is distorted and melts into fantasy. Things can no longer be taken for real and the playwright, Pierre Gringoire, homeless, poverty stricken and chased in the middle of the night by a trio of leprous beggars, can no longer believe where he is.

> Gringoire, more and more affrighted, held by the three mendicants as by three pairs of pincers and deafened by the crowd of vagrants that flocked barking round him – the unlucky Gringoire strove to muster sufficient presence of mind to recollect whether it was Saturday (witches' day) or not; but his efforts were vain; the thread of his memory and his thoughts was broken; and, doubting of everything – floating between what he saw and what he felt – he put the insoluble question to himself – 'If I am I, are these things then real? If these things be real, am I really I'? (Book 2, Chapter 6)

Forced into the Court of Miracles, the kingdom of 'Argot', to plead for his life before Clopin Trouillefou, the king of the beggars, Gringoire has run smack bang into the city of dreadful night, a phantasmagoric place he has arrived at 'walking, not in the Styx, but in the mud'. Things are turned on their head and the procession of Quasimodo dressed as the Fool's Pope leads to the parallel universe of the labyrinth of the beggars's dominion. Such a city becomes both real and visionary, both bricks and mortar and a product of our imagination, something both to live in and 'reconstruct in thought'. Here are all the pestilential and dead cities of the later Symbolists – Bruges, Brussels, Prague and Venice, as well as the night-time maze of Jack the Ripper's East End. It is where Poe's unknowable 'Man of the Crowd' forever guards his dark secret and where C. Auguste Dupin solves his crimes behind the shuttered windows of his crumbling mansion. It is a new thing – the spectral, haunted city.

London will be Thomas De Quincey's haunted city, a city where he first obtains opium from a druggist near the Pantheon on Oxford Street, where he sleeps on the floor of an attorney's house in Soho which he shares with a servant girl who believes a locked room contains the secrets of Bluebeard and where he encounters 'Ann' the 'streetwalker' with whom he falls in love but never learns her last name nor ever meets again. London, through the haze of drug memories,

becomes a fluid form, now clear and close, now receding. De Quincey
leaves Shrewsbury where he is lodging at 2 a.m. with the 'storm outside . . . raving' and the night as 'dark as "the inside of a wolf's
throat"', on the top of the mail coach which is cold and uninviting,
the journey, 'eight and twenty massy hours' continues until dawn
when he is deposited outside the General Post Office with 'London
expanding her visionary gates to receive [him], like some dreadful
mouth of Acheron'.

London becomes De Quincey's visionary city at once present and
imagined or 'recalled' in the way Romantic poets had imagined such
things might be recalled in the mind's eye almost 25 years prior to
The Confessions of an English Opium Eater appearing. Just before sleep
and in his mind's 'theatre', De Quincey would first project the
waking visions that would haunt his dreams, dreams that were
enhanced by opium because De Quincey believed that the drug was
more effective in that regard than eating raw meat as the painter
Fuseli was said to have done.

During 1817, such projections became nightmarish and were
increasingly filled with 'deep-seated anxiety and funereal melancholy'
associate with 'chasms and sunless abysses' where 'the sense of
space, and . . . time, were both powerfully affected. Buildings, landscapes . . . were exhibited in proportions so vast as the bodily eye is
not fitted to receive. Space swelled, and was amplified to an extent of
unutterable and self – repeating infinity'. De Quincey's scenic fantasies expand as organisms 'with the . . . power of endless growth and
reproduction'. In short, they are a type of culture-borne bacilli whose
form is 'architectural'. Such architectural and 'non-Euclidian' spaces
would also form the basis of H. P. Lovecraft's mythology in the 1920s,
itself the nightmare distortion of New York City.

Architecture becomes terrifying. One day, the two most famous
English drug addicts of the nineteenth century, Coleridge and De
Quincey, were looking over a copy of *Piranesi's Antiquities of Rome*
Coleridge paused and recounted a vision related to the book's
author.

> Coleridge, then standing by, described to me a set of plates from that
> artist, called his *Dreams*, and which record the scenery of his own

visions during the delirium of a fever. Some of these (I describe only from memory of Coleridge's account) represented vast Gothic halls; on the floor of which stood mighty engines and machinery, wheels, cables, catapults, etc., expressive of enormous power put forth, or resistance overcome. Creeping along the sides of the walls, you perceived a staircase; and upon this, groping his way upwards, was Piranesi himself. Follow the stairs a little farther, and you perceive them reaching an abrupt termination, without any balustrade, and allowing no step onwards to him who should reach the extremity, except into the depths below. Whatever is to become of poor Piranesi, at least you suppose that his labours must now in some way terminate. Bur raise your eyes, and behold a second flight of stairs still higher, on which again Piranesi is perceived, by this time standing on the very brink of the abyss. Once again elevate your eye, and a still more aerial flight is descried; and there, again, is the delirious Piranesi, busy on his aspiring labours: and so on, until the unfinished stairs and the hopeless Piranesi both are lost in the upper gloom of the hall. ('The Pains of Opium')

London spaces, architectural distortion, drugged and feverish nightmares and Piranesi on the edge of the abyss, frozen forever in ontological and existential limbo – such is the new gothic nightmare: the distorted city of Victor Hugo walked through by the madman of Edgar Poe.

Unlike Hugo whose long life would take him to 1885 and the brink of the modern age, Poe was to live only a few years more before his own death in a New York gutter helping to rig an election in 1849, but it was in Poe that the spark generated in Britain would flourish for a brief time across the Atlantic before again returning albeit in modified form to its British origins. For the most part, Poe's innovations in the genre were ignored, his party pieces like 'The Raven' embraced. By the 1840s, the gothic had been domesticated. No more barren castles; instead, lonely farmhouses, windswept heaths, ruined cottages and mist swirling around bleak ancestral piles would take the place of high gothic thrills. Such thrills were now to be sublimated to dramatic stories of unfortunate women and doomed love affairs in which the gothic was an atmosphere for social interaction.

In 1847, Charlotte Bronte used the gothic as a hinge to clarify Jane Eyre's childhood isolation from the Reed family. In her reading of *Bewick's History of British Birds*, Jane is fascinated not by the ornithological details, but by the introduction and vignettes that suggest gothic anxieties. It is not bird imagery that is highlighted here, but 'picture[s] that tell a story' and that story is of Shelleyan Arctic 'death-white realms' and border ballad fears.

> . . . and yet there were certain introductory pages that . . . I could not pass quite as a blank. They were those that treat of the haunts of sea-fowl; of 'the solitary rocks and promontories' by them only inhabited; of the coast of Norway, studded with isles from its southern extremity, the Lindeness, on Naze, to the North Cape –
>
> When the Northern Ocean, in vast whirls,
> Boils round the naked, melancholy isles
> Of farthest Thule; and the Atlantic surge
> Pours in among the stormy Hebrides.
>
> Nor could I pass unnoticed the suggestion of the bleak shores of Lapland, Siberia, Spitzbergen, Nova Sembla, Iceland, Greenland, with 'the vast sweep of the Arctic Zone, and those forlorn regions of dreary space – that reservoir of frost and snow, where firm fields of ice, the accumulation of centuries of winters, glazed in Alpine heights above heights surround the pole, and concentrate the multiplied rigours of extreme cold'. Of these death-white realms I formed an idea of my own. (Chapter 1)

In the abandoned apartments of Thornfield Hall, with their decaying and moth-eaten furniture, the horrors of a mock ghost story lie in wait.

> The furniture once appropriated to the lower apartments had from time to time been removed here, as fashions changed: and the imperfect light entering by their narrow casements showed bedsteads of a hundred years old; chests in oak or walnut, looking, with their strange carvings of palm branches and cherubs' heads, like types of the Hebrew ark; rows of venerable chairs, high-backed and narrow; stools

still more antiquated, on whose cushioned tops were yet apparent traces of half-effaced embroideries, wrought by fingers that for two generations had been coffindust. All these relics gave to the third story of Thornfield Hall the aspect of a home of the past – a shrine of memory. . . . [There is] a range of smaller apartments to the back; no one ever sleeps here. One would almost say that, if there were a ghost at Thornfield Hall, this would be its haunt.' (Chapter 11)

Yet, it is the very real madness of an imprisoned wife, a burnt and deformed Rochester and the unbending Christianity of St John Rivers in which the horrors (and the salvation) of the book lie.

Emily Brontë's *Wuthering Heights*, written in the same year as *Jane Eyre,* retains more of the gothic and therefore more of a new sense of that form of obsession that will transform Romanticism into romantic love. While a gothic atmosphere surrounds all the action, it is rarely evident in its raw state. One example is when Nelly Dean sings Walter Scott's ballad, 'The Ghaist's Warning' to Linton, in Chapter Nine; the song, concerning as it does the return from the dead of a mother to look after her children now in the clutches of a wicked step mother, is used for simple atmospheric effect and is neutral as a narrative device, something quite different from the authorial methods of Ann Radcliffe 50 years before. Nevertheless, the gothic is deployed in indirect ways throughout the novel from the random cruelty to animals by both the younger Cathy (Chapter 2) and Hareton (Chapter 17) to Cathy's hint that she is a witch when threatening Joseph.

'You scandalous old hypocrite!' she replied. 'Are you not afraid of being carried away bodily, whenever you mention the devil's name? I warn you to refrain from provoking me, or I'll ask your abduction as a special favour. Stop, look here, Joseph,' she continued, taking a long, dark book from a shelf. 'I'll show you how far I've progressed in the Black Art – I shall soon be competent to make a clear house of it. The red cow didn't die by chance; and your rheumatism can hardly be reckoned among providential visitations!'

'Oh wicked, wicked!' gasped the elder; 'may the Lord deliver us from evil!'

'No, reprobate! You are castaway – be off, or I'll hurt you seriously! I'll have you all modeled in wax and clay; and the first who passes the limits I fix, shall – I'll not say what he shall be done to – but, you'll see! Go, I'm looking at you!'.

The little witch put a mock malignity into her beautiful eyes, and Joseph, trembling with sincere horror, hurried out praying and ejaculating 'wicked' as he went. (Chapter 2)

And yet there is sufficient of the antiquarian gothic to supply details of Heathcliff's home (early Tudor dated to 1500) with its 'grotesque carving . . . wilderness of crumbling griffins, and shameless little boys' and to supply a description of Heathcliff himself as a hero straight out of *Melmoth* and who shares with Melmoth that despair which is embraced by 'death and hell' (Chapter 14). Lockwood even muses at the end of the novel that Heathcliff may have been demonic, something uneasily dismissed from his thoughts.

The light flashed on his features, as I spoke. Oh, Mr Lockwood, I cannot express what a terrible start I got, by the momentary view! Those deep black eyes! That smile, and ghastly paleness! It appeared to me, not Mr Heathcliff, but a goblin; and in my terror, I let the candle-bend towards the wall, and it left me in darkness. . . . 'Is he a ghoul, or a vampire?' . . . 'But, where did he come from, the little dark thing, harboured by a good man to his bane?' muttered superstition, as I dozed into unconsciousness. And I began, half dreaming, to weary myself with imaging some fit parentage for him; and repeating my waking meditations, I tracked his existence over again, with grim variations; at last picturing his death and funeral; of which, all I can remember is, being exceedingly vexed at having the task of dictating an inscription for his monument, and consulting the sexton about it; and, as he had no surname, and he could not tell his age, we were obliged to content ourselves with the single word, 'Heathcliff.' . . . If you enter the kirkyard, you'll read on his headstone, only that, and the date of his death. (Chapter 34)

It is, of course, the ambiguous end of the novel which is most indebted to its gothic heritage and which confirms and denies its supernaturalism at one and the same time.

But the country folks, if you ask them, would swear on their bible that he *walks*. There are those who speak to having met him near the church, and on the moor, and even within this house – Idle tales, you'll say, and so say I. Yet the old man by the kitchen fire affirms he has seen two on 'em looking out of his chamber window, on every rainy night since [Heathcliff's] death – and an odd thing happened to me about a month ago.

I was going to the Grange one evening – a dark evening threatening thunder – and, just at the turn of the Heights, I encountered a little boy with a sheep and two lambs before him, he was crying terribly, and I supposed the lambs were skittish, and would not be guided.

'What is the matter, my little man?' I asked.

'They's Heathcliff, and a woman, yonder, under t'Nab, he blubbered, 'un' Aw darrnut pass 'em.'

I saw nothing; . . . He probably raised the phantoms from thinking, as he traversed the moors alone, on the nonsense he had heard his parents and companions repeat – yet still, I don't like being out in the dark, now – and I don't like being left by myself in this grim house. (Chapter 34)

By the 1840s, the gothic was a respectable architectural and craft style. For the most part in literature, however, it was little more than last year's fashion, a thing to be remembered rather than read. In 1851, David Macbeth Moir could reminisce,

Horace Walpole had written his *Castle of Otranto* merely as a burlesque; but hitting the tone of the day, it had been read and relished as an admirable transcript of feudal times and Gothic manners; and his success taught Mrs Radcliffe and others to harp – and far from unpleasantly – on the same string. . . . nothing went down but *Udolphos* and *Romances of the Forest*, *Sicilian Bravos*, and *Legends of the Hartz Mountains*; corridors and daggers, moonlight and murdering, ruined castles and sheeted specters, gauntleted knights and imprisoned damsels. [Matthew Lewis] was the high priest of the intense school. . . . he wrote of demons, ghouls, ghosts, vampires, and disembodied spirits of every kind as if they were the common machinery of society . . . his every night was Hallowe'en or a Walpurgis

Night . . . Like the school of [Erasmus] Darwin, that of Lewis was
destined to have a day fully as remarkable for its brevity as its bright-
ness. . . . as the sacrifices of the high-priest ceased to ascend, the
worshippers gradually deserted . . . the young devotees . . . took, in
the maturity of intellect, to higher and more legitimate courses.[3]

Indeed, nothing was left but 'exquisite pleasantries'. By mid
century, the gothic was no more than a set of popular devices, a set
of generic markers for the most hackneyed thrills which would find
their readership no longer among the middle classes who could afford
the more costly volumes or had kept 'the blue books' from their
youth, but instead would reach to a wider, less literate working-class
mass readership. It was in 'bloods', 'penny dreadfuls' and 'shockers'
that the vampire and the madman, the werewolf and the spectral
monk would live again, and if they had not been reinvented in the
popular press the genre may well have died out.

Their reawakening comes as a consequence of a number of new
circumstances that occurred in publishing in the mid century. First
and foremost, many more young people were literate, having been
educated through charitable establishments; the population was rising; pulp paper was cheap; the steam press made publication simple
and efficient; part-work publication allowed sales to rise; a new generation of journalists had arisen willing to cater for the new mass
market; and above all, copyright laws were so lax as to allow plagiarism of almost any author who published in a mode too expensive
for a mass readership. Thus were working-class readers first introduced to Dickens. Popular consumerism saved the gothic which had
been a realm for middle-class readers or wealthy aristocrat authors.

Although the term 'penny dreadful' seems not to have been applied
to cheap serialized work until the 1860s, the idea of serialized part
works goes back a further 20 to 30 years when 'penny blood' tales
with their 'blood and thunder' story lines first entranced juvenile
readers (and, perhaps, many adults). Such tales were written quickly
and to deadlines by journalists whose aim was profit, not literary
quality. Nevertheless, although such writers made a living plagiari-
zing Dickens and any other popular but expensive book that was
proving readable at the time and such journalists wrote at speed

and in teams, it would be wrong to think that all their productive life was dedicated to producing second-rate hack work. Such writers although forgotten almost immediately after they died, were often talented writers of melodramatic thrills and were adept at witty dialogue and clever plotting. They were also excellent at reinventing stock situations.

It is a curious fact that more sense of the gothic comes through in the unconscious popular memory of such anonymous writers and their numerous 'forgotten' stories than from the classic authors. Everything in these cheap productions is sacrificed to effect, and as such, the narratives move with a pace and excitement missing in more literary attempts at the genre. All the paraphernalia of the gothic is here rehearsed and expanded; there are castles and German forests, pacts with the Devil, vampires a plenty, madmen and werewolves, deranged and debauched nuns, all the tortures of the Inquisition, cannibals and cannibalism, madhouses and grinning madhouse keepers, banditti, detectives and psychopaths. There could be no Dracula, no Mr Hyde, no Hound of the Baskervilles, nor even the filmic horror landscapes of the Universal movies of the 1930s without the suppressed memory of the 'bloods' of the 1840s.

The penny blood *Wagner the Werewolf* (alternatively, *Wagner the Wehr-Wolf*: 1846 to 1847) by George Reynolds, the pioneering journalist and social campaigner stands in the shadows behind Bram Stoker's *Dracula* just as surely as the more scholarly and academic *Book of Were-Wolves* (1865) by the Reverend W. Sabine Gould from which Stoker borrowed his 'facts'. It is clear from Dracula's physical appearance at the start of the novel, his command of Carpathian wolves and the episode with the escaped London Zoo wolf, Bersicker, that Stoker hesitated between a vampire and a werewolf for his model for the Count, a model which remained unresolved throughout the novel, and it was the emergence of the popular idea of the werewolf in this key period which caused the hesitation.

Even the fierce storms that ravage gothic landscapes got into the popular imagination through their depiction in tales which though sub-Radcliffe had long forgotten their debt. It must be said also that such storms are fiercer and more exciting than ever Radcliffe could produce. Here, for instance, is the prologue to *Wagner the Werewolf*.

The night was dark and tempestuous – the thunder growled around – the lightning flashed at short intervals – and the wind swept furiously along, in sudden and fitful gusts.

The streams of the great Black Forest of Germany bubbled in playful melody no more, but rushed on with deafening din, mingling their torrent-roar with the wild creaking of the huge oaks, the rustling of the firs, the howling of the affrighted wolves, and the hollow voices of the storm.

The dense black clouds were driven restlessly athwart the sky; and when the vivid lightning gleamed forth with rapid and eccentric glare, it seemed as if the dark jaws of some hideous monster, floating high above, opened to vomit flame.

And as the abrupt but furious gusts of wind swept through the forest they raised strange echoes – as if the impervious mazes of that mighty wood were the abode of hideous fiends and evil spirits, who responded in shrieks, moans, and lamentations, to the fearful din of the tempest.

It was indeed an appalling sight!

If werewolves were not to your taste, there were vampires aplenty. The most famous of all was Varney the Vampire, who made his appearance in the serial, *Varney the Vampire; or, the Feast of Blood* between 1845 and 1847, an anonymous work whose author or authors have been hotly disputed, but which was probably written by the hack journalist James Malcolm Rymer, whose prodigious work rate (there are 109 chapters to Varney [or 220 according to which printing]) allowed him to retire with a small fortune. The story features references to other vampire tales and in so one episode we meet 'Count Pollidori [*sic*]', a sly nod to Varney's origins. The tale mixes farce, melodrama, sensation and horror with information on vampires such as the use of the stake through the heart. Varney is resurrected several times, has sharp fingernails and pointed teeth and preys on female victims, a clear influence on Dracula with his violent and erotic bed-side manners.

The figure turns half round, and the light falls upon its face. It is perfectly white – perfectly bloodless. The eyes look like polished tin; the lips are drawn back, and the principal feature next to those dreadful eyes is the teeth – projecting like those of some wild animal, hideously, glaringly white and fang-like. It approaches the bed with a strange gliding movement. It clashes together its long nails that literally appear to hang from the finger ends. No sound comes from its lips . . .

The storm has ceased – all is still. The winds are hushed; the church clock proclaims the hour of one; a hissing sound comes from the throat of the hideous being and he raises his long gaunt arms – the lips move. He advances. The girl places one small foot from the bed on the floor. She is unconsciously dragging the clothing with her. The door of the room is in that direction – can she reach it?

With a sudden rush that could not be foreseen – with a strange howling cry that was enough to awaken terror in every breast, the figure seized the long tresses of her hair and twining them round his bony hands he held her to the bed. Then she screamed – Heaven granted her then the power to scream. Shriek followed shriek in rapid succession. The bed clothes fell in a heap by the side of the bed – she was dragged by her long silken hair completely on to it again. Her beautiful rounded limbs quivered with the agony of her soul. The glassy horrible eyes of the figure ran over the angelic form with a hideous satisfaction – horrible profanation. He drags her head to the bed's edge. He forces it back by the long hair still entwined in his grasp. With a plunge he seizes her neck in his fang-like teeth – a gush of blood and a hideous sucking noise follows. *The girl has swooned and the vampire is at his hideous repast!* (Chapter 1)

The story was an instant hit with a play running in Lambeth even before the conclusion of the serial. Yet, the success of werewolves and vampires was as nothing compared with the lasting impression given by a new style of villain inspired by real murderers, the real locations of the city of London and the growing interest in crime.

Sweeney Todd is one of the great characters of fiction and the book in which he first appeared, *Sweeney Todd or The String of Pearls*, one of the greatest of nineteenth-century narratives. It was produced by a series of highly talented but almost forgotten piece workers, who, nevertheless, were able to put together a story at once strange, farcical, ghoulish and wholly original, perhaps the only successful book produced by committee, nearer television soap opera or film than literature proper, which is not to say that it contains some of the finest melodramatic writing anywhere and that writing itself much indebted to Dickens with a cast of eccentric characters that includes the reverend Mr Lupin, Ben Bolt the Beefeater, Fungus the Doctor and Fogg the lunatic asylum owner of Peckhan Rye madhouse. Added to characters that might have stepped out of Pickwick Papers may be added Tobias, Sweeney's boy, Mrs Lovett, owner of the infamous pie shop, Johanna Oakley, the feisty cross-dressing heroine and Sir Richard Blunt and Colonel Jeffery, the first literary detectives, and you have a work of more than passing interest, not least of which because of the sheer bravado of the writing. So great is Sweeney Todd's impact on modern culture, in fact, that he steps out of the pages and into legend convincing many that he really existed, or at least, was based upon someone who did, a point played upon by the spoof preface to the 1850 edition.

The serial itself belonged to the stable of that prodigious publisher Edward Lloyd whose output of bloods allowed him in later life to start 'respectable' newspapers and retire on a fortune. In the meantime he had a living to earn and with writers like Thomas Peckett Prest (whose fate was to die in impoverished obscurity in Islington, in 1859, as an alcoholic) and James Rymer(who was more canny and died wealthy), he was able to publish plagiarized copies of Dickens and W. Harrison Ainsworth that sold as well as the originals. Blood and gore however were his speciality and on 21 November 1846, he started publishing a team-written tale called *The String of Pearls: A Romance* in his short lived *People's Periodical and Family Library*.

The tale remains remarkably un-gothic, it is too humorous and too cavalier for that, although the scenes underground in the pie shop cellars under St Dunstan's Church suggest all the trappings of the gothic labyrinth. Instead the priest of the old-style goth tale has been replaced with the detective and the monster replaced by a very human psychopath, himself an advance on the sort of ne'er do wells found in the Newgate Chronicle. More significant of all is that the story is set not in an imaginary Spain or Germany but in a wholly contemporary and recognizable London in which it foreshadows Dr Jekyll and Mr Hyde, Dracula, the adventures of Sherlock Holmes and the very real terrors of Jack the Ripper. The narrative was instantly plagiarized for the stage where it played in New York and London, Sweeney finally incarnate as 'the demon barber of Fleet Street' in the penny dreadful published by Charles Fox which appeared as late as 1885. This was not to be the last of the barber and he regularly appeared in pantomime, film, musicals and television throughout the twentieth century.

Alongside these often derivative but highly popular works was one that was wholly original, bizarre because it was aimed at children, and strangely inexplicable. A fantasy of children's fears, aimed at children – a type of dark adult humour pervading the whole. *Struwwelpeter (Shock-haired Peter)* was a slight book of strange cautionary poems written and illustrated by the anatomist and alienist Heinrich Hoffman who published the collection in 1845. Hoffman had been born in Frankfurt am Main in 1809, the same year as Edgar Allan Poe. He was the son of an architect and when he was of age he was sent to Heidleberg University where his sociable and clubby ways were a distraction from study. He moved to Halle and there took a medical degree. Moving once again to Paris to improve his surgical and anatomical skills, he took up residence in a pauper's clinic back in Germany and finally went to Frankfurt's lunatic asylum where his amateur knowledge of the illnesses of the mind nevertheless proved highly effective. Always imbued with a liberal good heartedness, Hoffman seems to have had a way with the 'cure' of schizophrenics, perhaps through the application of sympathetic methods of treatment.

Yet there was a baroque side to Hoffman's nature, something strange and dreamlike in his understanding of the psyche which foreshadowed Freud, but whose mystery is not fully explained by Freudian methods. His *Struwwelpeter* was conceived as a Christmas present for his son during 1844, but the nightmare visions of terrifying disasters and weird characters soon caught the attention of a publisher and then the general public. Sub-titled 'pretty stories and funny pictures', the poems are neither pretty in the obvious sense nor are the pictures funny in the least. There is latent cruelty here, sadistic imagining. The title poem describes, but never explains, the appearance of a strange boy with long black nails and weird hair. He is the bogey man and there is no salvation.

> Just look at him! there he stands,
> With his nasty hair and hands.
> See! his nails are never cut;
> They are grimed as black as soot;
> And the sloven, I declare,
> Never once has combed his hair;
> Anything to me is sweeter
> Than to see Shock-headed Peter. (*Struwwelpeter*)

In 'The Story of Little Suck-a-Thumb' the bogey man comes when mother goes out and puts paid to those masturbation fantasies that would obsess Freud, but seem hardly to explain or even come close to the fear caused by the horrific and disproportionate punishment meted out. Who or what is 'the great, long, red-legged scissor-man'?

> One day Mamma said "Conrad dear,
> I must go out and leave you here.
> But mind now, Conrad, what I say,
> Don't suck your thumb while I'm away.
> The great tall tailor always comes
> To little boys who suck their thumbs;
> And ere they dream what he's about,
> He takes his great sharp scissors out,
> And cuts their thumbs clean off – and then,
> You know, they never grow again."
>
> Mamma had scarcely turned her back,
> The thumb was in, Alack! Alack!
>
> The door flew open, in he ran,
> The great, long, red-legged scissor-man.
> Oh! children, see! the tailor's come
> And caught out little Suck-a-Thumb.
> Snip! Snap! Snip! the scissors go;
> And Conrad cries out "Oh! Oh! Oh!"
> Snip! Snap! Snip! They go so fast,
> That both his thumbs are off at last.
>
> Mamma comes home: there Conrad stands,
> And looks quite sad, and shows his hands;

> "Ah!" said Mamma, "I knew he'd come
> To naughty little Suck-a-Thumb." (*The Story of Little
> Suck-a-Thumb*)

Of course, in the hands of great writers gothic cliches could still be reinvented. When Dickens came to write *Great Expectations* between December 1860 and June 1861, he was able to manipulate elements of gothicism into the body of a book whose spirit was the very opposite of gothic gloom. Nevertheless, the book opens with the 'demonic' Magwich in the neglected graveyard where Pip is visiting the grave of his parents. Magwich rises from behind the headstone, half supernatural being of the marsh and half Frankenstein monster.

> 'Hold your noise!' cried a terrible voice, as a man started up from among the graves at the side of the church porch. 'keep still, you little devil or I'll cut your throat!'
> A fearful man, all in coarse gray [*sic*], with a great iron on his leg. A man with no hat, and with broken shoes, and with an old rag tied round his head. A man who had been soaked in water, and smothered in mud, and lamed by stones, and cut by flints, and stung by nettles, and torn by briars; who limped, and shivered, and glared and growled; and whose teeth chattered in his head as he seized me by the chin. (Chapter 1)

Yet read on and this, as yet, un-named creature of the marsh names an even greater monster than himself, one who eviscerates young boys as they hide in bed, but this comparison is so obviously exaggerated that it quickly takes on the grin charnel humour appropriate to Pip's final understanding of his relationship with Magwich. Pip is terrified of a villain straight out of the type of *Varney the Vampire*, melodramatic fiction that Dickens is utilizing only to debunk.

> There's a young man hid with me, in comparison with which young man I am a Angel. That young man hears the words I speak. That young man has a secret way pecooliar to himself, of getting at a boy, and at his heart, and at his liver. It is in wain for a boy to attempt to hide himself from that young man. A boy may lock his door, may be warm in bed, may tuck himself up, may draw the clothes over his head, may think himself comfortable and safe, but that young man

will softly creep and creep his way to him and tear him open.
(Chapter 1)

In this affectionately satirical way, Dickens also introduced his
version of the corpse bride, a character familiar from childhood
German nightmare tales which he mixes with Grimm's fairy stories.
Miss Haversham is both bride-corpse and Hansel and Gretel witch
rolled into one. Except, among her gothic trappings of dust and
decay she is, in the end, merely a tragic old woman.

I crossed the staircase landing, and entered the room she indicated.
From that room, too, the daylight was completely excluded, and it
had an airless smell that was oppressive. A fire had been lately kindled
in the damp, old-fashioned grate, and it was more disposed to go out
than to burn up, and the reluctant smoke which hung in the room
seemed colder than the clearer air – like our own marsh mist. Certain
wintry branches of candles on the high chimney-piece faintly lighted
the chamber: or, it would be more expressive to say, faintly troubled
its darkness. It was spacious, and I daresay had once been handsome,
but every discernible thing in it was covered with dust and mould,
and dropping to pieces. The most prominent object was a long table
with a tablecloth spread on it, as if a feast had been in preparation
when the house and the clock all stopped together. An epergne
or centre-piece of some kind was in the middle of this cloth; it was
so heavily overhung with cobwebs that its form was quite
undistinguishable; and, as I looked along the yellow expanse out of
which I remember its seeming to grow, like a black fungus, I saw
speckled-legged spiders with blotchy bodies running home to it, and
running out from it, as if some circumstance of the greatest public
importance had just transpired in the spider community.
    I heard the mice too, rattling behind the panels, as if the same
occurrence were important to their interests. But the black beetles
took no notice of the agitation, and groped about the hearth in a
ponderous, elderly way, as if they were short-sighted and hard of
hearing, and not on terms with one another.
    These crawling things had fascinated my attention, and I was
watching them from a distance, when Miss Havisham laid a hand
upon my shoulder. In her other hand she had a crutch-headed

stick on which she leaned, and she looked like the Witch of the place.

'This', said she, pointing to the long table with her stick, 'is where I will be laid when I am dead. They shall come and look at me here.'

With some vague misgiving that she might get upon the table then and there and die at once, the complete realization of the ghastly waxwork at the Fair, I shrank under her touch.

'What do you think that is?' She asked me, again pointing with her stick; 'that, where those cobwebs are?'

'I can't guess what it is, ma'am.'

'It's a great cake. A bride-cake. Mine!' (Chapter 11)

She dies in an explosion that is a reminder not only of the number of contemporary stories of self-combustion, but also of the stories of revenants that filled nineteenth-century narratives of ghosts and spirits.

I looked into the room where I had left her, and saw her seated in the ragged chair upon the hearth, close to the fire, with her back towards me. In the moment when I was withdrawing my head to go quietly away, I saw a great flaming light spring up. In the same moment, I saw her running at me, shrieking, with a whirl of fire blazing all about her, and soaring at least as many feet above her head as she was high. (Chapter 49)

Yet it is in the resolution of the story that Dickens finally dispenses with the gothic as a generic property and a philosophical proposition about human experience. It is in the very ruins of Satis House that Pip finally finds Estella and it is their implied relationship outside the pages of the book that will exorcise the baleful influence of gothic doom, not now romantic, but obsessive and stupidly dull. Instead of heralding the appearance of spectres and horrors, it is the ironic 'evening mists' of the ague-ridden marshes that dispel the gloom of gothicism and restore real human relationships.

I took her hand in mine, and we went out of the ruined place; and, as the morning mists had risen long ago . . . so the evening mists were rising now, and in all the broad expanse of tranquil light they showed to me, I saw no shadow of another parting from her. (Chapter 58)

In the mid-nineteenth century a revolution would take place in ordinary people's ideas of the supernatural and this would have profound affects on the gothic imagination. It was the appearance of spiritualism that would put back in the closet all the clanking ghosts in knightly armour and all the skeletal monks in their grottos.

Dickens was more interested than most in ghosts and supernaturalism. He had heard them at the knee of his nurse Mary Weller and enjoyed them as a boy in 'penny dreadfuls' and 'bloods'. Indeed, five ghostly anecdotes appear in *The Pickwick Papers* and ghost stories at Christmas became a regular Christmas treat throughout the 1840s (except 1847) and continued in *Household Words* from 1856. For the most part Dickens takes his ghost stories with a pinch of salt. The anecdote regarding Tom Smart's encounter with a ghostly 'queer' chair in Chapter 14 of *The Pickwick Papers* is treated humorously as is the meeting of the sexton Gabriel Grub and the Goblin King in Chapter 29 which is handled in the manner of Washington Irving. While the story of the madman from Chapter 11 is serious, it is, nevertheless, rather a tale of insanity and murder than ghosts, handled in the style of Dickens's youthful reading: a mixture of 'Newgate' confessional and *Melmoth the Wanderer*.

'Damm you,' said I, starting up and rushing upon him. 'I killed her. I am a mad man. Down with you. Blood. blood! [*sic*] I will have it!' . . . When I woke I found myself here – here in this gray [*sic*] cell, where the sunlight seldom comes, and the moon steels in, in rays which only serve to show the darks shadows about me, and that silent figure in its old corner. When I lie awake, I can sometimes hear strange shrieks and cries from distant parts of this large place. What they are, I know not; but they neither come from that pale form, nor does it regard them. For from the first shades of dusk till the earliest light of morning, it still stands motionless in the same place, listening to the music of my iron chain, and watching my gambols on my straw bed. (*The Pickwick Papers*, Chapter 11)

Nevertheless, Dickens remained a half believer in the spiritual world all his life, even mesmerizing a Madame de la Rue in Genoa during 1842, a woman whose dreams were full of demons.[4] He remained interested in dreams and nightmares and obsessed with the prospect of his own death throughout his life and regularly attended séances and table-turning sessions.[5]

Indeed, it is Dickens's own 'Christmas Carol' that has become the most famous ghost story of all. Published in 1843, it is not a real ghost story, and the supernatural occurrences are not really terrifying. Instead we get a sentimental moral tale of personal redemption set against the cruelty and greed of mere money making. Old Jacob Marley may appear on door knobs and trail a chain, but it is made of 'cash-boxes' and 'ledgers'; Scrooge may want to bury every well-wisher with 'a stake of holly through his heart', but people who like Christmas are not vampires and Scrooge is so used to apparitions by the end of the tale that the appearance of the 'last of the spirits', terrifying though it is, is merely a bagatelle compared with Scrooge's own moral salvation. The story ends not with the eerie, unsettling and supernaturally inconclusive, but instead with the cheery, 'God Bless Us, Every One!' Such mid-century bravado in the face of the supernatural would darken as the century progressed and when Dickens came to write 'The Signalman' (the tale of a spectral railway-man) in 1866, the circumstances of the story very much accorded with the later Victorian understanding of the genre.

Chapter Five
Dark Reflections in a Dull Mirror: Fuseli's The Nightmare and the Origins of Gothic Theatre

There was an astonished hush around the picture at the Royal Academy, the one with the swooning girl, the goblin and the black horse. Nothing quite like anything that had been seen before. It was disturbing, bizarre. What its meaning was, was unclear. It has remained unclear to the present day, refusing to be analysed, stubborn in its refusal to give up a message that seems always just beyond reach. It should have irritated Freud into action; he had a copy on the wall of his consulting room, but he ignored it and, like Poe's Raven on the bust of Pallas, Freud's print brooded over the inexplicable, reminding the psychoanalyst of his limits. The painting was *The Nightmare* by Henry Fuseli, a Swiss resident of London and the picture first went on view in 1782.

Johann Fuseli was originally from Zurich where he was born to a middle-class family on 6 February 1741 with the surname of Füssli, a name Johann later anglicized. His father had been a court painter, but decided that his son should be a Zvinglian minister, in which position he was ordained in 1761. Nevertheless, the young minister had less interest in religion than he had in literature and he took up writing, travelling Europe from Berlin to Rome and finally settling in London where his precocity was evidenced in his self-taught and growing ability in painting. Indeed, by the end of his life, and despite his rather quaint English, he had become a Keeper at the Royal Academy. He even earned himself a spot in St Paul's Cathedral when he died in 1825.

The Nightmare is a small picture, quite unlike Fuseli's other monumental historical and mythic efforts. It depicts a swooning woman lying on a divan or couch with her head and left hand drooping down. Beside the bed is a table upon which is a small bottle and jar. On the woman's chest and stomach sits an incubus which looks quizzically at the viewer with goblin eyes. The drapes behind the scene are blood red and through them a black horse with bulging, pupiless eyes thrusts his head. It is the incubus rather than the horse which is the 'nightmare' of the title – a strange creature from ancient Greece called a 'mara' or 'morra', an ancient version of a bloodsucking demon with obvious sexual connotations. The picture has never been fully explained. Byron once asked if the picture had a classical origin and was told that the whole thing only existed in '[Fuseli's] brain'. 'First I sits down', said the painter, 'Then I work myself up. Then I throw in my darks. Then I pulls out my lights'.[1] That was all the explanation that anyone got.

The Enlightenment explanation of nightmares suggested they were not the visitation of evil spirits, but the consequence of indigestion or sleeping in a poor posture. Fuseli's picture hinted at dark motives that were neither quite supernatural nor quite psychological, but a peculiar disturbing hinterland where desire and fear mixed.

The sensibilities of the eighteenth century were hardly likely to repeat themselves in the nineteenth, and yet surprisingly, *The Nightmare* was a popular print both in its own right and as a vehicle for satire. Rowlandson was first to parody the imagery in *The Covent Garden Nightmare* of 1784 to be followed by a variety of political and comic prints from 1794 to 1832 when R. Seymour produced a version celebrating the Bristol riots with an image showing an incubus sitting on Britannia. In Britain the copies were satiric, whereas abroad they were 'gothic'. The Symbolist painters adopted the imagery for their own erotic and Freudian nightmares at the end of the nineteenth century. In Max Klinger's *Dead Mother*, the corpse is surmounted by a baby looking out at the viewer. The picture, however, only achieves a mawkishness absent from its original model. The picture was also revived in the cinema, with versions of the general visual look of the painting being used by Carl Dreyer, James Whale and Ken Russell.

Fuseli could not repeat the trick and most of his other paintings are in the gothic taste for representing moments of great literature, especially if that literature was 'medieval' or Miltonic. His taste for strangely elongated women in pornographic poses or looking strangely vampiric remained popular with a small circle until the dream-like quality and slightly weird setting of his work started again to appeal to those like the Symbolists and Surrealists who were themselves looking for a vocabulary of the strange and occult. Fuseli's masterpiece was not to be repeated by others seeking Gothicism and the German painter Casper Friedrich chose to translate gothic idealism, with landscape, ruin and sunset rather than plumb the unconscious depths of fear. Thereafter, the gothic tone fades rapidly from European painting, if not from the dreams of British artists in love with medievalism, King Arthur, Ophelia, the Lady of Shallot and the imagination of those who called themselves Pre-Raphaelite.

Horror returned to painting only as psychological and sexual realism; Sigmund Freud and Joseph Breuer's *Study on Hysteria* published in 1895 and Emile Durkheim's *Study on Suicide* published in 1897 analysed and explained modernity's angst-ridden soul and gave expression to nightmares that might be painted or written up as literature. '[These] discoveries of our revolutionised modern emotional life', as Karl Scheffler called them in 1902, were the new doors to the irrational and repressed that Fuseli seemed to have tapped into years before. Yet now the whole of man's existence seemed to have turned inward. Edward Munch with his melancholia, parasitic vampire women and sick and dying children, and August Strindberg with his sexually neurotic women, his extreme artistic sensibility and his occultism seemed to sum up a type of despair, but this time it would be a heart sickness brought on by nature, not salved by it. 'Nature' was now full of 'arbitrary whims' and life 'an inferno' through which man walked in 'dazed amazement' whilst 'mocking insanity' and suffering 'pathological sexuality'.

'The spiritual fever' of the late nineteenth century was best caught in painting by Edvard Munch whose picture *The Scream* came about after an evening walk in early 1892.

> I was walking along the road with two friends. The sun set. I felt a tinge of melancholy. Suddenly the sky became a bloody red.

I stopped, leaned against the railing, dead tired, and I looked at the flaming clouds that hung like blood and a sword over the blue-black fjord and the city.

My friends walked on. I stood there, trembling with fright. And I felt a loud, unending scream piercing nature.[2]

A friend who had been with Munch in Nice recorded that

For some time Munch had been wanting to paint the memory of a sunset. Red as blood. No, it actually was coagulated blood. But not a single other person would see it the same way as he had; they would all see nothing but clouds. He talked himself sick about that sunset and about how it had filled him with great anxiety. He was in despair because the miserable means available to painting never went far enough. 'He is trying to do what is impossible, and his religion is despair,' I thought to myself but still advised him to try to paint it – and that was how he came to paint his remarkable *Scream*.[3]

From its inception the gothic was foremost a psychological, architectural, theatrical and visual statement about man's relationship to his surroundings. Gothic architecture was always meant to be theatrical, the remodelling of genuine older mansions and castles dramatized the everyday lives of the aristocracy both for themselves and for those looking up to their castellated walls or through their colour-stained and trellised windows. The style also allowed those whose money was newer enough to put on the pretences of old money as they painted their walls with fake escutcheons. The tournaments at places like Eglington were pure spectacle and all these manifestations of theatricality were themselves the inheritors of a literary gothic that delighted in the interplay of the special arrangements of architectural form and human engagement.

Having built Strawberry Hill in bricks and mortar it was Walpole's delight to demolish the edifice in print. Strawberry Hill was essentially a house in which to play and dream and Walpole's *Castle of Otranto* the literary embodiment of the acting out of the dramatic potential of an architectural style not fully realized in his home. In effect, the domestic comforts of real gothic architecture were matched by the phantasmagoric hallucinations of a literary

architecture where walls, towers, corridors and trap doors seem not
only to have sentience but whose modality was psychological.

Otranto itself begins in an architectural space violated by the
intrusion of a giant helmet which has been magically transported as
a vehicle of death.

> The company was assembled in the chapel of the castle, and every-
> thing ready for beginning the divine office, when Conrad himself was
> missing. Manfred, impatient of the least delay, and who had observed
> his son retire, despatched one of his attendants to summon the young
> prince. The servant . . . came running back breathless . . . his eyes
> staring, and foaming at the mouth. . . . The company was struck with
> terror and amazement. Manfred . . . asked imperiously, what was the
> matter? The fellow made no answer, but continued pointing towards
> the courtyard; and at last, . . . cried out, Oh, the helmet! the helmet!
> In the meantime some of the company had run into the court, from
> whence was heard a confused noise of shrieks, horror, and surprise.
> Manfred, . . . went himself to get information of what occasioned
> this strange confusion. . . . The first thing that struck Manfred's eyes
> was a group of his servants endeavouring to raise something that
> appeared to him a mountain of sable plumes. He gazed without
> believing his sight. What are ye doing? Cried Manfred. . . . Where is
> my son? . . . Oh my lord! The prince! The prince! The helmet! the
> helmet! . . . he beheld his child dashed to pieces. . . . in the midst of
> their senseless guesses a young peasant, whom rumour had drawn
> thither from a neighbouring village, observed that the miraculous
> helmet was exactly like that on the figure in black marble of Alphonso
> the Good . . . in the church of St Nicholas. (Chapter One)

Such transportations render the whole castle suddenly a prey to
every sort of weird manifestation. Indeed, very soon characters are
transported through the castle as if the familiar space of their home
was now rendered as entirely new, entirely strange and different,
a special place for gothic happenings.

> There is a chamber where 'nobody has dared to lie . . . since the great
> astrologer that was your brother's tutor drowned himself'. And there

are the apparitions; the fragmented giant or the walking portrait endower the building's 'soul'; when the 'soul' withdraws the material structure collapses and 'dies'. As the ghostly form of Alfonso the Good emerged from the castle, the walls . . . were thrown down with a mighty force! For three days the building has been the abode of a numinous presence. The haunted house is by definition a not-home, and *unheimlich* centre. . . . That 'long labyrinth of darkness into which Isabella ventured in the vaults of Otranto is the ancestor of Radcliffe's *Udolpho'* ('a strange rambling place', a place of 'proud irregularity').[4]

Gothic Romanticism and romantic gothicism especially were inherently melodramatic and sensational, apparently ideally suited for stage production. The times were fortuitous as the intimate Georgian theatres were closing and large play houses were opening, catering for the middle and lower classes as the aristocracy abandoned the theatre. These new play houses, often three times as big as their more intimate ancestors, also had bigger and better machinery, an essential part of the gothic, and new stage inventions, such a better trap doors, use of animals and fireworks suggested endless possibilities. These new possibilities made the stage ideal for spectacle and in so doing frightened off those playwrights who hankered for the older classical style of play; in broadening the appeal of melodramatic spectacle the gothic intrusion opened the stage to a succession of very effective journeyman playwrights who made no pretensions of their art.

Romantic poets such as Shelley and Byron who still took the stage seriously were often incompetent playwrights whose bombastic dynastic dramas were written for 'the mind' rather than the stage with unstageable theatrics or unacceptable themes, with Shelley relying on plagiarisms from *The White Devil* or *Macbeth*. On 26 April 1821 Byron wrote to Shelley about the Georgian taste for imitation.

You know my opinion of that second-hand school of poetry. You also know my high opinion of your own poetry, – because it is of no school. I read Cenci – but, besides that I think the subject essentially undramatic, I am not an admirer of our old dramatists, as models. I deny that the English have hitherto had a drama at all.

With attitudes like that coming from the leading author of his day how could any Romantic playwright succeed ? Yet Coleridge did find success with *Remorse* which with its medieval Spanish setting and its use of stage fireworks was a novelty at the time.

> The incense on the alter takes fire suddenly, and an illuminated picture of ALVAR'S assassination is discovered and having remained a few seconds is then hidden by ascending flames.[5]

It certainly seemed that the more stage effects one had in a gothic drama the more successful it might be and stage managers worked hard to perfect complex illusions to thrill audiences. Matthew Lewis's play *The Castle Spectre*, which first appeared in 1797 and was sold on his 'wicked' reputation, included scenes where 'an oratory is seen illuminated. In its centre stands a tall female figure, her white and flowing garments spotted with blood; her veil is thrown back and discovers a pale and melancholy countenance . . . a large wound appears upon her bosum'[*sic*].

Wordsworth's *Borderers* fared little better than most, although Byron, a member of the Drury Lane Committee of Management between 1812 and 1816 was (despite his gainsaying) actually able to write quite well for the new stage. His *Werner* contained a fair share of gothic trappings to capture the imagination of his audiences. Nevertheless, it was a minor literary figure who really captured the new taste for spectacle and melodrama, theatrical in ways that more lofty authors could not or would not envisage.

George Colman the Younger was the son of a successful playwright of light comedies. He soon realized the public's appetite for strong fare. One of his first adaptions was of William Godwin's *Caleb Williams* which he produced as *The Iron Chest*, reinforcing the wickedness of one of the main characters and strengthening the melodrama of a murderer undone by a revelation that was played to the hilt by actors such as Edmund Kean, Edwin Booth and Henry Irving. Colman was also exploiting the possibilities of Gothic stage machinery in Bluebeard which he put on at Drury Lane in 1798.

> SHACABAC [*sic*] puts the key into the lock; the Door instantly sinks, with a tremendous crash, and the BLUE CHAMBER appears

streaked with vivid streams of Blood. The figures in the picture over the door change their position, and ABOMELIQUE is represented in the action of beheading the Beauty he was, before, supplicating. The Pictures, and Devices of Love, change to subjects of Horror and Death. The INTERIOR APARTMENT (which the sinking of the door discovers) exhibits various Tombs, in a sepulchral building – in the midst of which ghastly and supernatural forms are seen – some in motion, some fixed – in the centre is a large Skeleton, seated on a tomb (with a Dart in his hand) and, over his head, in characters of Blood, is written 'THE PUNISHMENT OF CURIOSITY'.[6]

Thomas Lovell Beddoes, the last of the Romantics, was the son of Thomas Beddoes, a radical and a scientist who passed his interest in democratic politics and scientific enquiry onto his son. His equally illustrious mother Anna was the sister of Maria Edgeworth, the novelist, and the young Thomas was also the grandson of Robert Edgeworth, the educationalist and inventor. Thomas's father also knew Coleridge. At the early age of nineteen, the young Thomas had published a play and was being hailed as the next important dramatist. He worked on three more plays, but they were dropped in favour of a life in medicine, and Beddoes travelled to Germany to take up anatomical studies at Gottingen University.

Here he started writing a new form of play, *Death's Jest-Book*. While the genesis of the play, about crusaders, wicked dukes, beautiful maidens and sly Arabian banditti was a gothic-arabesque story about Egypt, black magic, graveyard resurrections and Kabbalistic folklore with a court fool in the style of Webster and a character called Homunculus Mandrake, a zany to a mountebank whose 'hobby' is the 'black art' and who is capable of becoming invisible, and even while the plot and language borrow heavily from *Hamlet*, *Othello* and *Titus Andronicus*, the substance of the plotting seemed all the while to remain ironic and detached in a way quite alien to the work of Shakespeare or of his contemporaries. In a fantastic scene in a ruined cathedral, Beddoes resurrects the *Dance of Death*, no longer in the spirit of Robert Blair and the Graveyard poets nor yet in the spirit of Gottfried Bürger, but now in the spirit of that black humour that believes in nothing and is born of a type of deep and cynical depression.

The Deaths, and the figures paired with them, come out of the walls, and dance fantastically to a rattling music, singing; some seat themselves at the table and drink and with mocking gestures, mask the feast, etc. (Song)

> Mummies and skeletons, out of your stones;
> Every age, every fashion, and figure of Death:
> The death of the giant with petrified bones;
> The death of the infant who never drew breath.
> Little and gristly, or bony and big,
> White and clattering, grassy and yellow;
> The partners are waiting, so strike up a jig,
> Dance and be merry, for Death's a droll fellow.
> The emperor and empress, the king and the queen,
> The knight and the abbot, friar fat, friar thin,
> The gipsy and beggar, are met on the green;
> Where's Death and his sweetheart? We want to begin.
> In circles, and mazes, and many a figure,
> Through clouds, over chimneys and cornfields yellow,
> We'll dance and laugh at the red-nosed gravedigger,
> Who dreams not that Death is so merry a fellow.
> [One with a scythe, who has stood sentinel, now sings:]
> Although my old ear
> Hath neither hammer nor drum,
> Methinks I can hear
> Living skeletons come.
> The cloister re-echoes the call,
> And it frightens the lizard,
> And, like an old hen, the wall
> Cries 'cluck! Cluck! back to my gizzard;
> 'Tis warm, though it's stony,
> 'My chickens so bony.'
> So come let us hide, each with is bride,
> For the wicked are coming who have not yet died. (Act 5, Scene III)

With Beddoes, everything seemed to turn to dust. He was, like his character Melveric, the Duke of Munsterberg, 'of the dead' but still living. A failed poet, failed dramatist and failed doctor, Beddoes had the psychological make-up of the last of an artistic type: idealistic, obsessive and manically depressive. His failure as a playwright and difficulties with friends and colleagues led to a suicide attempt in1848 while he was living in Basel; more rejection led to a successful attempt a year later. As a playwright, Beddoes was not only obsessed with the Jacobean sensibility, but also with the new revolutionary politics of Europe. He was pure goth, a medievalist whose literary medievalism was to be the equivalent of a type of architecture – a 'cathedral' of words built on the 'haunted ruins' of Elizabethan and Jacobean drama.

> Say what you will – I am convinced the man who is to awaken the drama must be a bold trampling fellow- no creeper into worm holes . . . These reanimations are vampire-cold. Such ghosts as Marloe[*sic*], Webster . . . are better dramatists . . . than any contemporary of ours . . .but they are ghosts.[7]

Yet how was he to 'revive' gothic drama with a modern sensibility. There had been no gothic drama before the eighteenth century. There were no models or models were of that projected imagination which found gothic landscapes in historical circumstances and in a past in which they never existed – the mere dreams of a gothic imaginings. Thus Beddoes saw his models, projected back into the past in order to correct the taste of the present. The work might have to wear antique clothes only the more to be contemporary. How was the gothic play to avoid anachronisms if the Elizabethan was its natural voice? It was a problem that would tax Beddoes to distraction, would so invade his anatomical studies that the language of playwrighting and the language of anatomy would mix in his correspondence; which would carry him into paranoia and death.

Beddoes ended up with a play that was static and unactable, in short a novel in verse, but he captured that new sense of nihilism that would slowly sweep revolutionary Europe. And he also expressed that emerging sense of helplessness which he felt as anatomy lessons showed that the afterlife was a fraud and all that was left was 'ever-dwindling life' where the living and the dead could become interchangeable; Wolfram resurrected from the grave, dead but 'alive' leads his killer, the Duke, Melveric, 'still alive, into the world 'o' th' dead'.

> Are you alone,
> Men, as you're called, monopolists of life?
> Or is all being, lying? And *what is,*
> With less of toil and trouble, more alive,
> Than they, who cannot, half a day, exist
> Without repairing their flesh mechanism?
> Or do you owe your life, not to this body,
> But to the sparks of spirit that fly off,
> Each instant disengaged and hurrying
> From little particles of flesh that die?
> If so, perhaps you are the dead yourselves. (Act 5,
> Scene III)

Things are turned on their head, 'tis satirical', but the satire is dark, humourless, suicidal. Like Antonin Artaud, Beddoes was seeking a pure theatre that could not exist and that had no language appropriate to it. By 1828, he had completed his 'Gothic-styled', Jacobean revenge 'tragedy-satire', but those he showed it to were unimpressed and suggested caution. Beddoes, stung and feeling rejected, spent the rest of his life revising the play. In self-pitying mood he wrote, 'of course no one will read it'. He already knew that his theatre was of the mind only. The play was published in 1850, a year after his death, but never acted.

It was, however, Matthew Lewis who understood the taste for gothic melodrama and stage effects the best. The career of Matthew Lewis is one of the most eccentric in English letters. His meteoric fame brought about by his famous novel and his plays was almost immediately eclipsed at his death amid accusations of blasphemy and condemnation as pornography. In his day he was praised by Byron, then trading ghost stories at the Villa Diodati, by Wordsworth and by Walter Scott. Everyone read his work. His novel, *The Monk,* nevertheless sank underground and stayed there for near on a hundred years, a work so seemingly disgusting that it was ignored by the polite society that had originally lionized its author. Coleridge, who admired Lewis in parts, displaying that awful priggishness that was to worsen in the coming century, was one of the first to call foul.

The horrible and the preternatural have usually seized on the popular taste, at the rising decline of literature. Most powerful stimulants, they can never be required except by the torpor of an unawakened or the languor of an exhausted, appetite. The same phenomenon, therefore, which we hale as a favourable omen in the belles letters of Germany, impresses a degree of gloom in the compositions of our countrymen. We trust, however, that satiety will banish what good sense should have prevented; and that wearied with fiends, incomprehensible characters, with shrieks, murders, and subterraneous dungeons, the public will learn, by the multitude of the manufactures, with how little expense of thought of imagination this species of composition is manufactured . . .

Figures that shock the imagination, and narrative that mangle the feelings, rarely discover *genius*, and always betray a low and vulgar *taste* . . . Not without reluctance then, but in full conviction that we are performing a duty, we declare it to be our opinion, that the Monk is a romance, which if a parent saw it in the hands of a son or daughter, he might reasonably turn pale . . . and though the tale is indeed a tale of horror, yet the most painful impression which the work left on our minds was that of great acquirements and splendid genius employed to furnish a *mormo* for children, a poison for youth and a provocative for the debauchee.[8]

The Monk, and Lewis's plays belong to a window in history that opened during the convolutions of the French Terror and were indirectly influenced by the writings of de Sade. This revolutionary and experimental window was to close as the Napoleonic wars progressed and as anything avant-garde was no longer seen as merely risqué but actually unpatriotic. This attitude simply worsened as time went by.

Matthew Lewis was born in London on 9 July 1775 as the eldest son of the Deputy-Secretary of War and the beautiful daughter of Sir Thomas Sewell of Stanstead Hall in Essex. The parents separated and their rift plagued Lewis all his life as did the constant nagging of his demanding mother. His father granted him a thousand pounds a year on his maturity and, as befit his class, Lewis lived the life of a leisured gentleman, a traveller and writer. In 1794, at the age of nineteen, he was sent to be useful at the embassy in the Hague, but found the whole thing a bore.

He travelled, met Goethe, translated Friedrich von Schiller, learnt German and wrote the first draught of a novel based loosely on his boyhood love of Walpole's *Otranto* and the more recent sensation of

Mrs Radcliffe's *Mysteries of Udolpho*. He wrote *The Monk* in a whirl-wind and 400 pages were finished in ten weeks. He travelled to London and published the novel in March 1790, to a hurricane of publicity: 'it was attacked, defended, parodied, plundered, drama-tises, opera'd, adapted, translated, imitated'.[9] Lewis was still nineteen, but his precocity was boundless. Poems and plays followed in quick succession, with his musical drama, *The Castle Spectre*, playing at Drury Lane in 1797 and the pseudo-Jacobean drama *Alfonso* at Covent Garden during 1802.

Nevertheless, Lewis who had now gained the sobriquet, 'Monk', which he rather enjoyed being called, was losing interest in literature. At the age of thirty-three, he declared that, 'the act of composing has ceased to amuse me; I feel that I am not likely to write better than I have done'. And so it was over. Lewis had been Member of Parliament for Hindon since he was twenty, the seat that by coinci-dence was William Beckford's old constituency, and by coincidence too Lewis was also homosexual and also made his money from the slave trade, but unlike Beckford, Lewis was modest in habits, a slight man with protruding eyes, he built no Fonthill Abbeys, but lived quietly at the Albany in Piccadilly and in a cottage at Barnes on the Thames where he would quietly entertain (without scandal) his long-time partner, William Kelly.

Like Beckford, Lewis had moral qualms about his plantation holdings and made two visits to his properties in Jamaica in 1816 and 1817. Here he began a new book called *The Journal of a West Indian Proprietor*, but he did not live to see it published, for on the return journey he died of yellow fever and was buried at sea on 14 May 1817, but his coffin being improperly weighted did not sink and was lost on the ocean in a grotesque parody of a gothic novel.

The Monk is full of those smoke and mirror effects beloved by the later Victorian stage, but in closet form, thrills for the mind's eye only. Such scenes are part spectacle and part erotic, psychological revelation, watered down versions of de Sade's manic theatricality.

> He fixed his eyes upon a picture of the Virgin, which was suspended opposite to him: this for two years had been the object of his increas-ing wonder and adoration. He paused, and gazed upon it with delight. 'What beauty in that countenance!' he continued after a

silence of some minutes; 'how graceful is the turn of that head!' What sweetness, yet what majesty in her divine eyes! How softly her cheek reclines upon her hand! Can the rose vie twith the blush of that cheek? Can the lily rival the whiteness of that hand? Oh! If such a creature existed, and existed but for me! Were I permitted to twine round my fingers those golden ringlets, and press with my lips the treasures of that snowy bosom! Gracious God, should I then resist the temptation? (Chapter 2)

The monumental Faustian climax of the whole book is of that kind of theatricality that still would remain near impossible to stage even today in film.

The Fiend answered by a malicious laugh:
'Our contract? Have I not performed my part? What more did I promise than to save you from your prison? Have I not done so? Are you not safe from the Inquisition – safe from all but from me? Fool that you were to confide yourself to a Devil! Why did you not stipulate for life, and power, and pleasure? Then all would have been granted: Now, your reflections come too late. Miscreant, prepare for death; You have not many hours to live!'
On hearing this sentence, dreadful were the feelings of the devoted Wretch! He sank upon his knees, and raised his hands towards heaven. The Fiend read his intention and prevented it –
'What?' He cried, darting at him a look of fury: 'Dare you still implore the Eternal's mercy? Would you feign penitence, and again act an Hypocrite's part? Villain, resign your hopes of pardon. Thus I secure my prey!'
As He said this, darting his talons into the Monk's shaven crown, He sprang with him from the rock. The Caves and mountains rang with Ambrosio's shrieks. The Daemon continued to soar aloft, till reaching a dreadful height, He released the sufferer. Headlong fell the Monk through the airy waste; The sharp point of a rock received him; and He rolled from precipice to precipice, till bruised and mangled He rested on the river's banks. Life still existed in his miserable frame: He attempted in vain to raise himself; his broken and dislocated limbs refused to perform their office, nor was He able to quit the spot where He had first fallen. The Sun now rose above the

horizon; Its scorching beams darted full upon the head of the expiring Sinner. Myriads of insects were called forth by the warmth; They drank the blood which trickled from Ambrosio's wounds; He had no power to drive them from him, and they fastened upon his sores, darted their stings into his body, covered him with their multitudes, and inflicted on him tortures the most exquisite and insupportable. The Eagles of the rock tore his flesh piecemeal, and dug out his eyeballs with their crooked beaks. A burning thirst tormented him; He heard the river's murmur as it rolled beside him, but strove in vain to drag himself towards the sound. Blind, maimed, helpless, and despairing, venting his rage in blasphemy and curses, execrating his existence, yet dreading the arrival of death destined to yield him up to greater torments, six miserable days did the Villain languish. On the Seventh a violent storm arose: The winds in fury rent up rocks and forests: The sky was now black with clouds, now sheeted with fire: The rain fell in torrents; It swelled the stream; The waves overflowed their banks; They reached the spot where Ambrosio lay, and when they abated carried with them into the river the Corse of the despairing Monk. (Chapter 12)

Despite of or because of this unstageability, Lewis realized the full potential of the theatre for a new form of horror which could be communal in nature and which would pave the way for every thrill ride, chamber of horrors exhibit and even horror film to come. The new idea was simple, but remained unexpressed: terrors could now be shared with friends and horrors could be joined to amusement for the masses. His first theatrical attempt at the new theatre was *The Castle Spectre* of 1797 which set the standard for the sensational.

The folding-doors unclose and the oratory is seen illuminated. In its centre stands a tall female figure, her white and flowing garments spotted with blood; her veil is thrown back,. And discovers a pale and melancholy countenance; her eyes are lifted upwards, her arms extended towards heaven, and a large wound appears upon her bosom. ANGELA [*sic*] sinks upon her knees, with her eyes riveted upon the figure, which for some moments remains motionless. At length the spectre advances slowly to a soft and plaintive strain: she stops opposite to REGINALD'S picture, and gazes upon it in silence. She then turns, approaches, ANGELA, seems to invoke a blessing upon her, points to the picture, and retires to the oratory. The music ceases. ANGELA rises with a wild look, and follows her vision, extending her arms towards it. The spectre waves her hand; as bidding her farewell. Instantly the organ's swell is heard; a full chorus of female voices chant 'Jubilate'. A blaze of light flashes through the oratory, and the folding-doors close with a loud noise, ANGELA falls motionless on the floor.[10]

From now on every theatre would have to up its game with more spectacular effects and every melodrama would have to contain more and more sensational situations.

Chapter Six
Desire and Loathing Strangely Mixed:
Gothic Melodrama and The Phantom
of the Opera

Matthew Lewis had created a novelty that would be difficult to top. The public demanded more of the same. Theatre owners looked around for other thrills. They found these in writers such as August von Kotzebue, a writer, diplomat and spy whose own life was worthy of everything gothic and who was assassinated by Karl Sand in 1819. His *Die Spanier in Peru* played in England, but with Pizarro removed from his evident South American setting and gothicized to suit the English taste.

James Planché, on the other hand, took his cue from George Coleman and adapted *The Vampyre*, by John Polidori, inventing a new form of trap door on the way for greater vampiric thrills. Complex mechanisms had to be devised from scratch and one was the 'Vampire Trap' for the 1820 adaption. It used two spring doors that parted and immediately reclosed when an actor stood on them. The device could also, if placed in a stage wall, give the 'impression that a figure was passing through solid matter'.[1]

In his own short lifetime John Polidori had the good (and bad) fortune to become the secretary and companion of Lord Byron and the witness to the most famous of all gothic gatherings (the company which included both Mary Godwin and Percy Shelley), the one at the Villa Diodati, where after a reading of the collection of ghost stories called *Fantasmagoriana, ou Recueil d'Histoires d'Apparitions, de Spectres, Revenans*, etc., which were translated into French from the German, decided on the fateful plan of writing gothic tales.

If *Frankenstein* was the most famous result, the only other tale to be completed was Polidori's *The Vampyre*, the first rendering of the folk-tale vampire into a literary context and the first one to work the creature as a social (rather than village) parasite, 'dead' from ennui, immortal and sexually predatory. The vampire himself bears the name Ruthven (pronounced Riven), the name borrowed from Lady Caroline Lamb's roman a cléf about Byron, *Glenarvon*. On its publication 'The Vampyre' was first attributed to Byron, so great was his reputation for weirdness. Polidori was mortified. He was under Byron's shadow as it was and this misidentification of authorship seemed to cut deep. His correction seemed to bring little solace, and lacking further literary talent and with a fragile ego at best, the author, sinking deeper into his gambling debts, committed suicide in 1821 at the age of 26.

Why would one need theatre when the whole atmosphere of the Villa Diodati was histrionic, not to say verging on hysteria? Polidori recalled the sort of peculiarly charged atmosphere in his diary.

> *June* 18. Shelley and party here . . . Began my ghost-story after tea. Twelve o'clock, really began to talk ghostly. L[ord] B[yron] repeated some verses of Coleridge's *Christabel*, of the witch's breast; when silence ensued, and Shelley, suddenly shrieking and putting his hands to his head, ran out of the room with a candle. Threw water in his face, and after gave him ether. He was looking at Mrs. S[helley], and suddenly thought of a woman he had heard of who had eyes instead of nipples, which, taking hold of his mind, horrified him.

> > 'Then drawing in her breath aloud,
> > Like one that shuddered, she unbound
> > The cincture from beneath her breast:
> > Her silken robe and inner vest
> > Dropped to her feet, and full in view
> > Behold! her bosom and half her side,
> > Hideous, deformed, and pale of hue —
> > A sight to dream of, not to tell!
> > And she is to sleep by Christabel!'[2]

Meanwhile, Plaché sensing the public's appetite for sensational subject matter continued looking for more melodramatic material after his success with Polidori's short story continuing with an adaptation of Der Freischutz (by Johann Aspel and Friedrich Laun) and was copied in his turn by Edward Fitzball, who reworked the German tale in the style of the old story of 'the Flying Dutchman'.

In France, Charles de Pixerecourt had started to create 'Bastille' epics that were soon imitated by British playwrights minus the political sentiments, but high on gothic stagecraft. Indeed, the debt to continental French and German theatre is greater than to any borrowings from Shakespeare. Even the word 'melodrama' originated on the Continent where it meant a passage from mime to music in France and meant the dialogue in German opera which was spoken to music rather than sung. Yet in both cases the influences seem to have been gothic in origin. Nevertheless, it would be another parallel invention that would show the real power of gothic stage projection.

While theatre owners were trying for ever more extravagant stage effects, others were using the theatrical backdrop itself to thrill audiences, by the manipulation of the special effects wrought by light on canvas. These were the first real experiments with a 'cinematic' sense. The first of these new 'dioramas' came to London's Regents Park in 1823 having successfully run in Paris the year before. The idea for the diorama was Louis Dageurre's, who was at that time just emerging as a theatre set designer and looking for a commercial business based on his ability to paint very large canvasses that used changing light to create various effects. Charles Bouton put up half the cash and his brother-in-law John Arrowsmith designed the hall, complete with a revolving auditorium in which the paintings, which were seventy by forty five feet, were exhibited. This first attempt at a cinema-style show was also the precursor of theme park attractions and was used to excite popular emotion and sentimentality rather than the historical and intellectual response garnered from the equally popular panoramas which exhibited historical events.[3]

The diorama was employed to exhibit landscapes in changing moods of light and shade as well as playing to the insatiable taste for ruins: 'a Gothic Cloister in decay' was the highlight of 'Ruins in a Fog' exhibited in 1825 and this success was followed by 'Interior of the Cloisters of St. Wandrille, in Normandy' whose 'mouldering silence' seemed to have also thrilled audiences. Such success spawned imitators. The 'British Diorama' followed at the Royal Bazaar in Oxford Street and boasted better effects produced by gas, a gimmick which, of course, ended in a fire when some turpentine ignited. There were other wonders to be seen, especially travelling magic lantern shows, the 'cosmorama, pleorama and myriorama as well as the more overtly gothic phantasmagoria'.[4]

The phantasmagoria magic lantern played to the eighteenth and nineteenth-century sense of novelty and drama. It lasted in one form or another from the 1790s to the 1850s and thrilled audiences with its mix of 'moving' slides, smoke, light effects and (added) sounds. Although magic lantern shows had existed since the seventeenth century, it was not until the 1760s in Germany that a coffee house proprietor called Johann Shropfer was able to convert his billiard hall into a more profitable 'séance chamber' perfected and streamlined with smells and even electric shocks. It was, however, Paul de Philipsthal, a magician working in Berlin and Vienna, who coined the term 'phantasmagoria' in the 1790s and from then on such shows took off, often placed within ruins to heighten the effect. Etienne Gaspard Robertson's elaborate high jinks toured Spain, Russia and America and were so successful that Philipsthal took his own show to the Lyceum in London in order to plug a gap in demand.

If these type of shows were considered passé by middle-class audiences in the 1820s, they nevertheless continued to amuse and frighten customers in provincial towns and in rural communities when travelling carnivals of itinerant showmen passed. The shows were even celebrated in a poem by Henry Lemoine called 'The Phantasmagoria' and published in the *Gentleman's Magazine* (no 72) in 1802.

> Behold expand the mimic scenes that show
> Transparent objects from the realms below,
> Whose fleeting forms, invisible by light,
> Delusive on our optics steal at night;
> So steals the Sorceress from her mystic cell,
> Calling forth Spectres, and invoking Hell; . . .
> Quick in succession magic shades invite
> Alternatively to torment or delight.

An awful sound proclaims a spectre near,
And full in sight behold it now appear;
Drawn from her head the mournful shroud depends,
Beneath her feet the winding garment ends;
Her lucid form a ghastly paleness wears,
Her trembling hand a livid taper bears,
In rueful order fun'ral torches pass,
Reflected through the Abbey's painted glass . . . .
Such are the forms Phantasmagoria shows.

By the 1860s, there was plenty of gothic action on stage. Alongside plays about gambling, boxing, domestic affairs, Irish emigrants and the New World could be found *The Changed Heart*, a drama in three acts with a prologue by J. Parselle which was licenced in January 1860 for performance at the Surrey and included references to drink, aristocracy, secret marriage, murder, duelling, letters, prison, convents, kidnapping, impersonation, royalty, bigamy, forgery, poison and female villains. *A Tale of Two Cities* by Tom Taylor (based on Dickens's story) promised the French Revolution, the Terror, narcotics, death, murder, peasants, prison, body-snatching and insanity. *Holly Bush Hall*, a drama in three acts by J. Mordaunt and based on the serialization by James Rymer had gipsies, ghosts, murder, police, dreams and ruins. *Manuel of Spain, or, The Mounted Brigands of Valentia*, a drama in two acts by R. Phillips had all the old-fashioned gothic tropes including bandits, Spanish characters, the Inquisition, prison and death while *The Secret Marriage, or, The Soldier, the Monk and the Assassin* which was performed at the Victoria on 5 March contained Italian settings, murder, mountains, Catholic monks, nuns, secret marriage, duelling, disguise and convents. *The Avenging Spirit* had fortune-telling, superstitions, witches, Jews, murder, execution, concealed identities, castles, ghosts and suicide while *Deeds of Darkness* by William E. Suter included treason, political revolution, castles, executions, impersonation, suicide, spirits, spectres and prison.

Suter was prolific with two other plays showing in 1860, one was *The Poisoner of Venice* performed at the Queen's Theatre on 8 December 1860 and again in 1861 which contained a stock of poisoners, aristocrats, spies, disguises, concealed identities and assassins while the second, *The Red Bridge* had bankruptcy, murder, illness and madness, ghosts, a transformation scene, visions and plenty of supernatural scenes. *False and True, or, The Brigands of Palermo*, a drama in two acts which played at the City of London Theatre had brigands, an Italian setting, orphans, wills, illegitimacy, starvation, kidnap, murder, superstitions, alchemy and dubious doctors. *The Oath and the Hour, or, The Venetian's vengeance*, drama in two acts again produced by Suter continued these themes but added disguise, Venice, exile, assassins, murder, magic, and water scenes. *Cagliostro the Magician, or, Oppression and Reprisal*, a drama in two acts by C. A. Clark gave the gothic a veneer of historical respectability. Performed at the Grecian Saloon on 27 September, the play included scenes of Paris and fashionable balls as well as magic, fortune-telling, mesmerism and treason.

Plays only peripherally gothic would also employ gothic machinery. There was *Christmas Eve, or, A Duel in the Snow* which played at Sadler's Wells and still need the obligatory ghost. *The Abbé Vaudreuil and the Court of Louis 15*, a drama in one act by H. R. Addison, even included the appearance of the Devil. The provinces had their fair share of gothic melodrama too. *Rose Graham, or, The Lass of Gowrie* played at the Theatre Royal, Swansea on 26 March 1860 and included among its Scottish and cockney characters a sprinkling of executions, insanity, superstition and ghosts.

Satire could always rely on the gothic for a smile. *Lurline, or, The Rhine and its Rhino* was a burlesque performed at the Britannia and had fun with German legends, water scenes, nymphs, the Rhine, ridiculous nobility, castles, magic, popular song and imps. Other burlesques followed. *The Raiment and Agonies* of that most amiable pair *Raymond and Agnes, or, The crime Stained Bandit and the Nun and the bleeding buzzum* by F. Marchant was based on the novel *The Monk* by Lewis and made the most of Madrid, convents, drink and drunkenness, bandits, murder and nuns. 'Monk' Lewis was box office again in 1860' 'Bianca the Bravo's Bride', an opera in four acts by J. P. Simpson with music by W. H. Balfe played at Covent Garden on 6 December 1860. It was based on Lewis's novel *The Bravo of Venice. Raymond in agonies, a bit of fun with Harlequin and the Bleeding Nun* was a pantomime by Thomas Mowbray performed in the Soho Theatre. Other more gothic tales also suggested self-parody.

Dinorah, or, The Demon's Treasure, a new romantic drama adapted from the opera had a fair share of spirits, madness, mountain settings, wizards, superstition, visions, fire, demons and spirits as did the extravaganza *The Sylphide* by William Brough and *Almina*, an opera in three acts by A. Lanzieres set in the middle ages.

Yet one offshoot of the gothic was making headway in the 1860 season and that was the dramatization of police and detection. *A Fairy Tale*, a comic drama in two acts by J. M. Morton included spies, alchemy, gambling, police and narcotics all set among gothic trappings. *The Woman in White* by Wilkie Collins and possibly adapted by J. M. Ware was playing at the Surrey while *The Thief-taker of Paris, or, Vidocq*, by F. Marchant was based on the French chief of police, Eugène François Vidocq, who had published his memoirs in 1828.

In 1861, an aficionado of terror may have looked forward to a rich crop of horrors in the London theatres. It would have been a mistake, as the taste for gothic thrills in the romantic mode seems to have been evaporated. Some remnants still remained, *The Syren of Paris* was a production by the ubiquitous Suter, but his style of show was numbered. There was also *The Devil's Compact, a Legendary Drama* or the more promising *The Angel of Death*, a play in four acts by George Conquest (or possibly even Suter or J. T. Douglass) and re-titled *Twelve o' Clock and the Spirit of Death* some time later to give it another airing, but neither version seems to have been staged.

The taste for the gothic, it would seem was now subordinated to domestic drama and sensational murder. Even in the provinces the new taste found favour. *The Woman in White* arranged by W. Sidney played at the Theatre Royal, Norwich. The turn to the sensational is best shown in the numerous versions of *The String of Pearls* based on the story of Sweeney Todd which had first appeared in the 1840s and was adopted for the stage in 1847 by George Pitt who had had to come up with a new trap door attached to the barber's chair in the process. The play has gone through numerous incarnations (including its revival as a gothic film by Tim Burton in 2007) and was played as the last histrionic gothic style melodrama well into the twentieth century by actors such a Tod Slaughter.

The death of old-fashioned gothic melodrama was completed by 1862. Some odd remnants still found an audience as they would continue to do at the 'gaffes' or unlicensed shows in shacks and tents across Britain. *Black Band, or, The Companions of Midnight* was a standard drama in three acts adapted by Robert Clark Allen, but it was probably a comedy as Allen was a 'comedian'. There was the promising *Ghost Hunter, or, The Colleen Dhas* by George Conquest based on a novel written ten years earlier and there was *The Necromancer*, a play by M. J. B. Howard (probably based on the novel by Peter Teufeld), but there was also *The Phantom* (an adaptation of Planché's adaptation of Polidori's *The Vampyre*), a drama in two acts by Dion Boucicault, the most successful of nineteenth-century theatrical playwright–entrepreneurs and someone used to stage machinery. The 'Corsican' trap had to be devised for Boucicault's adaption of Alexandre Dumas's *The Corsican Brothers*, which he brought to the stage in the 1850s. It involved

> An ascending track, on which a wheeled cart could be run, rising up out of the stage through a 'bristle' trap – a trapdoor covered with bristles painted to match the scenery. Once on the stage and in view, the track was covered by a sliding arrangement reminiscent of that of a roll-top desk; . . . nothing was seen except the ghost rising up through the floor and gliding across the stage.

Boucicault also played *The Vampire* for a new audience at the Princess's on 14 June 1852, and late produced it as *The Phantom*, at Wallack's Theatre, New York, in 1856.

On the whole, however, playgoers wanted the excitement of murder, sensation and the new spiritualism. *The Ghost of Cock Lane*, played during the summer season of 1862, 'under the management of Mr. William Travers . . . [it] was founded on the well known subject or tradition that caused such universal excitement' as the play bill announced. The play was based on a well-known ghostly fraud. Other plays were more sensational. *The Gypsey [sic] of Edgware, or, The Crime in Gill Hill Lane* by Henry Young was so gruesome and so offensive to the Lord Chamberlain that he refused a licence even though the crime inspired 17 proposed plays.

By 1863, there was little left of the theatrical gothic. There were, it was true, still plays with titles that smacked of older thrills such as *Night, or, The Perils of the Alps* by J. T. Douglass or *The Burgomaster's*

Daughter subtitled *The Fog Fiend and the Fairy Mountain*, but it was also called *The Barge Master's Daughter*, a somewhat less enticing name. *The Bridal Phantom, or, The Secret of Life* by G. Conquest was merely billed as a romance, hardly the stronger fare that had been available only three years previously, although the drama, *Lucy of Lammermoor*, was based on Sir Walter Scott's novel *The Bride of Lammermoor*. There were also revivals of *Spring-Heeled Jack* and *The Demon of the Drachenfels*, albeit in one act.

Indeed, in the penny gaffs, small illegal (that is, unlicensed) theatres built out of canvas or matchwood across London, Liverpool and Glasgow, juveniles (for they catered mainly to youngsters) might still thrill to adaptations of penny dreadfuls such as *Varney the Vampyre*, but the days of illegal theatres were also numbered. In effect, they represented the last repositories of the spirit of the first gothic thrills almost 80 years earlier.

What replaced the gothic in respectable theatres was Victorian domestic sensation. *Lady Audley's Secret* was written and produced by the ubiquitous Suter who having smelt the wind moved to another form of melodrama. There was more than one version of Mrs Braddon's shocker that year, one by George Roberts and another by C. H. Hazelwood. *The Detective, or, A Ticket of Leave* was another drama of everyday life by C. H. Hazelwood.

Plays about spiritualistic interests also start to come to prominence. *The Spirit Warning*, a mystic drama in two acts by John Brougham was put on at the Lyceum. *The Ghost! the Ghost!! the Ghost!!!; or, The Late Awful Rise in Spiritism* by Tom Taylor was licensed on 31 August 1863 for performance at the Olympic while *The Haunted Man* possibly by B. Webster junior played in June 1863 at the Adelphi. It was itself based on an earlier version of two of Dickens's stories: *The Haunted Man* and *The Ghost's Bargain*. It certainly seems as if gothic thrills remained few and far between during the later 1860s to their sudden revival in the later 1880s.

If gothic was inherently theatrical, and the proof could be found in *Otranto*, *Vathek*, *The Monk* and a host of minor tales and adapted folk legends, the most theatrical staging of all was opera, inherently 'gothic' in its mode of presentation. In 1706, the English critic John Dennis argued that opera threatened the implicitly masculine tradition of British drama, and that music was 'effeminate' and hence threatening to cultural order, especially to the hierarchies of social class and gender. In fact, he concluded, 'Nothing is so Gothick as an Opera', using 'Gothick' in its sense of 'barbarous'.

> Curiously, by the nature of opera it subverted the rationaliy that ordinarily organized a sense of reality. Opera took its eighteenth century audience into a world where everyone felt the need to express themselves in song. There's little speaking and in this fantasys world we are told of gods and heroes derived from classical mythology and Italian Renaissance romances. The gothic style of literature which emerged less than a century later seemed equally to attack those wishing to maintain an ideal of 'realism'. Instead the idea of 'consistency' was substituted. By way of *The Castle of Otranto*, 'the operatic' migrated into English sensibility. By such a definition opera might be considered 'Gothick'; the genre of gothic was also distinctly 'operatic' not only 'extravagant', but also 'flagrantly artificial', 'flamboyant', 'passionate', 'irrational', and 'exotic'.[5]

The possibilities of 'gothic' opera in the Arabesque style was first exploited by Amadeus Mozart *in The Magic Flute* (1791), but the gothic was subordinated to the fairy-pantomime, albeit with Masonic undertones. Carl Maria von Weber was one of the first fully to exploit the machinery of the genre in his opera of 1821, *Der Freischutz* ('The Marksman'; literally 'Free Shooter') in which he used a Faust type legend of a haunted huntsman which he had found in *Der Gespents-terbuch* ('The Ghost Book') by Johann Aspel and Friedrich Laun who had already supplied the basis of Planché's drama. Weber had to invent a musical language for the libretto which was suitable to invoke terror.

> I had to remind the hearer of those 'dark powers' by means of tone color and melody as often as possible . . . Naturally it had to be a dark, gloomy color – the lowest register of the violins, violas, and basses, particularly the lowest register of the clarinets, which seem especially suitable for depicting the sinister, then the mournful sound of the bassoon, the lowest notes of the horns, the hollow roll of drums or single hollow strokes on them.[6]

On the other hand, the Italians who might claim a monopoly on operatic scenarios had little experience of a sensibility that was inherently 'northern', but Donizetti's adaptation of Sir Walter Scott's novel *The Bride of Lammermoor* (1819), which was staged as Lucia di Lammermoor in 1835, included variations on the corpse bride and had a mad scene borrowed from Macbeth. The overall colour of the orchestration is appropriately dark. The prelude begins with a choir of four horns in B-flat minor, immediately establishing the sombre character of the work. It is followed by a chorus of men only, and solo passages by the lower-voiced principals. The first lightness of colour is Lucia's soprano voice and it isn't heard until the second scene. Again, a tonal palette was required. Donizetti wrote much of the score in minor keys, something not commonly done at the time. Lucia's first aria is in D minor and although it doesn't remain in that key for long it establishes the haunted, melancholy character of the heroine. The eerie timbre of the armonica (a glass harmonica) used during the mad scene created an aura that evoked the supernatural vein that runs throughout the opera. Use of funeral music in the final scene also ends the opera on a note of morbidity.

Wagner's *The Flying Dutchman*, based on the legend of 'the Wandering Jew' followed in 1843. In 1833, Wagner had already written additional music for a performance of the opera *Der Vampyr* by Heinrich Marschner, itself yet another adaption of John Polidori's *The Vampyre*. In the 1820s, 'Flying Dutchman' plays were performed across Europe, and in 1839 – the year Wagner reached London – Captain Frederick Marryat's Dutchman novel *The Phantom Ship* was a bestseller. An opera on the subject of the Flying Dutchman and his 'phantom ship' with a notion of capitalizing on the success of the Parisian revival of Weber's 'Der Freischutz' in 1840 and recent French interest in spectral themes of the Gothic and fantastic inspired Wagner's own attempt at the tale.

Perhaps most influential of all was Gounoud's *Faust*, which was performed during June 1863 at Her Majesty's Theatre, Haymarket and was based on Goethe's story. It followed Gounoud's earlier attempt at a gothic story, *La Nonne sanglante* ('The Bleeding Nun') of 1854. *Faust* had first been performed in Paris on 19 March 1859 and it was in its Paris setting that it was later revived as the central thematic music of the silent movie *The Phantom of the Opera* starring Lon Chaney Senior.

The original novel was by Gaston Leroux, a successful journalist, born in Paris on 6 May 1868. Leroux, bespectacled and over-weight,inherited a small fortune, but was careless of his wealth and lost most of it so that in his early twenties he was forced to earn a living by writing newspaper articles. Nevertheless, he also learnt the lessons of the new taste for gothic in Britain which had subsumed the monstrous, supernatural and sensational elements of the genre and rewritten them into the tales of sociopaths, megalomaniacs and detectives. In 1907 Leroux took the hint and began to produce detective stories such as *Le mystère de la chambre jaune* ('The Mystery of the Yellow Room'), in 1908, but it is for *Le Fantôme de l'Opéra* ('Phantom of the Opera'), written in 1910, that he is remembered outside France.

In it, Leroux managed to combine a romantic love story with the tale of Erik, the phantom of the Opera, a sociopath, mad genius, unrecognized artist and megalomaniac whose lifestyle epitomizes the gothic of Edgar Allan Poe. 'I remember', says Christine Daaé, that 'his hands smelt of death', a fitting charnel odour for someone who lives in a set of rooms 'set off [with] funereal upholstery' and who sleeps in an 'open coffin' when not working at 'the organ' composing his 'Don Juan Triumphant'. Curiously it is Erik's lair with its coffin, organ and drapes, deep under the Opera, situated next to a torture chamber and amid the catacombs where the Communards died, that has influenced the way many of us still imagine the gothic and that has formed the basis of many a movie and musical. The entrance of the phantom at the masked ball is one of the great 'events' in gothic literature.

> It was a man dressed all in scarlet, with a huge hat and feathers on the top of a wonderful death's head. From his shoulders hung an immense red-velvet cloak, which trailed along the floor like a king's train; and on this cloak was embroidered, in gold letters, which every one read and repeated aloud, 'Don't touch me! I am Red Death stalking abroad!'. ('Phantom of the Opera', Chapter 9)

It was Leroux's good journalistic sense that allowed him to see the essentially theatrical style of the gothic and thence to set his narrative actually in a theatre, but he was also writing on the brink of the age of film, indeed was a film maker himself and this too may have had an effect on the tale that has had as much influence in the cinema as *Frankenstein* or *Dracula*.

Chapter Seven
Do You See It?: The Gothic and the Ghostly

The theatre flourished and gothic entertainments were to last, in fits and starts, into the 1920s, but the literary gothic tale was another matter and it had to be re-invented, as we have seen, as the domestic ghost tale, giving dusty gothic props one last exceptional outing. It could not have happened without a radical shift in people's attitude to the dead, no longer skeletal and other but now spiritual and familiar. In its origins this new movement of thought contained a confused belief that a veil had been rent in consciousness (first hinted at by mesmerism) and that the spirit world was now within touch. In the same way that electricity remained for many years a mysterious force, so too the 'advances' in 'spiritism' suggested possibilities that hinted at a vast invisible liquid aether suffusing everything and harness-able by a few highly tuned minds. Yet it soon became clear that this aether was also the gateway to the dead and that the parlour tricks of the new clairvoyants were the first stages in contacting those who had 'passed over'.

For writers in the mid-eighteenth century, ghosts were not merely tangible, but they could speak and interact with the living as reanimated corpses or skeletons. It was enough to put fear into the heart of the most hardened sceptic. Immanuel Kant would have none of it and he set about attacking the leading philosopher of the spirit world, Emanuel Swedenborg in his *Geisterseher* (translated as *Dreams of a Ghost or [Spirit] Seer*) of 1766. Yet, even Kant who dismissed individual ghost encounters as superstitious and delusional nonsense believed in the totality of the phenomena, as he was later to make clear in his inaugural University lecture of 1770.

The same ignorance makes me so bold as to absolutely deny the truth of the various ghost stories, and yet with the common, although queer, reservation that while I doubt any one of them, still I have a certain faith in the whole of the taken together.[1]

Walpole in *The Castle of Otranto* conjures one such stage ghost to deliver a prophesy as part of the plot.

The marquis was about to return, when the figure rising, stood some moments fixed in meditation, without regarding him. The marquis, expecting the holy person to come forth, and meaning to excuse his uncivil interruption, said, Reverend father, I sought the lady Hippolita. – Hippolita! Replied a hollow voice: camest thou to this castle to seek Hippolita? – And then the figure, turning slowly round, discovered to Frederic the fleshless jaws and empty sockets of a skeleton, wrapt in a hermit's cowl. Angels of grace, protect me! Cried Frederic recoiling. Deserve their protection, said the spectre, Frederic, falling on his knees, adjured the phantom to take pity on him. Dost thou not remember me? Said the apparition. Remember the wood of Joppa! Art thou that holy hermit? Cried Frederic trembling – can I do aught for thy eternal peace? Wast thou delivered from bondage, said the spectre, to pursue carnal delights? Hast thou forgotten the buried saber, and the behest of heaven engraven on it? I have not, I have not, said Frederic – But say, blest spirit, what is thy errand to me? What remains to be done? To forget Matilda! Said the apparition – and vanished. (Chapter 5)

Such ghostly presences owed their origins to Shakespeare's ideas of the revenant: Hamlet's father and Banquo; or they torment the villain as in Richard III. They inhabited a far land dreamt of by Milton in *Paradise Lost*. They also owe something too to those graveyard spectres which more and more amused the bored writer of the period. In *Vathek* the 'ghouls' of the cemetery even have amorous liaisons! The early gothic 'ghost' is part of the architecture of terror, rattling its chains in torment as do the ghosts of Elvira and Antonia revisiting the tortured Ambrosio in *The Monk*. They appear at moments of high drama, or when conscience is finally pricked. Above all, they are present as solid creatures with solid aims, brought back by the earthly actions of the protagonists, conjured from the past by bad conscience.

They may be called up, but only by the spells of those fictional monsters whose models are the witches of the 'Scottish play'.

Yet attitudes were rapidly changing. A mere 100 years after *Otranto* there was no room for rattling chains and cowled skeletons. Instead, ghosts started to become aetherial, or worse, the merest hallucinations of the psychologically scarred as they appear in Henry James's *The Turn of the Screw*. In 'Green Tea' by Sheridan Le Fanu, the 'ghost' is a haunting by the alienated self, not a skeleton monk. Written in 1872 as part of a sequence of short stories gathered under the title *In a Glass Darkly*, the tale is related to the investigations of Dr Martin Hesselius, an expert in 'metaphysical medicine' and a follower of Immanuel Swedenburg who believes,

> That the essential man is a spirit, that the spirit is an organized substance, but as different in point of material from what we ordinarily understand by matter as light or electricity is; that the material body is, in the literal sense, a vesture, and death consequently no interruption of the living man's existence, but simply his extrication from the natural body – a process which commences at the moment of what we term death, and the completion of which, at the furthest a few day's later, is the resurrection 'in power'. (Sheridan Le Fanu, 'Green Tea')

Horrors now lay not in mouldering castles but in the mind itself symbolized by the ambience of 'the dark house'. The haunted and suicidal Reverend Jennings, the central figure of 'Green Tea' exists within the space of a 'perfectly silent room, of a very silent house, with a peculiar foreboding; and its darkness, and solemn clothing of books . . . helped this sombre feeling'.

The ghost was now the hallucination that kills or drives you to madness, the demonic presence of past lives and past sins and they remained so into their Edwardian heyday and right through until the 1920s when Hugh Walpole wrote the ghost tale, 'The Snow'.

> She knew the woman was not there. But if the woman was not, how was it that she could discern so clearly the old-fashioned grey cloak, the untidy grey hair and the sharp outline of the pale cheek and pointed chin? Yes, and more than that, the long sweep of the grey dress, falling in folds to the ground, the flash of a gold ring on the

white hand. No. No. No. This was madness. There was no one and nothing there. Hallucination . . . She moved and the figure was gone.

They could be conjured now, not by the potions of witches brews, but by the far more dangerous expedient of the black mass, the ghost may have ceased to rattle chains and moan, but it now seemed to issue from realms both more terrifying and more real.

By the Edwardian period ghosts were quaint amusements, the more sceptical the protagonist the more horrible his discomfort. Writers were content if ghosts and mental states coincided as if scepticism itself conjured demons, which a writer such as M. R. James was happy to exploit in order to keep the frisson of indecision in the introduction of paranormal activity.

By the 1930s, ghost hunting was little more than a pastime for enthusiastic cranks as Harry Price, the famous ghost hunter, reported on one of his endless ghost-hunting expeditions to Borley Rectory in Essex, 'the most Haunted House in England'.

In case the reader may wish to know what a psychic investigator takes with him when engaged on an important case, I will enumerate some of the items included in a ghost-hunter's kit.

Into a large suitcase are packed the following articles: A pair of soft felt overshoes used for creeping, unheard, about the house in order that neither human beings nor paranormal 'entities' shall be disturbed when producing 'phenomena'; steel measuring tape for measuring rooms, passages, testing the thickness of walls in looking for secret chambers or hidey-holes; steel screw-eyes, lead post-office seals, sealing tool, strong cord or tape, and adhesive surgical tape, for sealing doors, windows or cupboards; a set of tools, with wire, nails, etc.; hank of electric flex, small electric bells, dry batteries and switches (for secret electrical contacts); 9cm. by 12cm. reflex camera, film-packs and flash-bulbs for indoor or outdoor photography; a small portable telephone for communicating with assistant in another part of building or garden; note book, red, blue and black pencils; sketching block and case of drawing instruments for making plans; bandages, iodine and a flask of brandy in case member of investigating staff or resident is injured or faints; ball of string, stick of chalk, matches, electric torch and candle; bowl of mercury for detecting tremors in room or passage or for making silent electrical mercury switches; cinematograph camera with remote electrical control, and films; a sensitive transmitting thermometer [etc, etc].[2]

What people now feared was the preternatural moving of inanimate objects by poltergeists.

Whereas the ordinary ghost of our story-books is a quiet, inoffensive, timid, noiseless, and rather benevolent spirit, with-usually-friendly feelings towards the occupants of any place where it has its abode, the Poltergeist is just the reverse. According to the many reports of its activities, in all lands and all ages, the Poltergeist is mischievous, destructive, noisy, cruel, erratic, thievish, demonstrative, purposeless, cunning, unhelpful, malicious, audacious, teasing, ill-disposed, spiteful, ruthless, resourceful and vampiric. A ghost *haunts;* a poltergeist *infests.*[3]

Everything could be haunted and everything could take on a life of its own.

The phenomena our observers were able to confirm included footsteps and similar sounds; raps, taps and knockings; displacement of objects; 'clicks' and 'cracks'; sounds as of a door closing; knocks, bumps, thuds, humping or stamping; dragging noise; wailing sounds; rustling or scrabbling noises; 'metallic' sounds; crashing, as of crockery falling; wall-pencillings; 'appearance' of objects; luminous phenomenon; odours, pleasant and unpleasant; sensation of coldness; tactual phenomena; a sensation of a 'presence'; and a fulfilled prediction. One observer says she saw the 'nun'.[4]

What made a good ghost story? Price's story of Borley seemed to contain the definitive recipe: a coach and *headless* horseman; a ghostly nun who walked the grounds (waiting for her lover?); an old, decayed and isolated rectory (without electricity and with deep, dark and damp cellars that held a terrible secret); psychic occupants; bizarre occurrences (the appearance of a monster insect in one episode and of an old coat in another); bells that rang without human agency; messages from the dead (via suburban planchette readings); a legendary past (of monasteries and nunneries and a secret tunnel); flying bricks, vanishing and reappearing household utensils and 'apports' (a French medallion and a gold wedding ring). All this on what appeared an almost daily basis taking place in and around a 'cold' spot outside 'the Blue Room'. . . . Into this dramatic setting steps the one person able, like Holmes, to put the thing into perspective: the ghost hunter.[4]

For psychologists such as Carl Jung, the supernatural could be explained using psychoanalysis. In 1948, he announced with the authority of the sage that 'spirits appear to be "psychic phenomena whose origins lie in the unconscious" and that "the communication of spirits" are statements about the unconscious psyche'.[5] Even a terrifying encounter in the 1920s, while staying at a friend, in which Jung awoke to find the 'head of an old woman' with a glaring 'right eye' and 'the left half of the face missing' beside him on the pillow, was explained by the idea of 'hypnagogic hallucination', the self-projected memory vision of Jung's day-to-day work.[6]

Change in sentiments regarding otherworldliness and therefore in the gothic came in the mid-nineteenth century and nowhere was this change of attitude more evident than in the occurrences of 14 March 1855 in Hartford, Connecticut. A group of believers which included a journalist from *The Hartford Times* had gathered to hold a séance. At the centre of the events that unfolded was an extraordinary person: Daniel Home. As the party looked on, the supernatural, with all its gothic trappings, seemed to enter the airless room.

> The table-cloth was plainly lifted up, on the side opposite the medium, and in the full light of the lamp. It presented the appearance of something under it, for it moved about under the cloth . . . Soon after this, the thing, (whatever it was) . . . reached forward and touched one of the party . . . the hand – if it was a hand, left its protection of the table-cloth, and commenced touching the party in succession . . . But nothing could be seen![7]

To add to the marvels of the night a heavy guitar was then carried by something invisible to the door where it started to play, after which a 'heavy mahogany chair' was dragged around and the guitar levitated by 'the invisibles'. Then a pencil was thrown on the table whereupon it was taken up by the unseen hand from the table-cloth and it 'began to write'. By now the company was not only convinced that unseen forces had crossed into the material realm through a 'medium', they were also considerably rattled, for 'the hand . . . came and shook hands with each one present. [The] journalist felt it minutely . . . it was soft and warm. IT ENDED AT THE WRIST'[*sic*].[8]

The horror story had entered the drawing room. No longer would ghosts clank around ruined castles, for the ghostly had entered the domestic space of the country villa and gentleman's apartment. The gothic had become middle class.

Some years earlier in August 1852, in the house of a wealthy Connecticut silk weaver something took place which convinced witnesses that Home was indeed guided by spirits from another dimension. After a display which included the sounds and feelings of a recent shipwreck in which some relatives of one of the sitters had died,

> Mr Home was taken up in the air! [one of the guests] had hold of his hand at the time, and . . . others felt his feet – they were lifted a foot from the floor. He palpitated from head to foot apparently with the contending emotions of joy and fear which choked his utterance. Again and again he was taken from the floor, and the third time he was carried to the lofty ceiling of the apartment.[9]

Daniel Dunglas Home, born in Scotland to a clairvoyant mother, but now domiciled in the United States was the most famous psychic of his day. William Thackeray saw and believed as did Elizabeth Barrett Browning, Robert Owen, Mrs Trollope, the Pope (he was expelled from Rome as a necromancer), the Tzar of Russia and the Empress Eugenie of France; Charles Dickens remained sceptical, but would not give up attendance at séances; Napoleon III, Leo Tolstoy and Robert Browning hated him while Charles Darwin was eager to put him to the test.

This celebrated friend of the powerful began his career with a vision, just like his mother. One night he saw 'in a cloud of bright-ness' a childhood friend who had died three days earlier. 'The ghostly figure made three circles in the air with his hand and the hand began slowly to disappear, then the arm, and finally the whole body melted away'. The vision left Home paralysed for a while. Unlike his mother, Home would become, not just another local village wise man, but one of the first trans-Atlantic celebrities.

Despite the importance of science and technology in the Western world and the advances of rational thought, a general belief in the paranormal remained both widespread and deeply felt. Curiously, this shift in attitudes towards the dead was the product of the neuroses of a technological modern society. If there is a story to be read in this ethereal realm, it is not that of the eternal return of the non living, but rather the narration of a progressive and inclusive modernity in which supernaturalism was an integral part of the contemporary experience of the Victorian mind.

The modern form of spiritualism that evolved in the Victorian era represented a decisive break from all previous supernaturalism: a revolutionary leap from an essentially archaic, religious belief system concerned with the limits of sin and redemption (and *fear* of the dead) to one that was, in most of its features materialist, religiously ambivalent or agnostic (and fascinated with the dying and the dead). The development of carefully constructed mourning rituals and the belief that the dead were only 'asleep' and not departed went hand in hand with a new gothic monumentality in funereal sculpture and private cemetery gardens. In many of its more theorized aspects it was engaged in an aggressive debate with Darwinism or the consequences of Darwinism, and Darwin himself took a lively interest in the doings of clairvoyants. This 'revolution' was driven by the belief that contact with the dead and other disembodied spirit entities was a desirable thing. It was in direct opposition to the archaic belief that such contact should be feared and shunned and practitioners treated as necromancers.

The new 'rational' supernatural was believed to go beyond religion and science and explain both. Although this advance was supposedly based on 'natural law' and a type of spiritualized universal mechanics, it was founded on one central dogmatic assertion: *survival after death* as proven beyond doubt through the increasing activities of mediums. The medium was to spiritualism what the sensitive was to mesmerism. The meaning of this new area of speculation was summed up in a sermon preached after the death of the actress Anny Ahlers (who died in suspicious circumstances in 1933). The sermon was given by her husband:

I believe that we can and do have communication, in God's providence, and under God's care and protection, with those who have gone on before . . . If we believe in religion at all, we know that the unseen state is a reality. The subject can be approached from the point of view of faith or from that of science. By blending the two, the faith of the one is strengthened and the science of the other is helped.

Spiritualism proves that those who pass on are subject to growth, and that they advance sphere by sphere upwards and onwards. At first, a spirit is earthbound. Gradually, he [*sic*] goes on and becomes acclimatized to the unseen. After learning he goes on until at last he becomes a leader and a teacher. Spiritualism is a science, not a speculation.[10]

This seemed not to be a debate between faith and reason, but rather two forms of logic based on quite unrelated conceptual systems. Indeed, most writers in the occult insisted upon the conspiratorial nature of both conventional science and established religion which (against the evidence of history) had worked together in order to *conceal* a set of truths they only dimly understand but which they, nevertheless, fully comprehend would destroy their power should such truths be revealed to a wide public. 'Illuminated knowledge' would, clairvoyants believed, soon replace both science and religion; séances and clairvoyancy were the portals to a new revelation.

If science emphasized effect (not self-based) then 'magical' encounters emphasized affect (where subjectivity is a necessary corollary of determination: the self as conduit). Magical encounters were suffused with an overabundance of affect where a 'fact' in the world was determined by the presence of subjectivity and then returned as an effect (bells ringing, levitation, spirit hands). Spectators at such events were not mere onlookers, but witnesses of a new revelation of history in which time itself was abolished and with it the linear idea of events.

Such hallucination and its experience 'in the world' aspired to the conditions of history and yet was excluded not only by outside derision but by its own incapacity to conform to historical determination (nor yet to the theological determination of the miraculous – of which it falls short). Excluded from history although experienced as an event, the supernatural was relegated by its own processes and procedures to pseudo-history and the marginal, *confronting* history but incapable of being incorporated within it. Supernatural experience occurred *within* history but lacked significance: the effort of becoming an event was too great for the weight of its signification, leaving it only a mere anecdotal status.

It is this dislocation that makes the hallucination an event but prevents it from becoming history. Instead all is determined by a certain *scenario*, a theatre of staging, witnessing and participation at once cerebral and visceral. This scenario, according to its script, setting and direction, creates a framework whose dynamic tends towards zero: a trajectory out of time altogether into the ritualistic and mythic.

The decisive break in the history of supernaturalism occurred with the advent of spiritualism in 1848. While revolution disturbed Europe (and Marx mused in gothic metaphors over the 'spectre' of communism), John Fox, his wife, Margaret, and daughters Margaret and Kate moved into their new home in Hydesville, New York State. Within weeks the family had become the victims of strange rapping noises. One night, one of the daughters challenged this phenomenon with the words, 'Here, Mr. Splitfoot, do as I do' (the reference to the devil was soon conveniently forgotten), after which time the sisters became the centre and the controllers of the weird activity.

It might have been expected that the happenings at Hydesville would have quietly passed into one of the more bizarre backwaters of history, especially since the sisters were exposed by three professors from the University of Buffalo on 17 February 1851 who 'proved' the noises were those of cracking knee joints and both sisters themselves made and then retracted statements about fraudulent practice, but this was not to be the case, for their own brand of non-denominational mysticism and inspiration was steeped in the peculiarly hysterical and histrionic atmosphere of American religious practice and participated in the millennialism and apocalyptic imagination of New York State. On precisely the day of the first Fox phenomena it was claimed by Andrew Jackson Davis 'The Seer of Poughkeepsie', a self-taught healer and mystic, that a voice had spoken to him, proclaiming 'Brother, the great work has begun.' The Fox sisters and their small house became the centre of a cult and they had found their John the Baptist.

By the 1850s there was a positive epidemic of spiritualistic phenomena and mediums flourished on both sides of the Atlantic, mainly led by American spiritualists and charismatics or British spiritualist preachers who chose to settle in the United States such as Emma Britten, the Bang Sisters of Lily Dale near Buffalo, Thomas Lake Herm and Daniel Dunglas Home himself. It was the feats of levitation by Home that inspired Henry Sidgwick and Frederick Myers among others to found the Society for Psychical Research in 1882. Myers was particularly interested in telepathy while Edward Gurney and Eleanor Sidgwick produced work with titles such as *Phantasms of the Living* and *Phantasms of the Dead*, works that insisted on the peculiar, but ordinariness of what was observed.

From a quite different starting point, Mary Baker Eddy had, in 1879, founded the first 'Church of Christian Scientist' whose ambiguously and oxymoronically named system became the other part of the evangelical appeal of spiritualist belief. By the early twentieth century, Lily Dale had become spiritualism's largest summer camp, its focal point the now moved and resurrected cottage of John and Margaret Fox! Meanwhile Christian Science had taken on the trappings of respectable religious belief.

All this activity in the realm of this 'new' supernaturalism (the term was retained until the Second World War when it was replaced by discussion of the paranormal) might have remained at the level of popular superstition and arcane parlour tricks – might have remained simply a fashionable scandal – had it not been for the fortuitous conjunction of a certain expression of nonconformist belief, Christian Science and Theosophy. With these, the new occult gained its creed and its geography and it was into these that believers were able to insert their own personal and idiosyncratic narratives.

Helena Petrovna Blavatsky, better known as Madame Blavatsky, began her rise to fame after visiting the Eddy Farm (home to Mary Baker Eddy's daughter and scene of extraordinary mediumistic performances by her grandchildren) in Vermont in 1874. With some psychic ability and much personal presence she was taken up by one Colonel Olcott and together they formed a 'Miracle Club' followed by the Theosophical Society, which they founded in 1875 with William Quem Judge. Inspired first by the mysterious entity 'Tuit Bey', Blavatsky moved on to India where further inspirational entities led her to complete an occult cosmography described in *Isis Unveiled* (1877) and *The Secret Doctrine* (1888).

Despite the scorn of theosophists for Darwin (Madame Blavatsky kept a stuffed baboon dressed as a Darwinian professor in her apartments) theosophical spiritism follows the logic of materialism. Despite the debates that flared up in the late nineteenth century, spiritualism was never able to demonstrate the distinction between spirit and matter nor clarify their interconnectedness. Colonel Olcott (who influenced Blavatsky) could never decide if his belief system was scientific or spiritual. Unlike science, spiritualistic knowledge aimed to provide a particular form of ontology based on the conjunction of personality and death. In this model of evolution death is demoted to a peculiarly minor stage of life:

> Death does not say farewell to man as an individual; death heightens his individuality; death is one more rung in the ladder of his individual evolution and he emerges from death as an individual with his consciousness intact, with his memory in no way impaired, with all the faculties of mind and spirit ready to give him a larger service, because they are freed from the limitations of a physical body with its cramping, restricting, five poor senses.[11]

Theosophy's immense success at the end of the last century was due in part to its own logic which was at once laudable and reasonable as well as inherently revolutionary in its democratic and pluralistic vision of one human family. It stood for the formation of a universal human brotherhood without distinction of race, creed, sex, caste, or colour; the encouragement of studies in comparative religion, philosophy and science, and the investigation of unexplained laws of nature and the powers latent in man.

These general principles coalesced, however, with the ideas of survival after death, disembodied spirit guidance, contact by select illumination, out of body travel, psycho-kenesis, automatic writing, space travel, mystic and occult brotherhood. These further principles were indispensable to theosophy despite its attempt to differentiate itself from spiritualism as a general set of vaguely located beliefs. Thus, Theosophy 'sought to replace the *belief system* of the Christian religion and the *knowledge system* of modern science . . . with a spiritual knowledge that was free from associations of guilt and which did not carry within it a moral imperative. Theosophy transmuted scientific knowledge into an echo of spiritual knowledge.'

Mary Baker Eddy, meanwhile, joined her own belief in the healing powers of 'truth in Christ' to the strictly materialistic methods she had learned from her mentor Phineas Quimby. After Quimby's death in 1866, she added a theological gloss to his ideas and made them her raison d'etre. At one point she even created a 'metaphysical college'. Moreover, despite her attempts to differentiate her belief system from spiritualism in general and materialism in particular she still reproduced much that was central to the emergence of modern supernaturalism. Her arguments often differed only in the degree of phrasing from much that preceded them. Christian Science rewrote Christianity from a natural or rational perspective and rethought science from a metaphysical perspective.

The new arts were not immune from the influence of the spirit world. Photography, that most scientific of art forms, was soon to be put to use in trying to capture the aetherial world of spirits conjured by the occultists. In photography it was felt that the fleeting and invisible would become visible and permanent. In capturing the spectral on what was already a spectral apparatus (later Sir Arthur Conan Doyle would hope to talk to spirits through the telephone), photographers would redeem their medium from one that was only good for recording the mundane. It happened as an accident, when William H. Mumbler caught the fleeting trace of a (real) women on his photographic plate, but others thought that this was the way into the spirit world. The loss of life in both the Commune of Paris and the Civil War in America prompted collusion with mediums as well as experimentation with the medium.

Spirit photography took off in America, wafted to France and thence to Britain. It was most popular during the 1860s to 1870s and it curiously accompanies that other foray into the unknown, the pornographic photo. Both were aimed at large commercial profit, and while some photographers were genuinely interested in ectoplasm and spiritualism most were happy to produce spoof photos of shrouded spectres and ectoplasmic extrusions. The use of white sheets to produce 'ghosts' as well as the use of 'ghost stamps' (a technical device to distort a normal picture by adding a light source not present) kept an avid public more than happy. The exhibitionist spirit medium 'Eva P' sat for nude for photographs with ectoplasm coming from her vagina and sliding over her breasts creating in so doing a spectacular and legitimated pornographic theatre of which photography became the accomplice.

The powerful combination of nonconformist religion and theosophy or similar doctrines created a new area of popular culture – essentially modern, American and plebeian, which found a quick and easy acceptance in Britain. It is this Anglo-Americanism which dominated the modern popular revival of belief in the occult and which grew independently of the more aristocratic and arcane European versions which owed many of their ideas to this side of the Channel. Indeed, the Anglo-American version of spiritualism often merged and subsumed independent European Romantic magical and spiritual traditions which appeared to develop independently, but when investigated more closely, were tied to developments that may be considered broadly Anglo-American, or which are associated with European émigré culture in anglophone countries.

A pattern of plebian revelation had already established itself in the wanderings of American 'holy men' and seers and their fundamentalist followers. Most famous of all of these revelation narratives was Joseph Smith's vision of the 'angel', the cornerstone of Mormonism:

On the evening of the . . . twenty-first of September [1823] . . . I betook myself to prayer and supplication to Almighty God . . .

While I was thus in the act of calling upon God, I discovered a light appearing in my room, which continued to increase until the room was lighter than at noonday, when immediately a personage appeared at my bedside, standing in the air, for his feet did not touch the floor . . .

He said there was a book deposited, written upon gold plates, giving an account of the former inhabitants of this continent, and the source from whence they sprang. He also said that the fulness of the everlasting Gospel was contained in it, as delivered by the Saviour to the ancient inhabitants;

Also, that there were two stones . . . and the possession and use of these stones were what constituted *Seers* in ancient or former times; and that God had prepared them for the purpose of translating the book. (*Book of Mormon*)

It is only in the 'library' of the mind (the often encountered 'psychic library') that Smith could find those suitable books that were readable only by the light of illumination. Here also were stored Blavatsky's *Book of Dzyan* and Edgar Allan Poe's books of occult knowledge as well as those strange inventions, books whose very presence sends men mad – the strange play *The King in Yellow* invented by Robert Chambers and, of course, *the Necronomicon* of H. P. Lovecraft.

Spiritualism was a product of the mid-nineteenth century with its emphasis on individualism, populist mass culture, democratic inclusion, market choice, religiosity and revolutionary dreaming. It found a ready home in Victorian Britain, first as the answer to middle-class social and religious qualms and then later as a compensation for working-class poverty and exploitation. One commentator (Ronald Pearsall) has noted that spiritualism 'was the first popular movement to be imported from the United States' into Britain, a movement not only 'tailor made for the nineteenth century' but inherently tied to an entrepreneurial and acquisitive age.

> [The Victorians] wanted marvels and wonders . . . and because Victorian England [and America] was a capitalist country subsisting on the laws of supply and demand, they got them.[12]

Right from the beginning,

> The entrepreneurs were cashing in on the occult mood. In Florence 'guaranteed' turning tables were being sold with the tag 'It Moves!' In London, crystal balls were all the rage, and the 'original' was bought by Lady Blessington from an 'Egyptian magician', though she admitted that she never got the hang of it. An optician in London was turning them out by the dozen. Lord Stanhope said, 'Many people use the balls, without the moral courage to confess it'.[13]

Most spiritualists and clairvoyants were earning a living by theatrical performance or after dinner performances in the private houses of the wealthy as was the case with Ira and William Davenport from Buffalo, New York and their 'spirit cabinet' or John Henry Anderson, the 'Wizard of the North' whose theatrical events were the talk of London, or indeed the entrepreneurial European wanderings of Douglas Home himself.

> The séance becomes the defining *scene* of spiritualist activity. The spiritualist salon is filled with mediumistic levitation; kinetic movement of objects; raps and taps, cracks and whistles, snatches of birdsong and spirit voices; spirit drawing and writing; ectoplasmic extrusions and floating trumpets; the appearance of spirit bodies or dematerialised hands or limbs; the sudden appearance of rings, coins, flowers or sugar plums. (Florence, 1869)[14]

As real bodies dematerialized in séances and on photographic plates, the nineteenth-century American holding company took on legal flesh and bones. This was the materialization of Frankenstein's monster in reality. Not made of the remnants of the graveyard, nevertheless real and immortal, the creation of the legal profession.

> In America the corporation would have a fertile new life. Since corporations, the creatures of government, could be made immortal and could be given whatever powers the lawmakers wished for them. Sir Edward Coke, seventeenth-century champion of common-law rights against a tyrant-king, warned that corporations 'cannot commit treason, nor be outlawed nor excommunicated, for they have no souls.' Corporations [in the United States] . . . would spread over the land, and finally permeate every citizen's daily life. . . . The corporation had many advantages over the enterprising individual. . . . A creature of the law, it was immortal. . . . Lawyers presided over the mysteries of corporation law. Property became a new realm of the occult.[15]

Secret business trusts in the USA, when outlawed, metamorphosed in the hands of managing lawyers (of whom the chief magician was Rockefeller's Samuel C. T. Dodd) into the 'holding company' of which Standard Oil was the first in 1899. A paper delivered at the annual meeting of the American Bar Association in 1900 proclaimed, 'there is . . . complete freedom of contract; competition is now universal, and as merciless as nature and natural selection'. Far removed (at least on paper) from human (i.e. fallible) interference, the 'immortal' but 'soulless' corporation retained the same rights as actual humans, but avoided the responsibilities. The corporation was entirely the creation of law: an animus without anima moving with its ghostly presence through American history defended by the 6th and 14th Amendments and protected by 'due process', enjoying the rights of a 'natural person' but without substance or consciousness yet endowed with an immutable and immortal purposive 'will'. The corporation had rights in exact proportion to its non-materiality. Here was a new *spectral* economic and legal body against which popular and populist refusals were to little avail.

Borrowing a gothic metaphor, Karl Marx described the haunting 'spectre' of communism in *The Communist Manifesto* which was the ghostly double and terrifying nemesis of that other spectre: money. Money was both the alchemical principle of transubstantiation and the principle of eternal production. 'It is as though, for example, the discovery of a stone granted me possession of all the sciences, irrespective of my individuality.' Money was the *élan vitale*, the new linking force within society and capable of infinite and eternal transformation. Ironically, it was money which combined the material and spiritual universes through its infinite power of reproduction. 'All commodities are perishable money', said Marx and 'money is *imperishable* commodity'.

It is no surprise that belief in the world of spirit, a belief conditioned essentially by social disenchantment should cause disenfranchised groups to attempt to unite that belief with political and economic arguments derived from utopian socialists. For a time in the nineteenth century there was certainly debate and bridge building between both spiritualists and socialists and many utopian socialists were also in the spiritualist movement especially in Britain where many of the founders of the Labour Party were spiritualists. Spiritualism's egalitarian nature also allowed women to participate and created ground for temperance and suffrage debate.

Socialism and spiritualism form two means by whereby the masses make their revolt. Both provide for refusal and rebellion and both lead to a restored harmony, 'on the other side' – the other side of capitalist history. If the socialist revolution itself led to emancipation from the thrall of history, then for the spiritualist that emancipation or release came through death. The twin knowledge of death and of history, their secret occulted meanings revealed, allowed those who understood to rise above the mundane and achieve full consciousness. Such consciousness was the result of understanding the hidden processes of life and its universal or cosmic determinants.

Socialism, theosophy and psychology may have entered the consciousness of many in the late nineteenth century, but atavism was not so easily disregarded. Edith Wharton, thinking back to a period of childhood illness in the 1870s could vividly remember the delirium brought on by 'typhoid fever' combined with reading 'robber stories' and tales of 'ghosts' which 'brought on a serious relapse' from being haunted by 'formless horrors . . . like some dark undefinable menace, forever dogging my steps, lurking and threatening'. So bad were these waking nightmares that up to her late twenties she was unable to sleep in a room she knew contained a book of ghost stories. So fearful was she and so superstitious of the results that the ghost books in the library had to be burnt before she could effectively sleep at night. Demons could be in the room or in your head as Henry James conceded when he wrote *The Turn of the Screw* where the governess is 'mad' but the ghosts exist. Such thinking was formalized partially in Darwinian terms by Sigmund Freud from the 1890s who considered such conditions of terror the outcome of repressed and inherited thoughts, something he did not come to formulate until the essay 'The Uncanny' of 1916.

Yet was the fear of the supernatural merely an hallucination emanating from our own bodies or repressed thoughts? For many thinkers such explanations would not wash, or at the least would simply add a gloss to fears that were real because they existed in the world not in the head. The orientalist and horror writer Lefcadio Hearn, for instance, had this explanation of cosmic dread in 1900. Unlike Freud, Hearn located our darkest nightmares in the fear of contact not with what is familiar but with that which is forbidden, the ontological and atavistic fear threatening the integrity of both body and soul.

> What *is* the fear of ghosts among those who believe in ghosts? All fear is the result of experience, – experience of the individual or of the race, – experience either of the present life or of lives forgotten. Even the fear of the unknown can have no other origin. And the fear of ghosts must be a product of past pain.

Probably the fear of ghosts, as well as the belief in them, had its beginning in dreams. It is a peculiar fear. No other fear is so intense; yet none is so vague. Feelings thus voluminous and dim are super-individual mostly, – feelings inherited, – feelings made within us by the experience of the dead . . .

Nowhere do I remember reading a plain statement of the reason why ghosts are feared. Ask any ten intelligent persons of your acquaint-ance, who remember having once been afraid of ghosts, to tell you exactly why they were afraid, – to define the fancy behind the fear; – and I doubt whether even one will be able to answer the question. The literature of folk-lore – oral and written – throws no clear light upon the subject. We find, indeed, various legends of men torn asun-der by phantoms; but such gross imaginings could not explain the peculiar quality of ghostly fear. It is not a fear of bodily violence. It is not even a reasoning fear, – not a fear that can readily explain itself, – which would not be the case if it were founded upon definite ideas of physical danger. Furthermore, although primitive ghosts may have been imagined as capable of tearing and devouring, the common idea of a ghost is certainly that of a being intangible and imponderable.

Now I venture to state boldly that the common fear of ghosts is *the fear of being touched by ghosts,* – or, in other words, that the imagined Supernatural is dreaded mainly because of its imagined power to touch. . . . And who can ever have had the sensation of being touched by ghosts? The answer is simple: – *Everybody who has been seized by phantoms in a dream.*

Elements of primeval fears – fears older than humanity – doubtless enter into the child-terror of darkness. But the more definite fear of ghosts may very possibly be composed with inherited results of dream-pain, – ancestral experience of nightmare. And the intuitive terror of supernatural touch can thus be evolutionally explained.

('Nightmare Touch')

Unlike De Quincey, Coleridge or Fuseli, Hearné never did wish for bad dreams. His dreams seem indeed to replicate Jonathan Harker's fears on first seeing Dracula crawl down his castle wall.

They were not like any people that I had ever known. They were shadowy dark-robed figures, capable of atrocious self-distortion, – capable, for instance, of growing up to the ceiling, and then across it, and then lengthening themselves, head-downwards, along the opposite wall.

And like Harker, Hearn waits for the,

Ghastly footfall. Then, without a creak, the bolted door would open, – slowly, slowly, – and the thing would enter, gibbering sound-lessly, – and put out hands, – and clutch me, – and toss me to the black ceiling, – and catch me descending to toss me up again, and again, and again. . . . In those moments the feeling was not fear: fear itself had been torpified by the first seizure. It was a sensation that has no name in the language of the living. For every touch brought a shock of something infinitely worse than pain, – something that thrilled into the innermost secret being of me, – a sort of abominable electricity, discovering unimagined capacities of suffering in totally unfamiliar regions of sentiency.

It may be doubted whether the phantasms of any particular night-mare have a history older than the brain in which they move. But the shock of the touch would seem to indicate *some point of dream-contact with the total race-experience of shadowy seizure*. It may be that profun-dities of Self, – abysses never reached by any ray from the life of sun, – are strangely stirred in slumber, and that out of their blackness immediately responds a shuddering of memory, measureless even by millions of years. ('Nightmare Touch')

This fear of the touch of the ghostly dead emerges elsewhere too,

For some minutes he lay and pondered over the possibilities; then he turned over sharply, and with his eyes open lay breathlessly listen-ing. There had been a movement, he was sure, in the empty bed on the opposite side of the room. Tomorrow he would have it moved, for there must be rats or something playing about in it. It was quite now. No! the commotion began again. There was a rustling and shak-ing: surely more than any rat could cause.

I can figure to myself something of the Professor's bewilderment and horror, for I have in a dream thirty years back seen the same thing happen; but the reader will hardly perhaps, imagine how dread-ful it was to him to see a figure suddenly sit up in what he had known was an empty bed. . . .

Somehow, the idea of getting past it and escaping through the door was intolerable to him; he could not have borne – he didn't know why – to touch it; and as for its touching him, he would sooner dash himself through the window than have that happen. . . .what he chiefly remembers about it is a horrible, an intensely horrible, face of *crumpled linen*. . . . There seemed to be absolutely nothing material about it save the bedclothes of which it had made itself a body. (M. R. James, 'Oh, Whistle, and I'll Come to You, My Lad')

Terrors there may have been, but there was also consolation in ghost stories. The development of the 'traditional' ghostly tale went hand in hand with a nostalgia that was most distinct during the late Victorian and Edwardian periods for the very landscape of a 'lost' England and Anglo-Saxonism vanishing under the weight of modernity. England now became 'olde' England, a haunted landscape with mock Tudor revival buildings, tourist guides to the quaint and forgotten and tea rooms for cyclists. Surprisingly this older forgotten world was discovered in motor cars and charabancs – England had become a gigantic ghostly palimpsest available to the inquisitive and adventurous tourist of whom Rudyard Kipling was one of the first.

A day in the car in an English country is a day in some fairy museum where all the exhibits are alive and real and yet none the less delightfully mixed up with the books. For instance, in six hours, I can go from . . . the Norman Conquest and the Barons' War into Richard Jefferies' country, and so through the Regency . . . in England the dead, twelve coffin deep, clutch hold of my wheels at every turn, till I sometimes wonder that the very road does not bleed. That is the real joy of motoring – the exploration of this amazing England.[16]

For adventurous visitors who strayed off the beaten track the charm of the English manor house or castle was encapsulated both in ruin and in ghostly presences which still haunted its ancient battlements, but this time merely for an ornamental and picturesque purpose.

The two towers are crowned by turrets, named the watch and signal turrets. A moat surrounds the castle, and was spanned by a drawbridge, the vertical slits on each side of the central recessed window being fitted with levers for raising and lowering the bridge. Over the archway are the arms of the Fiennes family, a wolf-dog with its paws on a banner and three lions rampant. If we were to pass through this gate we should find the ruins of an immense castle, a veritable town. . . . The ghosts of its great owners seem to haunt the scene of their former splendour, and one noted uneasy spirit inhabited Drummer's hall, and marched along the battlements beating a devil's tattoo on his drum. But perhaps he was only a gardener in league with the smugglers, and used this ghostly means for conveying to them a needful signal. Ghosts often frequent the old houses of England and our artist's sketch of the haunted house, Harvington Hall, Worcestershire, which looks delightfully picturesque in the moon-light, certainly suggests the appearance of a ghostly resident or visitor.[17]

Such ghosts no longer fed the thrills of the gothic imagination, they no longer clanked and screamed. Instead they were imbued with psychic energy of a preternatural type and as such remained behind as spiritual reminders of our buried history and tradition, something not to be tampered with nor questioned, yet now charming and inviting rather than alarming reminders of psychic and cultural repression.

We know of such a house in Lancashire, which, like Harvington Hall, is encircled by a moat. It contains a skull in a case let into the wall of the staircase. This skull has been cast into the moat, buried in the ground, and removed in many other ways; but terrible happenings ensue: storms rage and lightnings flash, and groans are heard, until the skull is brought back to its niche, when peace ensues. . . . These ancient traditions, ghosts and legends, add greatly to the charm of our old houses.[18]

Chapter Eight
It's Alive: The Rise of the Gothic Movie

Ghosts were all very well, but monsters were better. During the Christmas period of 1887 the Gaiety Theatre put on a 'melodramatic burlesque' (a musical pantomime) of *Frankenstein* by 'Richard Henry', the combined pen name of Richard Butler and H. Chance Newton who were well known for writing amusing and light-hearted spoofs. Music was by Meyer Lutz. The play was in three acts and six scenes, including 'a laboratory' and the Italian Alps, all of which were interspersed with comic songs and slapstick. Frankenstein was played by Miss Nellie Farron and the monster by Mr Fred Leslie, while an unlikely vampire count called Visconti was played by Mr E. J. Lonnen. It is interesting that by the last quarter of the nineteenth century the idea of putting vampires and Frankenstein in the same environment was so established that it needed no explanation.

Act One began in the village of 'Villasuburbia' in the 'Pass of Pizzicato' complete with its 'local inn keeper', 'the village is vexed with vampires' and 'bandits have banned its inhabitants'. Into this scenario we are introduced to 'a patent mechanical man' and 'the sudden appearance of the monster'. Songs are sung to continue the narrative as the audience is introduced to both 'Frankenstein', 'the vampire's victim' and a passing 'witch'. As the curtain falls a 'lovely woman' is spied in the distance. Act Two begins with the monster 'ordering a bride' and the reappearance of the vampire now dressed as a 'fire brigadier' and a 'dispensing doctor'; the whole act culminating in the imprisonment of the monster and the song 'Honeymoonshine' which bring the curtain down. Act Three was set in London's 'clubland' and began with a satire on the 'special constable' and the recent disturbances in Trafalgar Square and ended in the Arctic with a song called 'Iceberglary'.

During 1888, there were two versions of *Dr Jekyll and Mr Hyde* playing in the West End of London. One was an authorized version written for the Lyceum, the theatre managed by Henry Irving and the other was at the Opera Comique where the tale was played as a 'harlequinade' starring David E. Bandmann. Both plays (00014) were from the same script by Richard Mansfield who had had great success in Boston and New York. The Bandmann version was immediately targeted as a plagiarism and subject to a lawsuit by Longman, the publishers of the original novel, who were seeking an injunction to stop production, a long and complex procedure which rarely halted illegal copies. This must have failed because a journalist from *The Sunday Times* compared the plays and found Mansfield's version merely 'dull' and Bandmann's 'ludicrous' (12 August 1888), but *The Times* was already prejudiced against Robert Louis Stevenson as an author who they thought a 'scribbler' only capable of 'pot boilers' (29 July 1888). *The Graphic* was kinder to Mansfield's Lyceum version, finding in his performance something that was 'at once human and supernatural' (11 August 1888) and that his transformation into an 'unearthly creature' sent a 'a thrill not of horror, but of awe and wonderment' through the audience. If *the Illustrated Sporting and Dramatic News* thought the Lyceum production lacked 'explanation, logic [and] justification' (18 August 1888) as they thought did the original, this seemed not to put off audiences who were so keen to know how Mansfield succeeded in his transformation scenes that magazines ran features on them.

Dr Jekyll and Mr Hyde remained a favourite with theatre audiences (temporarily being halted after the Jack the Ripper murders) and in early 1910, there was a new version produced at the Queen's Theatre, Shaftesbury Avenue where the manager was Henry Irving's son H. B. Irving. Stevenson had actually suggested a play version to Henry Irving who had turned him down. The play itself was written by J. Comyns Carr with H. B. Irving playing Dr Jekyll and was preceded by a sketch called 'The Plumbers'. By the twentieth century the idea of psychological realism (or maybe the prurient interest in drug abuse) may have created the respectability that made the show, 'Play of the Month' in *Playgoer and Society* (29 January 1910).

Henry Irving was no slacker when it came to sensation and he had appeared in a series of plays throughout the late nineteenth century that put his stamp on the genre. It was Irving who starred in the most famous gothic melodrama of them all, *The Bells* adapted by Leopold Lewis from *The Polish Jew*, 'a dramatic study' by the French authors Erkmann and Chatrian and which managed to charm and shock audiences on both sides of the Atlantic during 1871 while proving itself the most popular British play of the time.

The play, told in three acts, concerns itself with the tale of Mathias (played originally by Irving), the happily married burgomeister of a little village in Alsace. There is a terrible snow storm on Christmas Eve, 1833. Christian, the young quartermaster of gendarmes is about to marry Mathias's daughter, the beautiful Annette. But the night is dark and the storm fearful, which brings the village folk to discuss the brutal murder of a rich Jewish merchant on an evening just like this some 15 years ago. Mathias, having come back from a visit to a fair where a mesmerist has been performing, silences the conversation for he is, the murderer, now grown rich on the proceeds of his crime, but also plagued by a bad conscience which manifests itself in hallucinations of the bells on the Jewish merchant's horse and in continuous bad dreams. The sense of dread is established by the presence of the murdered man who waits silently at the back of the stage.

The JEW . . . suddenly turns his face, which is ashy pale, and fixes his eyes sternly upon [Mathias, who] utters a prolonged cry of terror. (*The Bells: A Drama in Three Acts*, Act One)

The final act was written so that Irving could give full vent to his histrionic acting skills. It is almost totally taken up with Mathias's nightmare dream of retribution, in which dream he is put under hypnosis by the mesmerist, and unable now to avoid confessing his crime, is condemned to death. He wakes and is found by the villagers, but he is raving and raving this time about the hangman's noose, just as before about the monstrous bells; he dies and the curtain falls. The play would be both prophetic and influential. The guilt-ridden anti-hero may have looked back to the melodramas of the previous

40 years, but the setting, with its burgomaster, gendarmes, inn keepers, peasants and storm looked forward to the atmosphere of films like *The Cabinet of Dr Caligari* as well as the opening of the horror films of James Whale and Tod Browning in the 1930s; the moment the merchant enters the inn snow covered, a stranger, would be also reproduced by Hammer films throughout their own oeuvre. Nevertheless, the play would be one inspiration for another masterpiece of the gothic.

Indeed, it would be the flawed masterpiece by Henry Irving's stage manager Bram Stoker that would become the staple of theatre and film. *Dracula* was published as a novel in 1897, but gained no real attention.[1] The book made a modest return until film makers and theatrical impresarios saw its potential. Friedrich Wilhelm Murnau's film *Nosferatu* of 1922 broke copyright and was suppressed after Mrs Stoker sued. The book would remain a drawing room melodrama even in Tod Browning's official filmic version which had been written as a screenplay by John Balderston following Hamilton Deane's London production.

On Valentine's night, 1927, *The Vampire Play, Dracula* opened at the Little Theatre, John Street in the Strand and played for many months before transferring to the Garrick where it was equally successful. The play by Deane and H. L. Warburton starred Sam Livesey as Van Helsing, Bernard Guest as Jonathan Harker, Bernard Jukes as 'R. M.' Renfield and Raymond Huntley as Count Dracula. The play was in three acts with an epilogue and it consisted of the study of Jonathan Harker's house on Hampstead Heath; Mrs Harker's boudoir; again, the study of Jonathan Harker's house; and the coach house at Carfax (which was now set on Hampstead Heath rather than Purfleet as in the original book). Lucy was already 'dead' before the curtain rose, and as an amusing twist Deane introduced the action with a little humorous warning speech and a nurse waited in the foyer for those overcome with the vapours. The play was preceded by Isabel Hirstfield playing a selection from her repertoire on the piano forte and which continued during the interval.

Dracula caught the attention of both playgoers and critics despite its awful dialogue which was picked up by all the reviewers from *the Sunday Times* on 14 February and the *Morning Post* the next day to the *Observer* on 20 February. So risible was the dialogue that both the *Observer* and the *Morning Post* offered parodies:

> Mr Lomath pronounced the word 'personally' as if it were spelt 'Pahrs O Nally' and said 'Sahr Vis' when he meant 'service'. Miss Patrick talked about a dreadful 'Leth Are Gee' which afflicted her 'Leems'. (*Observer*)

Nevertheless, the *Tatler*'s critic reviewing the production at the Garrick on 14 December and while disparaging the play as 'sensational crock' and considering it 'crude' in execution, still found space to admire its shock value, shocks which sent those of a 'limited intelligence' on a visit to the foyer nurse. At the Little Theatre version, the critic admitted to the fact he they 'leaped out of [his] skin'. The reason for the terror, simply the excellent effects which consisted of

> The mysterious appearances of Count Dracula, with his white face, red eyes, and Satanic wig, the sudden blood-curdling screams from the lunatic asylum next door, the crashing of a picture from the wall, the opening of doors and the turning of chairs – all these disturbances leave their impression on the audience plunged for the most part in total darkness and half-choked at moments by that ghastly vapour which stole through the bedroom-window of the unfortunate Mrs Harker and indicated the coming of the disembodied were-wulf [*sic*] to suck the life-blood from his victim's throat.

Stoker had stumbled onto a mythic gothic character who rose above the circumstances of a rather old-fashioned epistolary novel and who was actually largely removable from the circumstances of the novel in which he featured. And yet Stoker had also revitalized a genre that was essentially moribund, having long since been replaced by tales of ghost-haunted country houses or hallucinating schizophrenics. By placing the story firmly in modernity with its references to shorthand, typewriters, dictating machines, train time tables and blood transfusions, Stoker effectively created the first real gothic monster who enters the space of the contemporary world from an ancient but as yet undead spot in the middle of the Hapsburg Empire.

'It is the nineteenth century up-to-date with a vengeance', muses Jonathan Harker 'and yet, . . . the old centuries . . . have, powers of their own which mere "modernity" cannot kill' (Chapter 3) This collision is dramatically described as Dracula exits his castle, the last great gothic castle in literature.

> What I saw was the Count's head coming out from the window. . . . I was at first interested and somewhat amused . . . But my very feelings turned to repulsion and terror when I saw the whole man slowly emerge from the window and begin to crawl down the castle wall over that dreadful abyss, *face down*, with his cloak spreading out around him like great wings. (Chapter 3)

The old novels set in medieval or sixteenth-century Spain or Italy were revived in the scenery of Transylvania, but also made redundant by the creation of the forbidding world of the Carpathian mountains with its own internal mythology and it is this self-contained (if slightly barmy) folklore, rather than the tale itself, which proved so effective. Indeed, folklore studies had only just become legitimate, the term itself not invented until 1846 . . . At the centre of this mythic world it isn't Dracula but Abraham van Helsing who calls the tune with his garlic and crucifixes, mad wife and intimate friend 'Arminius, of Buda-Pesth University' whose research in the old parchments of Hungary is the key to Dracula's identity. 'In the records are such words as "stregoica" – witch, "orgod", and "pokol" – Satan and hell; and in one manuscript this very Dracula, spoken of as "wampyr"'(Chapter 18).

Alongside Van Helsing, Dracula is the embodiment of this mythic world; he is at once satanic and earthbound, seductive and horrible, combining secret fears about imperial vunerability, the sexuality of the 'new woman' and male middle-class impotence when faced with the erotic horror of the psychic invasion of a vague mitteleuropean aristocracy which should somehow be dead, but remains parasitical 'undead' and materially alive in the streets of London; Dracula's natural abode is the silence of the crypt where his victims also 'live'.

> Suddenly . . . I thought I saw something like a white streak, moving between two dark yet-trees at the side of the churchyard farthest from

the tomb, at the same time a dark mass moved from the Professor's side of the ground, and hurriedly went towards it. Then I too moved; but I had to go round headstones and railed-off tombs, and I stumbled over graves. The sky was overcast, and somewhere far off an early cock crew. A little way off, beyond a line of scattered juniper-trees, which marked the pathway to the church, a white, dim figure flitted in the direction of the tomb. The tomb itself was hidden by trees, and I could not see where the figure disappeared. (Chapter 15)

Against this evil is pitted the practical world of daylight and the new world of American progress exemplified by Quincey P. Morris.

'What a fine fellow is Quincey! [exclaims Van Helsing] "a moral Viking". If America can go on breeding men like that, she will be a power in the world indeed'. (Chapter 13)

There was much subliminally subversive material in *Dracula* (the book written two years after Breuer and Freud's *Studies in Hysteria*), which could be exploited on stage or in film. *Dracula* was both an erotic adventure and a horror story and film makers soon understood the visual effect of dominant male leads and sexually potent female victims. It was both the erotic fear of and desire for 'bad' women who turn from good middle-class school marms (Mina) or marriageable upper-class 'gals' (Lucy) that, of course, make the novel more than just a horror tale. Here the seductive actions of the male vampire are matched by the equally seductive intrigues of those females freed from the restraints of middle-class culture. Ordinary women become 'voluptuous' vampires – both corpse brides and demonic sex sirens.

I was not alone. The room was the same, unchanged in any way since I came into it; I could see along the floor, in the brilliant moonlight, my own footsteps marked where I had disturbed the long accumulation of dust. In the moonlight opposite me were three young women, ladies by their dress and manner. I thought at the time that I must be dreaming when I saw them, for, though the moonlight was behind them, they threw no shadow on the floor. They came close to me and looked at me for some time, and then whispered together. Two were dark, and had high aquiline noses, like the Count, and great dark, piercing eyes, that seemed to be almost red when contrasted with the pale yellow moon. The other was fair, as fair as can be, with great, wavy masses of golden hair and eyes like pale sapphires. I seemed somehow to know her face, and to know it in connection with some dreamy fear, but I could not recollect at the moment how or where. All three had brilliant white teeth, that shone like pearls against the ruby of their voluptuous lips. There was something about them that made me uneasy, some longing and at the same time some deadly fear. I felt in my heart a wicked, burning desire that they would kiss me with those red lips. . . . The fair girl shook her head coquettishly, and the other two urged her on. One said:- 'Go on! You are first, and we shall follow; yours is the right to begin'. The other added:- 'He is young and strong; there are kisses for us all.' (Chapter 3)

To destroy such women is a duty and a perverse pleasure both for the slayer and the slayed – a carnival of loathing and lust.

The Thing in the coffin writhed; and a hideous, blood-curdling screech came from the opened red lips. The body shook and quivered and twisted in wild contortions; the sharp white teeth champed together till the lips were cut, and the mouth was smeared with a crimson foam. But Arthur never faltered. He looked like a figure of Thor as his, untrembling arm rose and fell, driving deeper and deeper the mercy-bearing stake, whilst the blood from the pierced heart welled and spurted up around it. His face was set, and high duty seemed to shine through it, the sight of it gave us courage, so that our voices seems to ring through the little vault. (Chapter 16)

It took approximately 50 years of retelling the story to familiarize audiences and readers with the essential characteristics of Dracula, the carnal needs of vampires, the paraphernalia to defeat vampiric attack and the necessity of Dr Van Helsing. None of these ideas had entered Harriet Shelley's head when on 20 November 1814, now largely estranged from her husband, whose all too frequent visits to the Godwins (and therefore Mary) had become scandalous, she wrote a letter to her friend Catherine Nugent in which she divulged that 'the man I once loved is dead. This is a vampire'. By 1960 the tale had been refined beyond the original novel into a mythic tale of twentieth-century fear and desire and in the twenty-first century the vampire is the most famous and strangely attractive of all gothic monsters, not because of the book, but because of film.

The very first horror film was intimately related to the phonograph (the recording and 'talking machine') that Van Helsing and Dr Seward use in their attempts to investigate Renfield and Dracula. The phonograph machine was actually invented in the workshops of Thomas Edison in 1877; the first horror movie, *Frankenstein* was made in Edison's studio in 1910. The phonograph was never popular as an aide to business as in *Dracula*, rather it was adopted for side shows and amusement arcades where it vied for attention with electric shock and X-ray machines. In early 1893, there was an even more exciting breakthrough. Phonograph distributors were invited to witness the first showing of motion picture on a kinetoscope – the picture was a sneeze by one of Edison's assistants. In 1894, the first kinetoscope parlour appeared in New York.

It was soon realized that such 'peep shows' appealed to a voyeuristic male audience and that it was an ideal medium for the thrills of sexual titillation. It was not too long before the improved medium of film was available for gothic horror which in essence shared much of the voyeuristic and titillating. One of these popular new attractions was *The Execution of Mary, Queen of Scots.* A royally robed and bound actor was led to the block and her head placed upon it. Edison then stopped recording, substituted a dummy and when it started again the executioner let fly. The head falls and rolls; the consternation of the original audience was reportedly dramatic of itself.

Edison made his fifteen-minute version of *Frankenstein* in his purpose-built film studio in the Bronx. It starred Charles Ogle as the monster. Make up was left to the actors and Ogle created his own wild-haired, shambling creation using the original costume worn by Thomas Porter Cooke in the 1823 Covent Garden production of *Presumption or the Fate of Frankenstein* as his model. Later James Whale would return to the look created by Ogle. The film itself dramatically curtailed the original story and left a narrative in which the monster is a projection of Frankenstein's distempered brain, finally defeated by the power of love. The film had special effects added and was tinted and was ready for audiences by 18 March 1910. Although popular with the critics, the subject matter was controversial enough

for Edison to put out a type of 'spoiler' in the *Edison Kinetogram* so
that audiences would not be morally outraged by the story of a man
who plays God.

> To those familiar with Mrs. Shelley's story it will be evident that we
> have carefully omitted anything which might be any possibility shock
> any portion of the audience. In making the film the Edison Co. has
> carefully tried to eliminate all actual repulsive situations and to
> concentrate its endeavors upon the mystic and psychological prob-
> lems that are to be found in this weird tale. Wherever, therefore, the
> film differs from the original story it is purely with the idea of elimi-
> nating what would be repulsive to a moving picture audience.[2]

By 1925, the horror film was quickly becoming established as the
central challenge to theatrical mayhem. Yet for a time the silent movies were complemented by a rather strange and aberrant form of
theatrical entertainment popular in Paris and which combined the
thrill of a side show with the moral landscape of criminality and vice.
This was the theatre of the Grand Guinol at 20 Rue Chaptal which
showed 'dramatic entertainment featuring the gruesome or horrible'.
It was a great success which capitalized on the naturalism of The
Theatre Libre's 'rosse' (crass or rotten) plays of the 1880s, plays about
the world of the 'apaches' or underclass of hooligans. By the 1890s,
the former police secretary and yellow paper journalist, Oscar
Metenier was turning out plays using real criminals and circus
strongmen. It was Metenier who coined the term grand guinol after
the British Punch and Judy show and the knockabout horror was
aimed at those audiences who liked 'country freak shows and wax
museums that featured chambers of horror and sensational crime'.[3]
André Lorde was in charge of the theatre between 1901 and 1925,
writing more than one hundred plays that featured murder, severed
limbs and guillotining and where effects were performed close to the
audience, but undetectable by them, thus enhancing the thrills with
inexplicable illusion.

   Horror-melodrama theatre faded with the advent of the talkies
(it did not vanish until the 1960s!), but it had time to profoundly
influence Tod Browning, one of the great horror directors in his
collaboration with one of the great horror actors, Lon Chaney.

Browning, a former magician, was attracted by the potential of the freak show and travelling carnival and although he was an expert on 'black' literature and the stories of Poe preferred to remain for the most part in the visual and visceral world of the 'carny', which indeed is the setting for *The Cabinet of Doctor Caligari*, a film that Browning was to see and admire. Browning's main love was criminality brought about by magicians and illusionists and those out to deceive.

> Mirrors, facial masks, concealed rubber pieces for wounds and burns, fake heads and limbs, all the paraphernalia of magicians, when expertly used –during moments of darkness or out of the spectator's view – created an atmosphere of sickening and eerie realism.[4]

This fascination with cinema as an extension of a theatre of illusion per se came to a climax in *Freaks* with its last shots of the woman-headed chicken, a 'character' that had interested Browning for many years. And yet *Freaks* also turns illusion on its head as Browning used real side-show entertainers for his film rather than have actors create them from make up and prosthetics. Even in *Dracula*, a rather pedestrian filmic version of the American adaption of the London stage play, Browning plays with the illusion of mirrors and of transformations. The minor characters of Renfield (played by a very camp Dwight Frye who steals the show) and the asylum guard (played by E. E. Clive with a dreadful cockney accent) seem a reminder of the vaudeville world, the world of knockabout and the side-show freakery of a perpetually 'grinning man' who eats insects.

Such terrors could not last long on a theatrical stage when faced by the communal experience of cinematic terror effects, continuous talking dialogue, and by the early twentieth century live gothic thrills were more and more to be found at the fair or in carnivals, in ghost rides, freak shows, the chambers of horror in the wax museum and increasingly in the fetishization of Hallowe'en celebrations. The communal memory of shared fear in a live theatre was not entirely lost on audiences, however, and when Carl Laemmle produced the cinematic version of *Frankenstein* in 1931, the film was prefaced by an appearance by Edward Van Sloan coming supposedly through the curtains and onto the stage of a 'live' theatre to warn the audience of the thrills to come.

In Europe, directors may have still used the theatre to supply story lines (as was the case with Robert Wiene's *Cabinet of Doctor Caligari*), but they had already begun to supersede the theatrical staginess of the original scripts with a radical approach to shooting scripts which were influenced (as indeed was the stage) by Expressionism, Surrealism, Cubism and the work of Dhiagalev and Les Ballets Russe. Gothicism would soon become a matter of a new *visual* language determined by set design, musical accompaniment and, above all, cinematography which managed to turn the mundane objects of horror cinema into alienated and spectral substances: doors open and shut on their own; coffin lids slide across the boxes containing the vampire or somnambulist; whole towns exist only as painted and bizarre designs; walls bend and distort, replicating the insanity of the main characters; shadows move of their own accord; coaches travel without drivers. Action was also stronger meat than in Hollywood. The Danish director Benjamin Christensen, for instance, was able to produce *Häxan, or Witchcraft through the Ages* in 1920 with scenes which involved hysterical nuns and devils simulating masturbation. His other movies, which used cutting and chiaroscuro to great effect reflected his own interest in the occult.

Above all, silent European cinematic gothic horror was exemplified in the body of the monster whether Max Shreck as Nosferatu, Max Nordau as the somnambulist Cesare, Robert Wiene as Dr Caligari or Rudolf Klein-Rogge, playing the inventor/magician C. A. Rotwang who brings the gothic into the heart of Fritz Lang's *Metropolis*. This is a weird world of shadow and light, theatrical make up and the stagy rhetorical gestures of silent film, but it is also a powerful world of floating images and of monsters who combine stillness with spastic urgency, their spectral gliding and glances to camera the basis of dreamlike fear.

The new sense of the visual was recognized by British and American film makers too. Indeed, the powerful and silent looks of Bela Lugosi and Boris Karloff straight to camera did more than enough to make their names as the greatest horror stars. Indeed, in his gaze, Bela Lugosi combined the erotic power of sensuality with a conviction of the absolute power of the will while Karloff offered an ambiguous mixture of malevolence and innocence. To heighten suspense, in *Frankenstein*, James Whale makes the audience wait through a whole comic scene before making them privy to the monster's appearance, and even this is given more impact by Karloff's entering backwards and then turning his gaze (filmed in three close-ups) full on the spectator, now made to wish they had not wanted to see what was forbidden by the intervening scene.[5]

In finding a language for the gothic, European film makers found that all the literary paraphernalia of the stage and of the literature that prefigured it were redundant when they came to be translated into visual images. They had to start with the essence of the cinematic and so the visual image predominated in place of the logic of a literary narrative. Where the literary was needed (especially in explaining vampire lore in an age not yet used to vampires) it simply slowed down the visual thrust of the movie as a whole. In finding a visual language for the gothic such cinematography found its own unique 'voice'. Such cinema productions were closer to the weird mental landscapes of the Brothers Grimm, E. T. A. Hoffman, Heinrich Hoffman or Hans Christian Anderson than they were to the world of English gothic, for despite *Nosferatu's* evident debt to Stoker's *Dracula*, it is a film conceived in a make-believe world of plague-bearing rats, crumbling Hanseatic towns and the atmosphere as well as the costume of the 1840s. The *Cabinet of Dr Caligari* is even less historically specific, creating a spatial never-never land or dreamscape in which the Hanseatic town is imagined as consisting of town clerks, policemen, murderers, bizarre side shows and lunatic asylums.

The Danish director Carl Dreyer, working at the start of the sound era was able to put together the remarkable *Vampyr*, a dream-like meditation on Sheridan le Fanu's 'Carmilla'. The tale had interested Dreyer as an experiment in a genre that Dreyer had not yet attempted and he sent his researchers out to find locations that were infused with Poe's sense of the outré. The film, which features a mad doctor; peasants with scythes who substitute for Death; a local river that is symbolic of the Styx and is cut with strange sound and lighting effects; with shadows that dance and play without accompanying bodies; with the astral projection of the main character, Allan Gray, whose adventures in the occult we are never sure are not simply hallucinations and with a village vampire drawn from quite other sources than *Dracula*; produces a weirdly alienating affect on the audience. Produced when Universal were making *Dracula*, the film dispenses with the narrative that is so necessary for the former film, instead opting for a visual language that also dispenses with linear narrative.

European experimentation was a challenge to Hollywood which controlled eighty per cent of world distribution. American directors were threatened by German and Scandinavian film making and needed to find filmic answers to European innovations. Indeed so serious was the threat of Europe taken that *The Cabinet of Dr Caligari* was refused a showing in Los Angeles following various protests from groups, which included the Motion Picture Directors Association.

James Whale's *Frankenstein* was the Hollywood answer to the German film threat. Whale's version of the story (also based on a play) used just enough of expressionism to give texture to an otherwise linear movie. He modernized the story to put it in a type of fantasized present (the 'thirties' with the period's 'raygun gothic laboratory') and managed to create an original monster in Boris Karloff. But the folkloristic setting sticks long in the mind. Here are Barons ('Henry' Frankenstein is a baron's son) and burgermeisters, happy dancing mittel-european peasants and a world of mad scientists, labs generating wild electricity, lightening storms and anatomical theatres where 'mad' brains are studied, and a very American lynch mob at the end. In *Bride of Frankenstein*, Whale made the monster talk and have feelings, added imagery of martyrdom and emphasized the idea of the shunned outsider, something which may have related to his own sexual bias. By creating sympathy for the monster, Whale then had to add another mad scientist, the evil, necrophile, camp and comic Dr Pretorius played to the hilt by Ernest Thesinger.

Sympathy for the monster was what Curt Siodmak created when he rethought the werewolf mythology for *The Wolf Man* in 1941.[6] And here is perhaps the first true American monster for, despite being written by a German refugee, the film's central character is the 'hero' Larry Talbot whose werewolfry is an accidental and unfortunate disease akin to schizophrenia (there is even a painted advert for 'Saneman Products'). Larry Talbot himself was played by no subtle Hungarian or well-educated Englishman but by Lon Chaney junior, whose bulky appearance, almost simple expression, love of girls and practical backwoods handyman skills made him the perfect American innocent abroad. Although the film is supposedly set in

Wales, it makes no concessions to Britishness and the police chief and final hunting party are pure American in look and origin, the whole plot rethinking and reworking older ideas and inventing a new folklore for the legend which even included an invented rhyme created just for the film, but taken by some as authentic werewolf folklore.

> Even he who is pure of heart
> And says his prayers by night
> May become a wolf when the wolfbane blooms
> And the moon is full and bright.

It is perhaps ironic that all the main Universal gothic monsters were the creations of Europeans and that even Norman Bates in his haunted motel was the part creation of Alfred Hitchcock, born to a grocer in Leytonstone, London. It was in Britain that for a short time in the 1930s, the old-fashioned gaffe melodrama, held brief sway in celluloid. Best known for his parts in *Sweeney Todd* and *Crimes in the Dark House*, the barnstorming actor Tod Slaughter kept the spirit of bloody melodramatic penny dreadfuls going almost single handedly with his perfect rendering of a mid-nineteenth century villain, ghoulishly 'te he he-ing' and brandishing his cut throat while waiting to 'polish off' his customers. In America the comic version of the style was still to be discerned in the characters of Mrs Whack and Mrs Moncaster whose gin-soaked knockabout forms the humour for the 1935 film *Werewolf of London*. The zombie movie, whose origins began in the 1930s with such films as *White Zombie* set in Haiti and starring Bela Lugosi, is also all-American in attitude and location, but its revival in the 1950s with its beleaguered humans and ravaged shopping malls owes more to science-fiction radiation scares and communist witch hunts than gothic sensibilities.

Although Hollywood even flirted with Sherlock Holmes as a gothic adventurer, it was in *Dragonwyck* (1946), starring Vincent Price and Gene Tierney and *Suddenly Last Summer* (1959), starring Elizabeth Taylor that American gothic as a black and white Hollywood landscape was fully and originally employed, and yet these films are 13 years apart. The gothic look had already migrated into the shadows and neon of film noir, the very genre itself realigning with American gangsterism. Thereafter, the gothic languished or retraced its glory days in endless clichéd remakes. It was momentarily reborn in Technicolor, a technique used by both the low-budget movies of Hammer Films (where Jimmy Sangster, Terence Fisher, Christopher Lee and Peter Cushing revived the Universal favourites), the Cold War horror of Roger Corman's Edgar Allan Poe-based B films as well as the derivative, but powerful Italian cinema of the 1970s.

Chapter Nine
After Midnight: Goth Culture, Vampire Games and the Irresistible Rise of Twilight

By the 1930s, film was the dominant medium and the literary gothic was confined almost entirely to the formal ghost story, which had survived until the 1920s in the hands of writers like Algernon Blackwood, who turned such tales into adventures featuring psychic detectives. Such literary excursions were a fading memory. The genre was revived in the supernatural thrillers of authors such as Dennis Wheatley, who based much of his horror on the occult personality of Aleister Crowley who was known as 'the Great Beast 666' and whose exploits have proved more interesting than the whole of the literature of the occult that came from the period. What did come from the 1930s and 1940s was essentially the occult set in modern surroundings and little effort or interest remained in the old stock gothic scenarios, except, as we have seen, for a brief period in Hollywood.

Nevertheless, the emergence of the new pulp magazine in the United States (replacing the older dime novel) provided a new creative space for the fantastic. *Weird Tales* appeared in 1920, but this would be of little significance if it was not for the importance of one of its contributors and its most illustrious editor, H. P. Lovecraft. Lovecraft combined the mystical tale of Arthur Machen with an emergent American-style science fantasy to create tales at once supernatural (reincarnations abound) and cosmological (the space creatures from whose abode the horror comes). Like Stoker and his 'Transylvania', Lovecraft created a whole 'horror lifestyle' and culture around 'Arkham' and the mythos of Cthulhu. Never aspiring to the status of art, Lovecraft's work has achieved the status of a cult with its own book of magic – the dreaded 'Necronomicon'.

Lovecraft also encouraged other writers, one of whom, the 17-year-old Robert Bloch, later wrote one of horror's most enduring scenarios (scenario – for it is Alfred Hitchcock's film that is remembered): the tale of Norman Bates and the Bates Motel – *Psycho*. Hitchcock's film recruited Freudian theory on behalf of horror effect and by so doing redirected the gothic imagination firmly towards the human-made-monstrous, its hero the marginalized, *sexually* deviant psychopath.

The gothic tradition has, except for certain notable exceptions, fallen out of favour, at least at the cinema, and horror movie directors have chosen to go the way of gore and mayhem rather than atmosphere. The notable exceptions are David Lynch, whose homage to the genre include the television show *Twin Peaks* and films such as *Mulholland Drive* and Tim Burton's *Sleepy Hollow* and *Sweeney Todd*. Lynch's working of the story of the Elephant Man created the same sympathy for the monstrously deformed as did Browning's *Freaks*, and Burton's creation of Edward Scissorhands is perhaps the first genuine contribution to the genre since Siodmak's *The Wolf Man*.

During the 1950s and 1960s, television embraced the gothic with both late night and children's programmes and by the 1970s and 1980s, amusement park rides and horror theatre (there was a *Psycho* show at Disney) were expanding, even if, more often than not in the pastiche form of such shows as *The Little Shop of Horrors* and *The Rocky Horror Show*. *Dance of the Vampires* (although written by an American) was a huge hit as *Tanz der Vampires* when it played in Vienna; in 2009, Andrew Lloyd Webber's revival of *The Phantom of the Opera* had been running for 22 years across the world and the strange grand-guinol London Dungeon Experience for 33; the London Tombs since 2008; the Chamber of Horrors at Madame Toussauds for a staggering two hundred; the ghost play, *The Woman in Black* by Susan Hill and adapted for the stage by Stephen Mallatratt has been playing since 1989.

Since the 1950's exploitation of radiation scares and with the emergence of weird science as an element both horrific and gothic by turns, the genre took on another dimension, now with one eye on the world of B movies and the other influenced by the possibilities of the grotesque presented by the violent new adolescent-directed

horror comics which were soon to be censored in both America and
Britain. This pungent mixture influenced the 'revival' of horror in
the 1970s and can be found in the early work of James Herbert
(*The Rats*), Stephen King (*Carrie*), Guy N. Smith (*Crabs* series) and
Richard Lewis (Spider series) and includes tales of psycho-killers
such as Ramsey Campbell's *The Face that Must Die* and of demonic
possession such as Peter Blatty's *The Exorcist*.

By the 1980s the extraordinary increase in horror fiction sales
embraced everything from revivals (Susan Hill's *The Woman in
Black)* to supernatural thrillers such as Graham Masterton's *The
Djinn* or James Herbert's *The Magic Cottage*, Stephen King's prolific
output, Clive Barker's tales of violent dissection and 'factional'
works such as Whitley Strieber's *Communion* or Jay Anson's *Amity-
ville Horror*. H. P. Lovecraft became a cult figure and even the
British pulp writer of horror and science fiction R. L. Fanthorpe
suddenly found renewed fame. Feminists too discovered a wealth of
talented Victorian and Edwardian women writers (especially
Charlotte Perkinds Gillman whose 'The Yellow Wallpaper' has
become a totemic text among academics) and Angela Carter
emerged as Britain's most important woman writer with her tales of
perversity and dark desire. Indeed, on a wave of psycho-sexual
debate the gothic itself seemed to lend itself to feminism as an ideal
vehicle for the notations of gender. The vampire too made a con-
spicuous reappearance in both films and novels. Equally from the
1970s, reputable novelists fell over each other to co-opt horror for
their purposes, ironically courting the horror form as assiduously as
Henry James had attempted to escape it.

For current readers Stephen King, Clive Barker and Anne Rice
(Rather bizarrely christened Howard after her father) are probably
three of most significant horror genre exponents, but to a large extent
their works represent opposite currents in popular taste. King is not
only one of America's most prolific writers, he is also the best-selling
American author of all time. His tales are often explorations of small-
town sensibilities into which horror is integrated as a plot device. As
such, one can see King attached not only to the horror tradition (but
outside the type initiated by Poe) but also to the grander literary
tradition of American letters (in which Poe must be included). King
is concerned with American values and (ironically) provincial insecu-

rity, his work is based on social relations and family ties and is both democratic and yet nostalgic and conservative. Despite his interest in film, King is himself nostalgic for print culture and the nature of authorship fascinates him, attitudes explored in both *The Dark Half* and *Misery*.

To a large extent British author Clive Barker rethought the horror genre in the 1980s and moved it away from the more traditional terrors of Stephen King and James Herbert, concentrating instead on radical and repressed elements such as sexuality, the body (and its fluids), sado-masochism and the goth sensibility. This approach may relate to the 'queer' sense of his own gay sexuality. Through his film making he has been able to create a whole pantheon of ghouls not related to vampires or Frankenstein's monster. 'Pinhead' is the most famous, being one of the race of 'cenobites' or 'engineers' who wait to be called across the threshold by the human race.

> The Cenobites, theologians of the Order of the Gash, summoned from their experiments in their higher reaches of pleasure . . . bones . . . needles. A jug of urine . . . on the left of the altar. (*The Hellbound Heart*, Chapter One)

Such creatures are the inheritors of the world of de Sade, taking pleasure to the ultimate ends of pain and perversion. The Cenobites exemplify this contradiction even in their appearance where even their clothes 'were sown both *to* and through [their] skin' . . . When [they] spoke the hooks that transfixed the flaps on [their] eyes . . . by an infinite system of chains . . . through flesh and bone alike . . . 'were teased . . . exposing the glistening meat beneath'. Barker mixes horror with the fantastic to create what he rather pretentiously calls the 'fantastique' or the 'dark fantastic'.

Such horrors are grand guinol in every sense, but they also acknowledge the soft-machinic body horror that has become the dominant theme of modern writing on fear. Nowadays, it is our rebellious bodies, taken over by vampires, zombified or otherwise tortured that scare us the most. Horror rather than the gothic and horror mixed with torture and extreme violence seem to be the fare of the twenty-first century. The body is split open and anatomized; our interiors have become the new architectural spaces of fear.

The body itself has taken on the sense of excess and disturbance that was once attached to buildings. What happens to the body is now explosive, filling the imagination with every squirm-inducing thought about blood, vomit and excrement. It is a long way from the original gothic intention and quite different from the graveyard poet's ideas of the clean skeletal corpse curiously devoid of grave worms. For the most part, violence only comes to bodies now while they are still alive.

The horror story (as opposed to the horror film) probably peaked some time ago, but by combining chillers with serial killing, Tolkien-esque plots, crime writing, vampire hunting or historical mystery there may be a revival. James Herbert looks back to older writers in the genre and reinvents them for a contemporary readership while Peter James mixes straightforward horror fiction with psychological crime fiction, technological plots and supernaturalism or the par-anormal. In this respect the gothic is more often nowadays to be found in the work of crime fiction authors rather than horror fiction writers especially in the books of Thomas Harris, where settings and the character of Hannibal Lecter seem again to epitomize a gothic sensibility.

> The fire lights glowed red in the Insect Zoo, reflected in ten thousand active eyes of the older phylum. The humidifier hummed and hissed. Beneath the cover, in the black cage, the Death's-head Moth climbed down the nightshade. She moved across the floor, her wings trailing like a cape, and found the bit of honeycomb in her dish. Grasping the honeycomb in her powerful front legs, she uncoiled her sharp proboscis and plunged it through the wax cap of a honey cell. Now she sat sucking quietly while all around her in the dark the chirps and whirs resumed, and with them the tiny tillings and killings. (*Silence of the Lambs*, Chapter Forty)

Harris has also been able to create a new monster who is both a psychopath in the serial-killer tradition and also oddly supernatural.

> Dr Lecter has six fingers on his left hand . . . His cultured voice has a slight metallic rasp . . . [his] eyes are maroon and they reflect the light in pinpoints of red. (Chapter Three)

Even secondary characters are imbued with gothic style characteristics.

> The chamber where Mason spends his life is quiet, but it has its own soft pulse, the hiss and sigh of the respirator that finds him breath. It is dark except for the glow of the big aquarium where an exotic eel turns and turns in an endless figure eight, its cast shadow moving like a ribbon over the room.
>
> Mason's plaited hair lies in a thick coil on the respirator shell covering his chest on the elevated bed. A device of tubes, like panpipes, is suspended before him.
>
> Mason's long tongue slides out from between his teeth. He scrolls his tongue around the end pipe and puffs with the next pulse of the respirator. (*Hannibal*, Chapter 6)

This is, however, no new idea and writers such as Cornell Woolrich and James M. Cain were experimenting with a hybrid of gothicism and crime as long ago as the 1940s. Here for instance is Cain in *Double Indemnity*, invoking the gothic and the gottic female.

> That was how I came to this House of Death, that your've been reading about in the papers. It didn't look like a House of Death when I saw it. It was just a Spanish house, like all the rest of them in California, with white walls, red tile roof, and a patio out to one side. [. . .]
>
> They've made a lot of that living room, especially those 'blood-red drapes.' All I saw was a living room like every other living room in California, maybe a little more expensive than some, but nothing that any department store wouldn't deliver on one truck, lay out in the morning, and have the credit O.K. ready the same afternoon. The furniture was Spanish, the kind that looks pretty and sits stiff. The rug was one of those 12 × 15's that would have been Mexican except it was made in Oakland, California. The blood-red drapes were there, but they didn't mean anything. All these Spanish houses had red velvet drapes that run on iron spears and generally some red velvet wall tapestries to go with them. This was right out of the same can, with a coat-of-arms tapestry over the fireplace and a castle tapestry over the sofa. (Chapter 1)

...

But there's something in me that loves Death. I think of myself as Death, sometimes. In a scarlet shroud, floating through the night. I'm so beautiful, then. And sad, And hungry to make the whole world happy, by taking them out where I am, into the night, away from all trouble, all unhappiness. (Chapter 2)

Yet it is the vampire who has proved the most enduring of all gothic monsters mutating and developing with each generation of writers. The change was started by Anne Rice who in the gay vampire Lestat not only created a back story for vampirism which proved highly effective and extremely contagious, but also set the narrative in the New World, and in doing so rewrote the vampire myth in terms of American modernity and cultural hegemony.

'It was detachment that made this possible, a sublime loneliness with which Lestat and I moved through the world of mortal men'. [. . .] 'This was new Orleans, a magical and magnificent place to live. In which a vampire, richly dressed and gracefully walking through the pools of light of one gas lamp after another might attract no more notice in the evening than hundreds of other exotic creatures – if he attracted any at all, if anyone stopped to whisper behind a fan, 'That man . . . how pale, how he gleams . . . how he moves. It's not natural' A city in which a vampire might be gone before the words had even passed the lips, seeking out the alleys in which he could see like a cat, the darkened bars in which sailors slept with their heads on the table, great high-ceilinged hotel rooms where a lone figure might sit, her feet upon an embroidered cushion, her legs covered with a lace coun-terpane, her head bent under the tarnished light of a single candle, never seeing the great shadow move across the plaster flowers of the ceiling, never seeing the long white fingers reached to press the fragile flame. (*Interview with the Vampire*, Part One)

Since 2000, there has been a virtual deluge of vampire-inspired novels. This has been particularly noticeable in the area of women's romance, especially in the Love Spell Book Club which promotes writers such as Lynsay Sands, C. J. Barry, Colleen Thompson (the slyly named), Nina Bangs, Kate MacAlister and Marjorie Liu, 'bringing a little magic' in the life of their readers. The love bites hardly stop there and other publishers such as Piatkus are in on the act with their own writers such as Maryjanice Davidson. In a series of books, humorously titled, *Undead and Unwed*, *Undead and Unemployed* and *Undead and Unappreciated* we follow the antics of Elizabeth ('Beth') Taylor who finds herself on a morgue slab one day, a vampire and a spinster, in search of a man and the perfect shoes. If one is not keen on straightforward romance there is Charlaine Harris's *Dead until Dark*, a Sookie Stackhouse mystery where a mind-reading waitress solves a series of psychopathic killings while dating one of the undead (filmed as 'True Blood' for television). Other stories include, *Living Dead in Dallas* and *Club Dead*. If the reader is in the mood for mystery there is also *Dead Witch Walking*, a police procedural where the main protagonist is an Irish-descended witch in a halter neck, who keeps charms on her handcuffs. She is an 'Inlander' who works in the vampire bars of Cincinnati looking for tax evading leprechauns and is partnered by Jenks, an actual fairy who likes imitating Billy Idol. We are told in the blurb that Harrison 'has been called a witch . . . has never seen a vampire . . . loves graveyards . . . and wears too much black'.

The vampire is now a firm favourite in the sort of jobbing pulp fiction written by Laurell K. Hamilton. Hamilton was born in Heber Springs, Arkansas but brought up by her grandmother in Indiana; Hamilton graduated in English and biology before embarking on her first mixed genre novel, *Guilty Pleasures* about the vampire hunter, 'Anita Blake'. Mixing genre expectations from science fiction, romance, erotica and horror and including a rewriting of the vampire myth and a female heroine created a new form, the vampire 'paranormal romance' whose main exponents are American and which owes much to the symbiotic relationship of popular film, television and books as well as to the advent of 'Slash' fiction (fan-based reworkings of stock characters). This new and problematic 'genre' is hard to categorize, sometimes being considered 'supernatural crime thrillers' and sometimes as horror.

In the twenty-first century, the Gothic has become a ubiquitous and invasive generic form, both parasitic and reinvigorating. Take for instance the 2009 bestseller, *Pride and Prejudice and Zombies* which combines violent horror and Regency gentility in a 'mashup' or 'recombination' spoof of both genres. The books that have spanned juvenile and adult reading, however, are those that have reinvented the figure of the vampire, now, by far, the major Gothic character. Indeed, vampires and Gothic settings dominate a large section of the adult and predominantly female romance market where they are figures of both male domination and of female empowerment. Vampires seem to have a versatility other monsters do not have and their protean nature allows them to appear in bars and nightclubs as well as high schools. No longer is the vampire confined to novels as a character, rather now they act as a type of narrative trope, differing as to the fictional context within which that trope is used.

One series especially has bridged the gap between juvenile and adult reading and between the Gothic and the Romance, creating fictional scenarios that appeal as much to young adult women as to teenage girls. The 'Twilight' series which began with the publication of *Twilight* on 5 October 2005 by author Stephenie Meyer tells the story of teenager Isabella 'Bella' Swan who falls for the charms of Edward Cullen, a vampire.[3] The tale mixes fantasies of high-school adventure, gang culture, teenage eroticism and ideas of the superhero and is, perhaps, a fitting series for post-feminist womanhood who still crave heterosexual desire and danger, the theme of blood being a simple metaphor for sublimated adolescent male lust and budding female sexuality. The world of the vampire has finally caught up with that of Romeo and Juliet. Vampires are now dash and cool.

Alongside the reinvention of European gothicism by American authors, there is also the creation of new gothic spaces that are indigenously American. This trend had begun with Washington Irving, Nathaniel Hawthorne and Ambrose Bierce, but it has taken root not in the 'crumbling' spaces of New England, but rather in the swamps or backwoods shacks of the south or the Texas/Mexico border, a mixture of latter-day cowboy weirdness, drug-store banality and small-town isolation. In recent years this has come to surpass all other forms of Hollywood horror with teenagers being regularly butchered on lonely back roads, in teen camp or on hikes in the woods and its literary importance may be seen in the critical praise heaped upon Cormac McCarthy, whose pioneering style and offbeat tales of degenerate life styles have caught the imagination of cultured readers who would not normally bother with horror titles.

> Here the walls with their softlooking convolutions, slavered over as they were with wet and bloodred mud, had an organic look to them, like the innards of some great beast. Here in the bowels of the mountain Ballard turned his light on ledges or pallets of stone where dead people lay like saints. (*Child of God*)

Just as America has invented new geographical locations for the gothic, so too American humourists such as Charles Adams and Edward Gorey have revisited the European landscape and reworked it as whimsy and this, in turn, has led to a growth in horror and gothic books for children, by such writers as Lemony Snicket (Daniel Handler) and R. L. Stine. R. L. Stine was born on 8 October 1943, but it was not until 1986 that Stine got his start as a horror author with his first novel *Blind Date*. Stine soon followed with four more and that year also co-created and worked as head author on the Nickelodeon television show *Eureka's Castle*. In 1989 he embarked on a new horror series, *Fear Street* for 8- to 12-year olds. In 1992 Parachute Press launched Stine's *Goosebumps* series. The series, much like *Fear Street* was a horror series geared towards young readers. Stine first published *Welcome to Dead House* in 1992, eventually writing 62 books for the *Goosebumps* series alone, culminating with *Monster Blood IV* in 1997. The books have been printed in 28 languages and to date have sold over 300 million copies worldwide.

Such developments keep the spirit of gothic alive but they cannot compete perhaps with the impact of horror films and television. Yet in recent years film and television have not been able to satisfy the growing desire of individuals to actually participate in the world of the gothic and experience gothic thrills first hand. In this, the tradition of Walpole and the gothic dilletantes who wished to live out their fantasies in the architecture of their homes is now followed vicariously by those who choose to dress 'goth' and dramatize their lives through music (exemplified by videos like Michael Jackson's *Thriller* or even the entire oeuvre of Meatloaf and groups like Metallica, Slipknot and Rammstein), gothic lifestyle (including gathering each year at Whitby – a central location of *Dracula*), computer games and role play dedicated to placating the ennui of life and based around the cult of the night and the images of death.

In the twenty-first century, it is the world of computer gaming that has most successfully revived the landscape of the Universal films and the vampire myth. Games such as *Resident Evil*, *Diablo*, *Silent Hill*, *Eternal Darkness* and *Doom* allow players the excitement of participating in worlds full of demons and vampires amid ruins and gothic chaos. So vivid can these games become that some of their creators try to build in the sort of mental confusion in their players that might be expected in real life encounters with monsters in order to enhance the imaginative and dream-like quality of play.

Dedication to gothic excess may be playful and theatrical or deadly and brooding, all clad in red and purple taffeta and velvet or dressed in rubber and leather for S&M play at the Torture Garden, the club which has pioneered the public experimentation with body image and sexual identity since its opening in 1990 – a very serious form of fancy dress. Such a club would have delighted William Beckford and tickled Byron's and 'Monk' Lewis's perversity. The club provides a space for 'a semi-public psychodrama of desire' in a space that is like 'entering a scene from a film, a fantasy, . . . anything you want it to be'.[1] It is a place to be, be seen and experiment with the body's limits in a safe environment where the boundaries of self may be explored and a new temporary identity emerge from those fragments of self which are presented to the mundane world. Here artifice is the real, if only for a moment as the outside world fades away in dance and conviviality.

And conviviality is what the players of Live Action Role Play (LARP) are seeking when they put on the costume and assume the persona of their favourite character of the night. LARPing was born out of the role playing games and *Dungeons and Dragons* encounters of the 1980s and consists of collective improvisational theatre played out by those who take their narrative themes from gothic fiction or Tolkienesque fantasy. Narratives often represent the battles about authority and legitimacy and have recently become standardized with rules of action provided by the game *Vampires: The Masquerade* or *White Wolf* in which 'clans' of vampires 'descended' from the biblical Cain, battle for supremacy. It is an escape into fiction and play rather than an escape from reality.[2]

Yet there are those who seek to go farther into their fantasy world and live as the characters that they have created. The craze for living as a vampire which is now popular across the globe is one such instance of the gothic invading reality. Nevertheless, many vampire life stylists consider themselves quite different from current goth culture. Watching vampire movies, dressing in vampire outfits, finding like-minded friends is what appeals to living vampires: 'it's all there – [it's] alluring, powerful and seductive. That's what being a vampire is all about'.[4]

Notes

Chapter One

1 Donald S. Johnson, *Phantom Islands of the Atlantic* (New Bruswick: Souvenir Press, 1997). Information from Chapter Two.
2 Peter Haining, 13.
3 Kim Ian Michasiw, Introduction, *Zofloya* (Oxford: Oxford University Press, 1997), xiv–xv.
4 Donald Tovey (ed.), 'Letters of Thomas Gray', vol. 1 (London: George Bell and Sons, 1900), 44.
5 For those visiting the Lake District during the periods of war when Europe was inaccessible a new word had to be found. 'Tourists' were those of middle-class background who travelled out of curiosity rather than undertaking the Grand Tour.
6 Kenneth Clarke, *The Gothic Revival* (London: John Murray, 1962), 14.
7 Ibid., 14.
8 Ibid., 15.
9 R. J. Smith, *The Gothic Bequest* (Cambridge: Cambridge University Press, 2002), 28.
10 Ibid., 40–1.
11 Ronald Hutton, *The Triumph of the Moon* (Oxford: Oxford University Press, 1999), 10.
12 Ibid., 9.
13 Ibid., 9.
14 Richard Norton, *Gothic Readings* (London: Leicester University Press, 2000), 355. A first-rate anthology of unusual quotes.
15 Ibid., 340.
16 Ibid., 282.

17 Ibid., 329.
18 Ibid., 362.

Chapter Two

1 Steven Connor, 'Sufficiently Decayed'. A talk given at the Frieze Art Fair, Regent's Park, London (15 October 2006).
2 Ibid., npn.
3 George Saintsbury, *The Cambridge History of English and American Literature*, volume XI. Ed. A. Ward and A. R. Waller (Cambridge: Cambridge University Press), 111.
4 Ibid., 111.
5 Mark Girouard, *The Return to Camelot* (New Haven, CT: Yale University Press, 1981), 40.
6 Ibid., 57.
7 Ibid., 61.
8 Ibid., 90–1.
9 Ibid., 6–7.
10 Collette Colligan, *The Traffic in Obscenity from Byron to Beardsley* (Basingstoke: Palgrave, 2006), 32.
11 Quoted in David Pirie, *A New Heritage Horror: The English Gothic Cinema* (London: I. B. Tauris, 2008) 25.
12 Ibid., 25.
13 Ibid., 96.
14 Giorgio Vasari, *Lives of the Artists*, vol. II. Tr. George Bull (Harmondsworth: Penguin, 1987), 109.
15 Michasiw, xiii.
16 John Cornwell, *Coleridge* (London: Allen Lane, 1973), 2.

Chapter Three

1 Jack Zipes, *Happy Ever After* (London: Routledge, 1997), 47.
2 *Percy Bysshe Shelley: The Critical Heritage*. Ed. James E. Barcus (London: Routledge, 1995), 51.
3 Mary Shelley may have had a faint memory of a work she had read or heard of from 1790. Francois-Felix Nogaret published *Le Miroir*

des evenemens actuel, ou la belle au plus offrant (*The Looking Glass of actuality, or Beauty to the Highest Bidder*) during the height of the French Revolution. The tale concerns a character called 'Frankenstein' and an automaton. As with Shelley's version the story is about the 'new man' to emerge from the Revolution. This tale only reappeared in 2009, when Professor Julia Douthwaite and Daniel Richter of Notre Dame University published their evidence in the July issue of *European Studies*.

4 Rupert Christianson, *Romantic Affinities* (London: Pimlico, 2004), 57–8.
5 Ibid., 58.
6 Norton, 300.
7 Christianson, 59–60.
8 Ibid., 71.

Chapter Four

1 Norton, 364–5.
2 I did not know if it was something in the turpentine or a defect in the canvas, but the more I scrubbed the more the gangrene seemed to spread . . .

> 'What a horrible color it is now . . . [it] resembles green cheese'.
> (Robert W. Chambers, 'The Yellow Sign')

3 Norton, 335–8.
4 Christine Baker, *Introduction to Best Ghost Stories: Charles Dickens* (London: Wordsworth, 1997), vii.
5 Ibid., viii.

Chapter Five

1 Nicholas Powell, *Fuseli: The Nightmare* (London: Allen Lane, 1973), 35.
2 Reinhold Heller, *Edvard Munch: The Scream* (London: Allen Lane, 1973), 65.
3 Ibid., 66.

4 Manuel Aguirre, *The Closed Space* (Manchester: Manchester University Press, 1990), 92.
5 George Rowell, *The Victorian Theatre* (Cambridge: Cambridge University Press, 1956), 34.
6 Ibid., 35.
7 Beddoes, xi.
8 Samuel Taylor Coleridge, 'Review of the Monk. A Romance', in the *Critical Review*, February 1797, 194–200.
9 John Beryman, Introduction to Matthew Lewis, *The Monk* (New York: Evergreen Books, 1952), 20.
10 Rowell, 44.

Chapter Six

1 Kyla Ward, 'Slayin'em in the Aisles', *Tabula Rasa* no. 6 (1995). Information about stage machinery mainly from this source.
2 From *The Diary of Dr. John William Polidori: 1816, Relating to Byron, Shelley.* Ed. William Michael Rossetti (London: Elkin Mathews, 1911), 96–135.
3 Sophie Thomas, 'Making Visible: the Diorama, the Double and the (Gothic) Subject', in *Praxis*, January, 2009.
4 Ibid.
5 Ann Williams, 'Lewis/Gounod's Bleeding *Nonne*: An Introduction and Translation of the Scribe/Delavigne Libretto' in *Praxis*, January 2008
6 These ideas were suggested by my student Annamaria Sofillas at New York University.

Chapter Seven

1 C. G. Jung, *Psychology and the Occult.* Tr. R. F. C. Hull (London: Routledge and Kegan Paul, 1977), 144.
2 Clive Bloom, *Cult Fiction* (Basingstoke: Palgrave, 1998), 212.
3 Trevor H. Hall, *Search for Harry Price* (London: Duckworth, 1978), 188.

4 Bloom, 211.
5 Jung, 138–9.
6 Ibid., 150.
7 Peter Lamont, *The First Psychic* (London: Abacus, 2005), 2.
8 Ibid., 2.
9 Ibid., 32–3.
10 Quoted in Hannen Swaffer, *My Greatest Story: Vol. 2* (London: Psychic Book Club, 1945), 25.
11 Peter Washington, *Madame Blavatsky's Baboon* (London: Secker and Warburg, 1993).
12 Ronald Pearsall, *The Table-Rappers* (London: Michael Joseph, 1972), 52.
13 Ibid., 53.
14 Ibid., 55.
15 Daniel J. Boorstin, *The Americans: The Democratic Experience* (New York: Vintage, 1974), 246.
16 Rudyard Kipling quoted in Peter Hunt, *An Introduction to Children's Literature* (Oxford: Oxford University Press, 1994), 96.
17 P. H. Ditchfield, *The Charm of the English Village* (London: Bracken Books, [1906] 1985), 37–8.
18 Ibid., 38.

Chapter Eight

1 The relationship between Renfield and Dracula in the book may have replicated, to some extent, the master/slave relationship that developed between Bram Stoker and Henry Irving; Stoker, a man with hidden and subversive desires may have written his own masochistic tendencies into the book. He certainly shares characteristics with Renfield, his own erotic dream of the 'brides' he gave to Harker and Van Helsing shares his first name. As for his masochistic and 'repressed' urges we simply have to look at the scene with Dracula and Mina. In some senses Stoker was both patient and psychologist for his own inner turmoil.
2 http://www.filmbuffonline.com/Features/EdisonsFrankenstein1.htm

3 Mel Gordon, *The Grand Guinol* (New York: Amok Press, 1988), 10.
4 Stephanie Diekmann and Ekehard Knorer, 'The Spectator's Spectacle: Tod Browning's Theatre', in *The Films of Tod Browning*, ed.
   Bernd Herzogenrath (London: Black Dog, 2006), 72.
5 It is amusing to think that Lugosi, who played a blood-sucking aristocrat most of his life, had been a communist during the Hungarian
   Revolution of 1919 and may have relished the thought of portraying the class enemy.
6 It would be overstating the case to say that the Universal Studios
   created the werewolf. They had been around in the Victorian
   consciousness for some years before. Since Sutherland Menzies's
   story, *Hugues the Wer-Wolf* of 1838 and Captain Marryat's *The White
   Wolf of the Hartz Mountains* of 1839, the werewolf had appeared
   sporadically in the literature of the Gothic. During the 1890s there
   was a veritable werewolf epidemic in fiction with 11 books appearing between 1899 and 1900, including work by Arthur Conan
   Doyle, Rudyard Kipling, Honoré Beaugrand and even William
   Butler Yeats. From the 1850s there was also a stream of non-fiction
   works, but it was the films above all that caught the imagination
   and made the werewolf genre so generally popular and so evidently
   visual. It was the combination of mythical transformation scene and
   tragic characterization that was essentially new and powerful on
   screen.

Chapter Nine

1 Powell, 4.
2 These ideas were suggested by Jake Griswold, a student at Notre
   Dame University.
3 85 million copies of the books have been sold by 2010 as well as
   spanning a highly successful film series
4 'Interview with Thunder Raven-Stoker' (*Metro*, 28 October 2008).

Primary Reading List

Early Gothic: Walpole to the Romantics

Burger, Gottfried, 'Lenora', tr. William Taylor, http://www.rc.umd.edu/rchs/reader/lenora.html.

Dacre, Charlotte, *Zofloya or The Moor*, ed. Kim Ian Michasiw (Oxford: Oxford World's Classics, 1997).

De Quincey, Thomas, *The Confessions of an English Opium Eater* (London: J M Dent, 1960).

de Sade, Marquis, *Justine, Philosophy in the Bedroom, & Other Writings*, tr. Richard Seaver and Austryn Wainhouse (New York: Grove Press, 1965).

Dyer, John, 'Grongar Hill', http://andromeda.rutgers.edu/~jlynch/Texts/grongar.html.

Evance, Susan, 'Netley Abbey', http://www.southernlife.org.uk/netley_abbey.html.

George Gordon, Lord Byron, 'The Giaor', http://readytogoebooks.com/LB-Giaour.htm.

Haining, Peter (ed.), *Great British Tales of Terror: Gothic Stories of Horror and Romance* (Harmondsworth: Penguin, 1972).

Haining, Peter (ed.), *Great Tales of Terror from Europe and America: Gothic Stories of Horror and Romance* (Harmondsworth: Penguin, 1972).

Hoffman, E. T. A., 'The Sandman', in *Tales of Hoffman*, ed. R. J. Hollingdale (Harmondsworth: Penguin, 1982).

Lewis, Matthew G., *The Monk* (New York: Grove Press, Inc., 1952).

Maturin, Charles, 'Introduction to First Edition', *Melmoth the Wanderer*, ed. Alethea Hayter (Harmondsworth: Penguin, 1977).

Peacock, Thomas Love, *Nightmare Abbey/Crotchet Castle* (Harmondsworth: Penguin, 1969).

Polidori, John, *The Vampyre and Other Tales of the Macabre*, ed. Robert Morrison and Chris Baldick (Oxford, Oxford World's Classic, 1997).

Praz, Mario (ed.), *Three Gothic Novels* (Harmondsworth: Penguin, 1986).

Radcliffe, Ann, *The Mysteries of Udolpho*, ed. Jacqueline Howard, (Harmondsworth: Penguin, [1794] 2001).

Scott, Sir Walter, *Ivanhoe* (Harmondsworth: Penguin, [1819] 1994).

Von Schiller, Friedrich, *The Ghost-seer* (London: Hesperus Press Limited, [1798] 2003).

Gothic Developed: Poe to the Brontes

Ainsworth, William Harrison, *The Lancashire Witches* (Manchester: Aurora Publishing, [1849] n.d.).

Anonymous, *Sweeney Todd or The String of Pearls* (London: Wordsworth Editions, 2007).

Beddoes, Thomas Lovell, *Death's Jest-Book* (Manchester: Carcanet, [1829] 2003).

Bronte, Charlotte, *Jane Eyre* (Harmondsworth: Penguin, [1847] 1978).

Bronte, Emily, *Wuthering Heights*, ed. David Daiches (Harmondsworth: Penguin, [1847] 1981).

Dickens, Charles, *Great Expectations* (London: Wordsworth Classics, 1993).

Dickens, Charles, *Best Ghost Stories* (London: Wordsworth Editions, 1997).

Hoffmann, Dr Heinrich, *Struwwelpeter* (London: Pavilion, 2002).

Hugo, Victor, *The Hunchback of Notre-Dame* (London: Wordsworth Editions, 1993).

Le Fanu, Sheridan, *In a Glass Darkly* (London: Wordsworth Editions, 1995).

Poe, Edgar Allan, Tales of Mystery and Imagination (London: Dent and Co, 1909).

Reynolds, George W. M., *Wagner the Werewolf* (London: Wordsworth Editions, 2006).

Rymer, James Malcolm, *Varney the Vampyre* (Berkeley Heights, NJ, Wildside Press, [1845–7] 2001).

Victorian and Edwardian Gothic: Stoker to Leroux

Asquith, Cynthia, *Shudders* (London: Hutchinson & Co, n.d.).

Chambers, Robert W., *The King in Yellow and Other Horror Stories*, ed. E. F. Bleiler (New York: Dover Publications, 1970).

Doyle, Sir Arthur Conan, *The Penguin Complete Sherlock Holmes* (Harmondsworth: Penguin, 1981).

James, M. R., *The Penguin Complete Ghost Stories of M. R. James* (Harmondsworth: Penguin, [1931] 1985).

Leroux, Gaston, *The Phantom of the Opera* (New York: Carroll & Graf Publishers, Inc., [1908] 1986).

Lewis, Leopold, *The Bells* (London: Samuel French, n.d.).

Stoker, Bram, *Dracula*, ed. Clive Leatherdale (Southend: Dessert Island Books, [1897] 2006).

Late Flowerings: James M. Cain to Stephanie Meyer

Austen, Jane and Seth Gordon-Smith, *Pride and Prejudice and Zombies* (Harmondsworth: Penguin, 2008).

Barker, Clive, *The Hellbound Heart* (London: Fontana, 1991).

Cain, James M., *Double Indemnity* (London: Pan, [1945] 1983).

Harris, Thomas, *The Silence of the Lambs* (London: Mandarin, 1991).

Harris, Thomas, *Hannibal* (London: Arrow, 2000).

Lovecraft, H. P. *The Haunter of the Dark* (London: Panther, 1963).

Lovecraft, H. P. *At the Mountains of Madness* (London: Panther, 1973).

McCarthy, Cormac, *Child of God* (London: Picador, 1989).

Meyers, Stephanie, *Twilight* (London: Atom, 2006).

Rice, Anne, *Interview with the Vampire* (London: Warner, 1976).

Woolrich, Cornell, *Night Has a Thousand Eyes* (New York: Ballantine Books, 1982).

Further Selected Readings in the Gothic

Aguirre, Manuel, *The Closed Space* (Manchester: Manchester University Press, 1990).

Baker, Dorothy Z., *America's Gothic Fiction* (Columbus, OH: The Ohio State University Press, 2007).

Bloom, Clive (ed.), *Creepers* (London: Pluto Press, 1993).

Bloom, Clive, *Gothic Horror* (Basingstoke: Palgrave, 2008).

Bottigheimer, Ruth B., *Grimms' Bad Girls & Bold Boys: The Moral & Social Vision of the Tales* (New Haven, CT: Yale University Press, 1987).

Botting, Fred (ed.), *Frankenstein* (Basingstoke: Macmillan, 1998).

Burke, Edmund, *A Philosophical Enquiry into the Origins of Our Ideas of the Sublime and the Beautiful*, ed. James T. Bolton (Oxford: Basil Blackwell, [1757] 1987).

Buse, Peter and Andrew Stott (eds), *Ghosts: Deconstruction, Psychoanalysis, History* (Basingstoke: Palgrave, 1999).

Byron, Glennis (ed.), *Dracula* (Basingstoke: Palgrave, 1999).

Cavallaro, Dani, *The Gothic Vision* (London: Continuum, 2005).

Chaplin, Sue, *The Gothic and the Rule of Law 1764–1820* (Basingstoke: Palgrave, 2007).

Darnton, Roger, *Mesmerism and the End of the Enlightenment* (New York: Schocken Books, 1970).

Davies, Owen, *The Haunted: A Social History of Ghosts* (Basingstoke: Palgrave, 2009).

L. Camp de Sprague, *Lovecraft: a Biography* (London: New English Library, 1975).

Defoe, Daniel, *Journal of the Plague Year*, ed. Anthony Burgess (Harmondsworth: Penguin, [1722] 1966).

Docherty, Brian (ed.), *American Horror Fiction* (Basingstoke: Macmillan, 1999).

Fisch, Audrey A., *Frankenstein: Icon of Modern Culture* (New York: Helm Information, 2009).

Fothergill, Brian, *Beckford of Fonthill* (Stroud: Nonsuch Publishing, 1979).

Gibson, William, *Neuromancer* (London: Harper Collins, 1984).

Halberstam, Judith, *Skin Shows* (London and Durham [USA]: Duke University Press, 1995).

Hearn, Lafcadio, *Nightmare Touch in Shadowings* (New York: Little, Brown and Co., 1900).

Herzogenrath, Bernd (ed.), *The Films of Tod Browning* (London: Black Dog, 2006).

Hill, Rosemary, *God's Architect: Pugin and the Building of Romantic Britain* (Harmondsworth: Penguin, 2007).

Hills, Matthew, *The Pleasures of Horror* (London: Continuum, 2005).

Hoffman, Dr Heinrich, *Struwwelpeter* (London: Pavillion books, [1845] 1997).

Horner, Avril and Sue Zlosnik (eds), *Le Gothic* (Basingstoke: Palgrave, 2008).

Horrells, Coral Ann, *Love, Mystery and Misery* (London: Continuum, 2005).

Houellebecq, Michel, *H. P. Lovecraft: Against the World, against Life* (London: Weidenfeld and Nicolson, 2006).

Hurley, Kelly, *The Gothic Body* (Cambridge: Cambridge University Press, 1996).

Hutton, Ronald, *The Triumph of the Moon* (Oxford: Oxford University Press, 1999).

Hutton, Ronald, *Blood Mistletoe: The History of the Druids in Britain* (Yale: Yale University Press, 2009).

Joshi, S. T., *H. P. Lovecraft: A Life* (West Warwick, RI: Necronomicon Press, 1996).

Joshi, S. T., *The Modern Weird Tale* (Jefferson, NC: McFarland, 2001).

Kayser, Wolfgang, *The Grotesque in Art and Literature* (Indiana: Indiana University Press, [1957] 1963).

Kilpatrick, Nancy, *The Goth Bible* (London: Plexus, 2005).

Lamont, Peter, *The First Psychic* (London: Abacus, 2005).

Leopold Lewis, *The Bells: A Drama in Three Acts* (London: Samuel French, n.d.).

Mack, Robert L., *The Wonderful and Surprising History of Sweeney Todd* (London: Continuum, 2007).

Morgan, Jack, *The Biology of Horror* (Carbondale and Edwardsville: Southern Illinois Press, 2002).

Norton, Richard (ed.), *Gothic Readings* (London: Leicester University Press, 2000).

Parramore, Lynn, *Reading the Sphinx* (Basingstoke: Palgrave, 2008).

Perry, Dennis H. and Carl R. Sederholm, *Poe, 'The House of Usher' and the American Gothic* (Basingstoke: Palgrave, 2009).

Pirie, David, *A New Heritage Horror: The English Gothic Cinema* (London: I. B. Tauris, 2008).

Punter, David, *The Literature of Terror* (Harlow: Pearson, 1980).

Punter, David (ed.), *A Companion to the Gothic* (Oxford: Blackwell, 2000).

Reynolds, Sir Joshua, *Discourses on Art*, ed. Stephen O. Mitchell (New York: Bobbs-Merrill, [1797] 1965) Discourse 1.

Richardson, Ruth, *Death, Dissection and the Destitute* (London: Routledge & Kegan Paul, 1987).

Rowell, George, *The Victorian Theatre 1792–1914* (Cambridge: Cambridge University Press, 1978).

Sage, Victor (ed.), *The Gothick Novel* (Basingstoke: Macmillan, 1990).

Schaeffer, Neil, *The Marquis de Sade: A Life* (London: Hamish Hamilton, 1999).

Smith, Joseph, *Book of Mormon* (Salt Lake City, UT: Church of the Latter Day Saints, [1830] 1998).

Smith, R. J., *The Gothic Bequest: Medieval Institutions in British Thought, 1688–1863* (Cambridge, Cambridge University Press, 1987).

Spadoni, Robert, *Uncanny Bodies* (California: University of California Press, 2007).

Todd, Janet, *Death and the Maidens* (Berkeley: University of California Press, 2007).

Walpole, Horace, Introduction to First Edition of The Castle of Otranto, 1764.

Wolfreys, Julian, *Victorian Hauntings* (Basingstoke: Palgrave, 2002).

Wordsworth, William, *Guide to the Lakes*, ed. Ernest do Selincourt (Oxford: Oxford University Press, [1835] 1906).

Index